WHEN LEAN ENTERPRISES COLLIDE

WHEN LEAN ENTERPRISES COLLIDE

Competing through Confrontation

ROBIN COOPER

HARVARD BUSINESS SCHOOL PRESS
BOSTON, MASSACHUSETTS

LIBRARY OF CONGRESS CATALOGING-IN-PUBLICATION DATA
Cooper, Robin, 1951–
    When lean enterprises collide : competing through confrontation /
    Robin Cooper.
        p. cm.
    Includes index.
    ISBN 0-87584-571-1
    1. Costs, Industrial—Japan—Case studies. 2. Japan—
Manufactures—Costs. 3. Production management—Japan. 4. Cost
control—Japan. 5. Competition—Japan. I. Title.
HD47.C638 1995
338.0952—dc20   94-47474
                                                               CIP

The paper used in this publication meets the requirements of the American National Standard for Permanence of Paper for Printed Library
Materials Z39.49-1984.

To my best friend, Helen Mayers Cooper

Competition is eternal.
There is no such thing as winning.
There is no end to the game.
Even if you compete and win today,
you must compete and win tomorrow.

Kuniyasu Sakai, Chairman Taiyo Kogyo

CONTENTS

Contents

PREFACE

The emergence of the lean enterprise has forever changed the way firms compete. With their adoption of just-in-time (JIT) production, total quality management (TQM), team-based work arrangements, and supportive supplier relations among other things, lean enterprises react much faster than their mass producer counterparts to changes in the competitive environment. These fast reflexes render the sustainable competitive advantages that mass producers have relied on virtually impossible to achieve. Instead, lean enterprises compete by repeatedly creating temporary competitive advantages. Because these enterprises are lean, they can deliver products with higher quality and functionality at lower costs than mass producers, which leads to improved customer satisfaction. These abilities have enabled lean enterprises to dominate many industries.

Because they do not have sustainable competitive advantages, lean enterprises are forced to seek out competition. They adopt a generic strategy of confrontation, that is, they compete head-on by selling equivalent products. When firms compete in this manner, three product-related characteristics play a critical role. These characteristics, known as the survival triplet, have internal and external forms. Internally, they are the product's cost, quality, and functionality. Externally, they are its selling price, quality, and functionality. While the selling prices of products can be disconnected from their costs temporarily, if the firm is to remain profitable in the long run, costs must be brought into line with selling prices.

This book, then, has three primary purposes: to introduce the concept of confrontation strategy, to explain the role of costs in confrontation strategy, and to describe the integrated cost management systems that have emerged in Japanese firms to manage costs across the value chain.

Although cost control is emphasized, this book is not specifically about cost management. Instead, it is about a philosophy of competition. The way in which Japanese firms manage costs is described in depth because it represents the missing piece of the puzzle of how lean enterprises compete. The findings in the book are based upon a five-year, in-depth study of twenty Japanese manufacturing firms. The firms were drawn from a number of different industries and varied in size from very large to quite small. Most were publicly traded, a few were privately owned, and all were lean.

In-depth interviews in English, with translator support as appropriate, were held with three to twelve individuals in each firm, including managers, design and manufacturing engineers, and blue-collar workers. Job titles ranged from general manager of product planning to manager of corporate planning to chief engineer to senior manager of group accounting. Copious notes and tape recordings of the interviews were used to prepare research cases of approximately 5,000 words each. The contact manager in each firm was then asked to review the cases. The cases were used as the basis for this book once the managers were satisfied that the cases were factually correct. It was the cumulative insights gained from all twenty companies that led me to derive the theory of confrontation and to understand the critical role played by integrated quality, functionality, and cost management systems.

Firms that want to compete in a confrontational environment must develop the systems, organizational context, and culture that are required to support the aggressive management of the survival triplet. It is critical that managers in these firms realize that all three (systems, organizational context, and culture) are necessary and must be in harmony for the successful adoption of confrontation strategy. To achieve this, firms must begin to integrate total quality management, product development, and cost management systems. While the integration of the three subsystems into a coherent program to manage the survival triplet will consume considerable resources, it is still necessary for firms to create the right organizational context through the development of self-directed work groups that are committed to a confrontation strategy. Without the commitment of its workforce, a firm will never develop the ability to manage the survival triplet aggressively. The key point is that firms must learn to view the process of managing the survival triplet as a total systems solution, not a collection of independent techniques either across characteristics of the survival triplet or within them. This, then, is the central message of this book:

> In industries in which lean enterprises are becoming dominant, only those firms that adopt a confrontation strategy *and* aggressively manage the survival triplet will survive.

Robin Cooper
Claremont, California, and Pointe Aux Barques, Michigan

ACKNOWLEDGMENTS

This book would not have been possible without the extensive commitment of a large number of individuals in different organizations. First and foremost, I owe an incalculable debt to the twenty Japanese firms and all of the people within them that gave so freely of their time. It is impossible to say how many individuals in those firms (some of whom I never even met) provided input to the research, but the number exceeds well over 150. To those individuals I give my warmest thanks. To give some idea of the effort required on their part it should be noted that a total of eighty-five days was spent visiting the companies. When the cases were written, over 1,500 outstanding questions had to be answered. At the end of the project, only seven remained unanswered and none of these were important. Every case was read at least three times and corrections and suggestions made after each reading. These suggestions helped to ensure the accuracy of the cases and the richness of my understanding of Japanese practice. I would particularly like to thank Toshiro Shimoyama, chairman and CEO of Olympus Optical Co., Ltd., for spending considerable time with me discussing the theory of the confrontation strategy.

I greatly thank Professor Takeo Yoshikawa of Yokohama National University who co-authored the cases on Isuzu Motors, Ltd.; Yokohama Corp., Ltd.; Kamakura Iron Works Co., Ltd.; and Nippon Kayaku. I would also like to thank those who were actively involved in the process of writing the book, Kathleen Gumbleton, Nilubol (Ni) Haruathaivijitchock, Saori Takahashi, Sarah Conner, Elizabeth (Liz) Stillman, and my secretaries Elizabeth Rowe and Juliene Hunter. Each provided unflagging energy to keep the project on course. Kathy worked with me for over a year as a research associate and kept me under control during the most hectic parts of the writing project. She provided many important suggestions that helped to shape this book. Ni and Saori kept control of all of the cases and ensured that the version that finally appeared in the book was the latest one. This was no small accomplishment as the twenty-three were rewritten at least partially five times while the book was being written. Sarah, a case editor at Harvard Business School case services, performed the invaluable and near endless task of editing over 700 pages of cases and teaching notes. Liz, a doctoral student at Claremont, voluntarily spent her pregnancy reading all of the material written and providing valuable feedback and endless encouragement. Elizabeth and Juliene kept the rest of the world off my back as much as possible for the seventeen months of writing. Without them, the project would have taken much longer.

The third set of individuals who gave me support was the reviewers. These included Shannon Anderson, Peter Drucker, Marc Epstein, Peter Fahquar, Karen Higgins, Norika Kameda, Robert Kaplan, Joseph Maciarello, and Cecily Raiborn. In addition, several members of Monitor Corporation, including Mark Fuller and Bruce Chew, provided feedback on the entire manuscript and the confrontation strategy in particular. The feedback that all of these individuals, particularly Cecily, gave me was invaluable in shaping the manuscript.

Clearly, this book could not have come about without the help of the institutions that supported the research. The first three years of the project were supported by the Harvard Business School's Division of Research. The last two years were supported by the Institute of U.S./Japanese Relations in the World Economy and the Claremont Graduate School. This was an extremely expensive undertaking, and I hope that all three institutions consider their money well spent.

Next, I would like to thank the people at the Harvard Business School Press. I owe a large debt to Carol Franco, who told me in our first conversation that I was wrong about the way I wanted to structure the book. She was right. The nature of this book is a direct outcome of that first discussion, and her expert judgement has helped immeasurably in shaping this book. I also want to thank her for the way in which she patiently listened to my cries of anguish and excitement during the eighteen months that it took to complete the manuscript. And, I want to acknowledge all the other people at HBS Press who have worked so hard to make this book a success.

Finally, I would like to thank my family for their support. I spent a total of eight trips—seventeen weeks—in Japan to complete this project. These absences placed a significant extra load on all of the members of the Cooper family. None of them complained about the trips, and all greeted me with loving enthusiasm when I returned. In addition, two summers (and the year in-between) were spent writing the book. I will never forget my children repeatedly asking me why I was working so hard on vacation. It was difficult to explain to them the excitement that drove me, and I can only hope that as they grow older they too will come to understand the unique challenge of research.

Last and by no means least, I want to thank my wife, Helen, for her never-ending belief in my ability to complete the "Japan project." Without her love, I would never have had the courage to write this book.

WHEN LEAN ENTERPRISES COLLIDE

PART ONE

COMPETING UNDER CONFRONTATION

Competition has become a treadmill of exhaustion from which there appears to be no escape.

Toshiro Shimoyama, Chairman and CEO
Olympus Optical Co., Ltd.

INTRODUCTION

There have been two major revolutions in manufacturing in the twentieth century. The first was the development of **mass production,** best exemplified by Henry Ford's Model T, and the second was the development of **lean production** by Toyota. Although it took both innovations only ten years to evolve and mature—mass production from approximately 1915 to 1925 and lean production from 1951 to 1961—their spread to other countries and industries occurred more slowly. Indeed, it is possible to identify firms that are lean but have yet to adopt all of the practices of lean production.

The slow spread of these innovations made subsequent changes in the competitive environment appear to be independent of the changes in production philosophy. Firms that adopted one or the other of the innovations saw the nature of competition shift only as other firms in the industry changed their production philosophy. This lag between the adoption of an innovation and a change in the competitive environment allowed managers to identify other reasons for the intensified competition they faced. New theories of competition emerged to describe how to compete in the new environment, but these theories did not identify the change in production philosophy as the primary driving force behind the new order. Thus, the slow spread of these innovations obfuscated the results of their adoption—change in the nature of competition. Mass producers compete differently from craft producers; lean producers compete differently from mass producers.

Before Henry Ford introduced mass production, the automobile industry was dominated by craft producers who sold their products at high prices with high quality and functionality. These firms were natural differentiators. Each firm had its own particular "look," and given the long design process, it was unusual for customers to shop around. With the introduction of mass production, however, Ford made it possible to produce a car at a low cost compared to the costs of craft producers. Because they could not match Ford's cost, craft producers directed their products toward upper-class customers, while Ford's mass-produced vehicles were designed for middle-class customers. Since the products were designed for different market segments, there was no competition. The firms that eventually emerged to compete with Ford, in particular General Motors, were forced to adopt their own versions of mass production. Even then, however, they could not match Ford's cost advantage. Thus, they were forced to find other ways to compete. Real competition emerged only when General Motors began to compete on the basis of functionality at prices close to Ford's. As more firms became effective mass producers, competition in the automobile industry shifted from competition between craft producers to competition between mass producers.

The competitive environment of mass producers supports the generic strategies of cost leadership and product differentiation. Both of these strategies are based upon the assumption that a firm can develop and sustain competitive advantages and, therefore, can avoid competition. By developing a sustainable cost advantage, the cost leader is able to offer products that are low in price and functionality. In essence, the cost leader avoids competition by saying, "Do not compete with me. If you do, I will drop prices even lower and render you unprofitable." In contrast, product differentiators develop sustainable advantages in product development. They offer products that have higher functionality but sell at higher prices. Thus, product differentiators develop unique products or services that closely satisfy customers' requirements. In essence, they isolate a section of the main market and state, "This is my territory. I am so good at what I do that attempting to compete with me is pointless."

In theory, then, cost leadership and product differentiation strategies in their pure forms create zones of no competition.

Consequently, it is unusual to see the best firms in an industry dominated by mass producers engaged in head-on competition. It is only the firms that are stuck in the middle that engage in this form of competition. These firms compete head-on because they have no sustainable competitive advantage and, therefore, cannot create barriers to competition. The only exception to this rule occurs when one firm decides that it can benefit from changing the status quo of the market. In order to gain market share, this firm will purposely enter into head-on competition with the best firms in the industry. Once the firm either has achieved its objective or has failed to do so, it returns to protecting the status quo. Thus, head-on competition is a transitory state for the best firms in the mass production era.

With the emergence and spread of lean production, the competitive environment has undergone a slow, steady transformation from competition between mass producers to competition between lean producers. Before managers can determine how their firms should evolve over the next decade, they need to understand that lean enterprises do not compete in the same way as mass producers. Unlike occasional head-on competition between mass producers, head-on competition between lean producers is continuous. Competition between these enterprises is based upon the assumption that sustainable product-related competitive advantages are unlikely to be developed. Since, in the eyes of these firms, there is no mechanism to avoid competition, they confront it and compete head-on. Confrontation is necessary because the reaction time of lean enterprises is fast enough to render product-related competitive advantages too fleeting to be sustainable. There is not enough time to educate the customer to the positive attributes of the new product before other firms have me-too versions. This difference in the attitude of lean producers toward competition renders many of the lessons learned about competition between mass producers obsolete.

All of the examples in this book are drawn from Japan. Japanese firms were chosen because they have extensive experience with competition between lean enterprises. This experience has given them time to develop and mature the systems they use to compete in a confrontational mode. If lean enterprises do compete using confrontational strategies rather than avoidance-based generic strategies, Western firms will be forced in increasing numbers to adapt to confrontational modes of competition. The insights gained from observing Japanese firms may help these firms adapt to this new form of competition. As noted in the preface, the evidence presented in this book is drawn from a multiyear, in-depth study of twenty Japanese manufacturing firms. Each firm was given several opportunities to review the cases created from the study. Of the twenty companies, nineteen approved at least one case. After reading the first draft of the case, the twentieth firm stated that it gave away too much sensitive material and requested that it not be published. The other nineteen firms approved a total of twenty-three cases. While there is no way to prove that there are no errors, it seems unlikely that any major errors have survived the review process. As a final check, every company was given the opportunity to review the appropriate sections of this book before publication. None found any major errors, all minor errors identified were corrected, and all approved publication. This book was written entirely from the case material and nonfactual insights. All factual evidence not included in the cases either by choice or company request was excluded from the book.

The nineteen firms that approved publication are listed below, and a brief description of each one appears in the Appendix.

Citizen Watch Company, Ltd.
Higashimaru Shoyu Company, Ltd.
Isuzu Motors, Ltd.
Kamakura Iron Works Company, Ltd.
Kirin Brewery Company, Ltd.
Komatsu, Ltd.
Kyocera Corporation
Mitsubishi Kasei Corporation
Nippon Kayaku
Nissan Motor Company, Ltd.
Olympus Optical Company, Ltd.
Shionogi Pharmaceuticals
Sony Corporation
Sumitomo Electric Industries, Ltd.
Taiyo Kogyo Co., Ltd. (The Taiyo Group)

Topcon Corporation
Yamanouchi Pharmaceutical
  Co., Ltd.

Yamatake-Honeywell Com-
  pany, Ltd.
Yokohama Corporation, Ltd.

Firms that adopt a confrontation strategy must become experts at developing low-cost, high-quality products that have the functionality customers demand. The cost, quality, and functionality expertise required for this must be used to form a coherent manufacturing strategy that is based upon developing products with the right level of functionality and quality at the right price. Consequently, firms adopting the confrontation strategy must develop integrated quality, functionality, and cost management systems. It is the integration of these systems that allows many Japanese firms to respond so quickly to changes in economic conditions and to match the innovative products of their competitors. If these systems were stand-alone systems, a fast response rate would not be possible. Unfortunately, in Western literature, the systems that have evolved to manage quality (typically described as "total quality management systems") and functionality (typically described as "time to market systems") have been described in isolation, and the systems that have emerged in Japanese firms to manage costs have almost been ignored. In a world of nonsustainable competitive advantage, however, costs have to be managed both aggressively and intelligently. A firm that fails to reduce costs as rapidly as its competitors will find its profit margins squeezed and its existence threatened. It is no longer enough to say, "Reduce costs by 10 percent across the board." Cost management, like quality, has to become a discipline practiced by virtually every person in the firm. Therefore, overlapping systems that create intense downward pressures on all elements of costs are required.

CHAPTER 1

CONFRONTATION STRATEGY

Imagine a world in which you are forced to compete with four to six technologically equivalent competitors. None of these firms, not even your own, has a sustainable competitive advantage. What would you do? In today's highly competitive environment, sustainable competitive advantages are like Nobel Prizes—extremely rare. They are rare because to achieve a sustainable advantage requires a complex clustering of events that together create an insurmountable barrier to emulation. Obviously, if a firm can see a way to create a sustainable competitive advantage, it should, just as any sensible individual should accept a Nobel Prize if it is offered to him or her. Unfortunately, as the level of competition increases, which it does when lean enterprises compete, it becomes increasingly difficult to maintain such an advantage. The central premise of this book is that when firms compete in a world in which sustainable competitive advantages become virtually impossible to achieve, then firms must stop avoiding competition and confront it.

COST LEADERSHIP, DIFFERENTIATION, COLLUSION, AND CONFRONTATION

There are two generic strategies that rely upon avoiding competition by creating sustainable competitive advantages. These generic strategies are **cost leadership** and **differentiation**. Firms adopt these generic strategies because they provide above average returns if they are successfully applied.

The firm trying to become the lowest cost producer in the

industry is following a cost leadership strategy. The critical advantage of this strategy is the ability to threaten other competitors with a price war if they do not behave. Competition is avoided by threat of retaliation. The cost leader will make above average returns when the other firms in the industry choose to become differentiators because then the cost leader can set prices that enable it to take full advantage of its cost efficiencies. Even if the differentiators fail to differentiate themselves successfully, they will create a price umbrella under which the cost leader can make profits. Thus, it is possible for the cost leader to be profitable in an unprofitable industry.

The firm seeking to create a unique position for itself in its industry is following a differentiation strategy. To be successful, the firm's unique position must be perceived as adding sufficient value to the customer in the form of products and services with higher quality and functionality that the additional costs of differentiation are more than offset by the increased price that the customer is willing to pay for the firm's products. The critical advantage of this strategy is that customers are so satisfied they see no reason to change suppliers. The differentiator makes above average returns when customers are willing to pay high prices for the products and services they receive. By charging more than the additional service costs, the differentiator increases profits.

Western strategic thinking so emphasizes competitive avoidance that it has become codified as strategic portfolio planning. Firms engaged in strategic portfolio planning try to identify their divisions or subsidiaries that have managed to differentiate themselves successfully or have become cost leaders in their industries. In order to create new stars, these firms support nurseries in which fledgling divisions and subsidiaries are protected as they try to develop their own sustainable competitive advantages. Divisions and subsidiaries that fail to create advantages, the "dogs," are either sold or liquidated. Divisions and subsidiaries that have created competitive advantages that are no longer considered sustainable are treated as cash cows. The only other way to avoid competition is to collude with your competitors. Collusion is only successful if all of the competing firms in the industry are willing to subject themselves to some form of central control. In Japan, this form of competition is called *dango* and is practiced in several industries, including construction. For this strategy to work, there must be no free market competitive pressures. For the most part, then, the *dango* strategy only succeeds in markets where there is no foreign competition. The strategy's inherent problem is that it does not foster learning. Firms adopting the *dango* strategy remain inefficient and noncompetitive in the global economy.

A generic strategy that does not rely on avoiding competition is **confrontation.** Firms that adopt a confrontation strategy do not attempt to collude with their competitors nor do they attempt to become cost leaders or differentiators. Instead, they compete head-on for their share of the market by developing and exploiting *temporary* competitive advantages. While they still try to differentiate their products by introducing new features or try to develop a price leadership position by dropping prices, they do not expect such actions to lead to a sustainable competitive advantage. Instead, they assume that their competitors will rapidly bring out products that are equivalent and match any price changes. The experience of Topcon, a Japanese manufacturer of advanced ophthalmic instruments, serves to illustrate the temporary nature of competitive advantages.

> The firm's early investment in the development of optomecha-tronics, a fusion of three separate technologies (advanced optics, electronics, and precision equipment processing), paid off in 1978 with the introduction of six highly successful products that relied heavily upon that technology. . . .
>
> Over the next two years, . . . the firm proceeded to take advantage of its technological lead over its competitors by introducing a steady stream of new products, each more advanced than its predecessor. . . .
>
> Within a few years, new competitors had entered that market; Nidek, Canon, and Nikon. . . . The entry of these three firms dramatically increased the level of competition in the ophthalmic market, which caused prices to fall and profit margins to shrink. By 1992, unless a new product contained significant tech-

nological innovations, adequate profits were extremely difficult to generate. Although each firm jockeyed for technical leadership, they were relatively evenly matched. In the early 1990s, Nidek probably had a slight advantage; however, Topcon did not consider this advantage significant. (Cooper, 1993o, 2–3)

Thus, even though Topcon developed truly revolutionary products, it was unable to sustain a competitive advantage for more than a few years. The critical point is not that firms have lost the ability to differentiate their products but that they have lost the ability to sustain those differences. This inability is evidenced by the rapid return of Topcon's profit margins to historical levels (see Figure 1-1).

The acceptance of the inability to create sustainable product-related competitive advantages leads firms to stop avoiding com-

Figure 1-1
Topcon's Operating Profits as a Percentage of Sales, 1967–1993

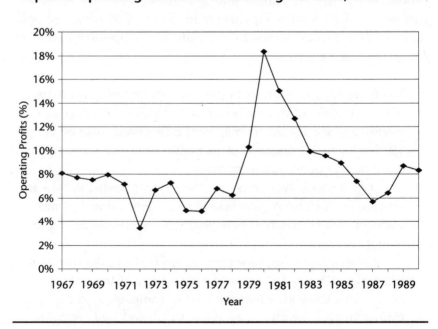

petition. Instead, they adopt a confrontation strategy, which leads invariably to direct, head-on competition. Unfortunately, a confrontation strategy is inherently less profitable than strategies that manage to reduce or avoid competition.

Of course, a firm may use a confrontation strategy for a subset of the market, if there is no overriding benefit from producing both high- and low-end products. A firm might, for example, sell only products below a certain price, leaving other firms to sell the high-end products. This is the way Canon competed for nearly two decades. It followed a confrontation strategy in the low and medium segments of the copier market and left the high-end market to Xerox, which was following a differentiation strategy. As Canon was able to reduce the perceived value of high-end differentiation, it expanded its market. Nor is it necessary for a firm to treat all of its markets in a confrontational style. If a significant technological or other sustainable advantage can be developed, then a differentiation or cost leader strategy may be more profitable. For example, Canon has significant advantage in laser engines for printers and Sony has the same for the lasers used in compact disc players.

Confrontation strategy usually does not allow niche firms (firms that produce goods for a specialized segment of a market) of any significant size to survive. As soon as the niche firm begins to generate decent profits, it attracts the attention of the confrontation firms that then introduce competing products. The niche player has problems surviving because of the scale advantages of the major players. Confrontation strategy not only removes niche players, it actively hinders their emergence. This practice is one of the major reasons that it is so difficult for firms (Western or Japanese) to enter new markets in Japan. Coca-Cola, for example, was able to enter the intensely competitive Japanese soft drink market because of its "niche" product (Coca-Cola) and enormous financial resources. However, to survive, the firm had to adopt a confrontation strategy and all that the strategy involved, including rapid product introduction to produce a "near seamless set of products."

STRATEGY AND THE ROLE OF THE SURVIVAL TRIPLET

Three product-related characteristics, known as the **survival trip-let,** play a critical role in the success of firms that have adopted a confrontation strategy. The survival triplet has an internal form that reflects the perspective of the producer and an external form that reflects the perspective of the customer. Internally, the three characteristics are the product's cost, quality, and functionality. Externally, these characteristics are selling price, perceived quality, and perceived functionality. (For ease of presentation in the rest of the book, the term *cost* will be used if the phenomenon being discussed is internal to the firm; if the phenomenon is external to the firm, the term *price* will be used for the cost-price charac-teristic.) While the selling prices of products can be disconnected from costs temporarily, if the firm is to remain profitable in the long run, costs must be brought into line with selling prices. Therefore, the survival triplet can be better represented as cost-price, quality, and functionality (see Figure 1-2). Here, cost-price is used to represent the long-term relationship between cost and price.

In the survival triplet, price is defined as the amount at which

Figure 1-2
The Survival Triplet

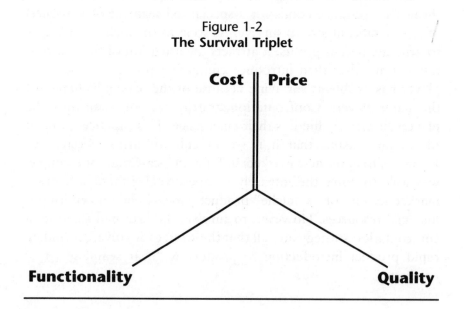

the product is sold in the marketplace in arm's-length transactions. In the highly competitive markets in which most Japanese firms compete, selling prices are set by the market, and cost is the value of the resources consumed to get the product into the hands of the customer. Cost includes all investment costs (such as research and development), all production costs, and all marketing and selling costs. Unlike price, it is not set externally but, like quality and functionality, has to be managed.

Quality is defined as performance to specifications, and functionality is defined by the specifications of the product. This definition of quality is more narrow than the definition often used in literature on quality, in which quality is defined to include the ability to design a product that meets customer requirements (quality of design). This more narrow definition allows quality and functionality to be treated as two separate characteristics.

Functionality is not a single dimension but rather multidimensional. Therefore, it is possible to differentiate products according to their functionality even when their prices and quality are identical. This ability allows a firm to compete using the functionality characteristic in three ways. It can, for example, differentiate its products vertically by accelerating the rate at which increased functionality is introduced. Olympus reduced the time it took to design a camera from ten years for the OM10 to eighteen months for a compact camera. Alternatively, a firm can differentiate its products horizontally by satisfying customers' preferences or taste, as opposed to offering increased functionality at increased prices. For example, one camera might have a 200 mm zoom lens but no antired eye flash while another might have a 150 mm zoom lens and an antired eye flash. Both products sell at the same price but attract different customers. Finally, a firm can change the nature of the functionality. Caterpillar competes by defining functionality as a complete solution to earth-moving problems, while Komatsu defines it as the functional ability of their bulldozers. This different view of functionality has allowed Caterpillar to outperform Komatsu in recent years.

When a firm competes using the survival triplet, it may find it beneficial to decompose functionality into a number of characteristics. That is, the firm may want to differentiate between the fundamental functionality of the product (for example, the ability of a bulldozer to move earth) and the service functionality (for example, the ability to guarantee forty-eight-hour delivery of spare parts anywhere in the world). These two dimensions can be called *product focus* and *customer focus*. Such a differentiation will permit a richer modeling of the competitive environment, allowing management to better understand the nature of the competition they face.

For the purposes of this book, however, the survival n-tuplet is kept as simple as possible (i.e., as a triplet) because it allows its role to be clearly illustrated. Splitting functionality into more than one dimension is less helpful in the explication of the general theory than it may appear at first. For one thing, the part breakdown of functionality will vary by firm and will be dependent upon a number of factors, including the nature of the product and the strategy the firm is following. For another thing, it is difficult to graph more than three dimensions. Keeping to three dimensions allows the survival zones to be graphed and understood. After all, the survival triplet is an intellectual construct, not an attempt to model reality. It gains its effectiveness through its simplicity.

The term *product* is used in two ways within the survival triplet. When describing events in current time it is the physical item that is sold. When describing future events it is the generations of products launched over time. In a discussion of Nissan, for example, the product may be the Nissan Sentra model that is currently sold by the firm or it may be the future stream of Sentra models that will be sold by the firm. The second use of the term allows the survival triplet to be modeled over time. For example, the second generation of a product may sell at the same price and have an identical quality level but provide the customer with higher functionality (see Figure 1-3). It is often expedient simply to plot one characteristic over time (see Figure 1-4).

The willingness of the customer to make trade-offs among the characteristics that make up the survival triplet defines a product's survival zone. For example, a customer may be willing to pay more for a product that has higher quality and functionality than for

Figure 1-3
**The Survival Triplet over Time
(Three-Dimensional View)**

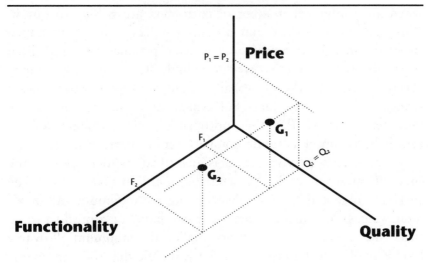

Figure 1-4
Functionality against Time

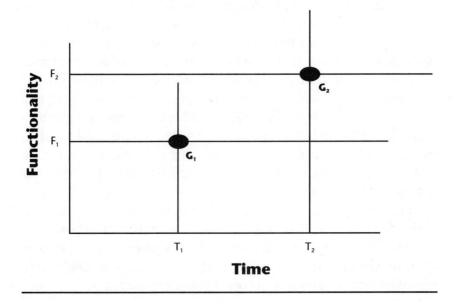

another product that costs less. A product is inside its survival zone when its continued production is justified by the number of customers who are willing to buy it; it is outside the survival zone when an insufficient number of customers are willing to buy it. Although each product that a firm sells has a uniquely shaped survival zone, most products in a given product line, and often most product lines in a product family, have similarly shaped survival zones. This similarity allows the development of coherent strategies for these products. Survival zones are important because they determine whether the appropriate generic strategy for the firm is based upon avoiding competition or confronting it.

A product's survival zone is identified by determining the **survival range** for each characteristic in the survival triplet. The survival range is defined by determining the minimum and maximum values that each characteristic can have for a product to be successful. For quality and functionality, the **minimum allowable level** is the lowest value of each characteristic that the customer is willing to accept regardless of the values of the other two characteristics. Below a certain level of functionality, for example, few customers are willing to buy a product no matter how low the price or high the quality.

The **maximum feasible values** for quality and functionality are determined by the capabilities of the firm. The maximum values are the highest values that the firm can achieve without inducing significant penalties in the other characteristics. For example, above a certain functionality level, products will have quality problems and will need to be priced excessively to make adequate profits. Low quality and high prices will result in too few customers being willing to buy the products. The maximum feasible value, then, represents the highest value that the characteristic can have with respect to the other two characteristics and still have the customer purchase the product.

The price characteristic is slightly different from the other two in that the customer determines the **maximum allowable price** and the firm determines the **minimum feasible price**. The maximum allowable price is the highest price the customer is willing to pay regardless of the values of the other two characteristics. The minimum feasible price is the lowest price the firm is willing to accept for the product if it is at its minimum allowable quality and functionality levels. While the customer views the critical characteristic as price, the firm views it as cost. The **minimum acceptable profit** at any price level transforms cost to price.

The survival zone is the volume created by connecting the three minimum values and three maximum values together. It is useful to plot the survival triplet of a product by assigning each characteristic to a separate coordinate. This permits the survival ranges for each characteristic to be plotted (see Figure 1-5).

Cost leadership and differentiation strategies are successful when the survival zone for a firm's products are large. Large survival zones occur when the difference between the minimum and maximum ranges is significant for at least two of the characteristics (see Figure 1-6). Confrontation strategies are successful when the survival zones are all small (see Figure 1-7).

As the gap between the minimum and maximum levels widens, the ability of firms to create distinguishable products that have high values on one characteristic and low values on the others increases. When the gap becomes large enough, firms must choose to compete on either the price characteristic or the other two

Figure 1-5
The Survival Zone

Figure 1-6
The Survival Zones of the Cost Leader and Differentiators

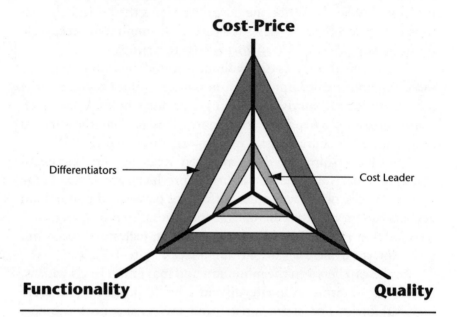

Figure 1-7
A Confrontational Survival Zone

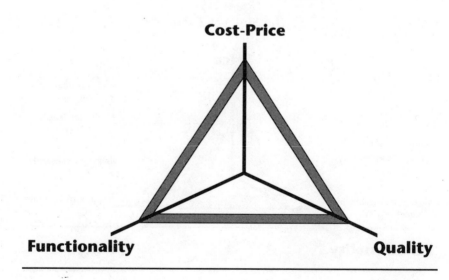

characteristics. Firms competing on the price characteristic are vying for a cost leadership position, while firms competing on functionality and quality characteristics have adopted differentiation strategies.

Firms successfully achieve cost leadership and differentiation strategies when they have developed sustainable competitive advantages for a significant portion of the products they sell. It is not possible to become a cost leader by simply being more efficient at manufacturing a single product nor is it possible for a firm to be considered a differentiator if only a few of its products are unique. Thus while the survival triplet operates at the individual product level, it is the cumulative effect of how the firm positions itself product by product that creates the generic strategy. Once enough products have achieved cost leadership or have been differentiated, the firm can create its market position in the eyes of its customers.

In this case, the survival ranges for all three characteristics are too small to support cost leadership and differentiation strategies. Firms attempting to establish cost leadership positions discover that they are forced to violate the acceptable minimums values for quality and functionality. Firms attempting to increase the quality and functionality of their products to differentiate them discover that the allowable values on cost-price are being violated. Finally, collusion strategies are adopted when the survival zone is large and competitors can be disciplined not to shrink it through independent actions.

Time is a critical component of the survival triplet. While all three characteristics have a time-based coefficient—the rate at which they can be improved relative to other competitors—the only one that is separately named is the time-based aspect of functionality, which is often called time-based competition. In terms of the survival triplet, time-based competition (fast cycle time) accelerates the rate of introduction of new functionality. Time-based competition is the rate at which functionality can be improved—a critical prerequisite for competition based upon product functionality—while time to market determines how rapidly the product can be introduced. While time-based competition and time to market are related, they are not the same.

The rate of change for one characteristic can affect the rate of change for other characteristics. By rapidly increasing product functionality, for example, it is sometimes possible to decrease the rate at which price reductions occur. On the other hand, by increasing the rate of price reduction, it is sometimes possible to slow the rate at which functionality has to be increased. Under confrontation strategy, the challenge is to increase the rate at which the three characteristics of the firm's products are changing (in the hope of leaving at least one competitor behind) without overshooting customer requirements or becoming unprofitable.

SURVIVAL ZONES AND THE AUTOMOBILE INDUSTRY

Using the language of the survival triplet, it is possible to explore how changes in the position and shape of survival zones of products have affected the nature of competition in the automobile industry. Before mass production, the automobile industry was dominated by craft producers who sold custom-built cars specifically designed to satisfy the customer. These firms were natural differentiators because each had its own particular look, and customers rarely shopped around. The survival zones of the products produced by these firms were relatively large; firms had to give the customer what he or she wanted. While there was some degree of freedom on price, there was little on quality and functionality (see Figure 1-8). No firm had the ability to produce an automobile with adequate quality and functionality at such a low price that customers would make trade-offs among the characteristics of the survival triplet. In more formal language, there was no cost leader.

With the introduction of mass production, Henry Ford made it possible to produce a car with acceptable levels of quality and functionality at a cost much lower than the costs of craft producers. However, his mass-produced vehicles were not aimed at the same market segment as the craft-produced vehicles. Ford developed a completely new market. While craft producers were after upper-class customers, Ford was after middle-class customers. Since the cars were designed for different market segments, there

Figure 1-8
The Survival Zone of the Craft Producers

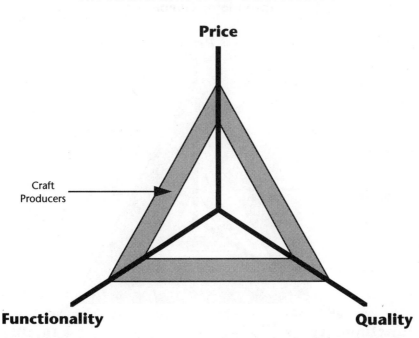

was no true competition between Ford and the craft producers. If the survival zones of the two types of vehicles are drawn on the same diagram (see Figure 1-9), the lack of competition is obvious. The two survival zones do not overlap at any point, indicating no competition between Ford and the other firms.

Real competition required the emergence of General Motors (GM). Recognizing that he could not compete head-on with Ford successfully, Alfred P. Sloan, GM's president, adopted the generic strategy of differentiation and began to compete on the basis of functionality rather than price (see Figure 1-10). Sloan achieved this objective through vertical product differentiation, i.e., by producing "a product for every purse" (Sloan 1963, 63). This strategy had two effects. First, it allowed the type of automobile owned to become a status symbol, which Ford, with only the Model T, could not do. Second, because prices were close to those of the Model T, it offered customers choices.

Figure 1-9
**The Survival Zones of the Craft Producers and
Ford Motor Company**

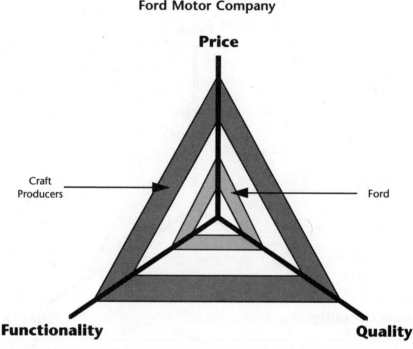

Craft
Producers

Ford

Price

Functionality

Quality

In theory, Ford could have remained the cost leader, forcing GM to occupy the differentiator position, if the firm had increased the functionality of the Model T at an adequate rate. However, Ford made a critical mistake and failed to do so. Over time, the gap in functionality between the lowest cost GM car and the Model T became too large. Customers became unwilling to sacrifice the functionality GM offered just to save money. In more formal terms, the survival zone of the cost leader collapsed, and the Model T fell outside its survival zone (see Figure 1-11). The result was a massive loss of market share for Ford, which it has never fully regained.

As GM, Ford, and other major manufacturers used vertical product differentiation to increase both their market reach and market share, they began to satisfy customers at higher and higher prices by introducing luxury models. This step forced the remain-

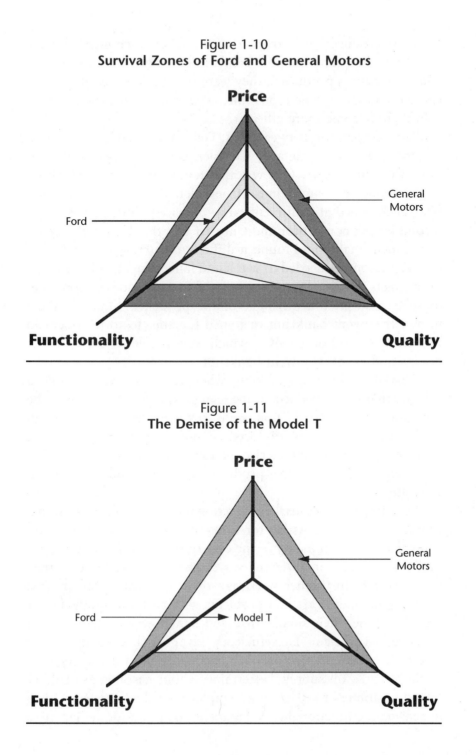

Figure 1-10
Survival Zones of Ford and General Motors

Figure 1-11
The Demise of the Model T

ing craft producers to retreat to even higher price niches, where they were, in effect, trapped. While these niches were too low in volume for mass producers, they were profitable for craft producers, who adopted, where possible, aspects of mass production to help them become more efficient.

The competition between GM, Ford, and other major American manufacturers, primarily Chrysler, continued in this vein for more than fifty years. GM was the dominant competitor with a large number of named lines (Chevrolet, Pontiac, and Oldsmobile), each aimed at a different range of price points. Ford was the second largest competitor and Chrysler was the third. Other firms were much smaller and found it difficult to survive as they lacked the deep resources needed to withstand failed models, a large range of products to spread the risk of model failure, and the economies of scale associated with high-volume products. Many of these firms either went bankrupt or joined together to form American Motors Corporation (AMC), which was unable to overcome its origins and eventually went bankrupt.

This situation changed only when the Japanese introduced vehicles that were produced using lean production techniques. The Japanese produced cars that were lower in cost and higher in quality than their mass-produced counterparts (see Figure 1-12). In the functionality characteristic, these cars were not different but equivalent. Therefore, mass producers and lean producers were in competition.

Because, as noted earlier, functionality is a multidimensional characteristic, it is possible for firms to launch products that are equivalent in functionality in the eyes of the customer but achieve that functionality in different ways. For example, because they were made from thinner steel than their American counterparts, the early Japanese cars had problems with rust and safety, but at the same time, their smaller size and lighter weight helped them be more fuel efficient. This efficiency advantage became important as OPEC gained control over the production of a major segment of the world's oil supply. Uncertainty about gasoline availability forced customers to place more emphasis on fuel efficiency, thus increasing the functionality of Japanese cars (without the Japanese

Figure 1-12
The Survival Zones of Mass Producers and Lean Producers

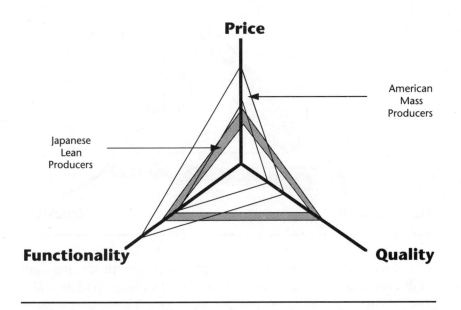

having to do anything). For the next few years, American firms expended considerable energy closing the quality gap. In contrast, Japanese firms spent their energy on increasing functionality (see Figure 1-13). As they pulled ahead on functionality and maintained their lead on price and quality, their products began to dominate those of American firms.

Customer loyalty and different product ranges protected mass producers from certain extinction, even though the products produced by the lean enterprises were superior in all regards to those made by the mass producers. Customer loyalty thus creates a region of relaxation in the survival zone of the product (see Figure 1-14). Such regions allow a firm to sell products that are technically outside their survival zones and still be profitable. However, relaxation regions are best viewed as temporary safety blankets as they typically disappear once a firm is forced to rely upon them.

The different product ranges of American mass producers

Figure 1-13
The Evolution of Japanese Automakers Survival Zones over Time

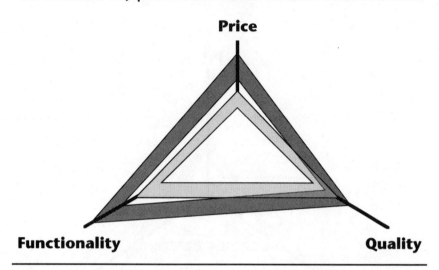

Price

Functionality   **Quality**

offered some protection because the Japanese were producing only small cars and not competing in medium and large vehicles. The Japanese market was dominated by small cars. Therefore Japanese firms had to gain reasonable market penetration and reputation in the American small-car market before they could begin to move into large vehicles. Once they had developed their reputation, they could afford to launch ever more upscale models and challenge the entire American market. Fortunately for American firms, by this time they, themselves, had become sufficiently lean to be able to produce cars that were either at or close to parity with their Japanese counterparts.

The final chapter in the story of the evolution of competition in the automobile industry involves the craft producers that remained in the industry. The ability of the lean enterprise to make products economically at lower volumes than a mass producer allowed the Japanese to compete with the craft producers for their niches. Firms such as Mercedes and BMW are now forced to confront the Lexus and Infiniti class of automobiles. Although brand names will offer some protection for a while, they will not provide a sustainable competitive advantage over the long run.

Figure 1-14
The Role of Brand Loyalty

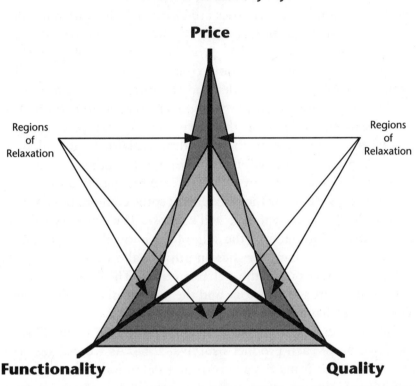

Price

Regions
of
Relaxation

Regions
of
Relaxation

Functionality

Quality

The evolution of competition in the automobile industry high-lights several important lessons about competing using the survival triplet. First, if the survival zones of two products do not overlap, the products will not compete with each other because they are designed to satisfy different market segments. Second, if the two survival zones overlap on one characteristic but not the other two, the products will not be in competition as long as each product is superior to the other on one of the other characteristics of the survival triplet. Again, the products are designed to satisfy differ-ent market segments. If, however, the survival zones overlap on two characteristics, the story is more complex. If the product that is superior on the third characteristic is sufficiently different in at least one of the other characteristics that customers can differentiate between the products along that characteristic, the two products will not be in competition. If, however, the differences in the two overlapping characteristics are insufficient for differentiation, the two survival zones will collapse into one. The collapsing of survival zones indicates that products that were not in direct competition previously are now competing with each other. For example, while the cost leader and the differentiators are not in direct competition, they are in indirect competition. If the cost leader can either increase the price gap or narrow the quality and/or functionality gap, then the differentiators' survival zones will collapse and they will risk failure. On the other hand, if one or more differentiators can either increase the quality and/or functionality gap or narrow the price gap of some combination thereof, the cost leader's survival zone will collapse. The new survival zone will be defined initially by the sum of the allowable ranges on the two overlapping characteristics and by the allowable range of the superior product on the third characteristic. The superior product will be inside its survival zone and the inferior one will be outside. This is what happened to the Model T.

Indirect competition plays an important role in establishing the position of each product's survival zone. As we will see later, many Japanese firms have very broad definitions of competitive products (Olympus views portable compact disc players as competitive products because they vie for the same money in the customer's pocket). Thus, five major factors shape the position of a product's survival zone: customer preferences; the differential ability to manage the survival zones of the firm; competitors; so-called noncompetitors in the same industry; and finally, competitors for the same funds. Firms must remain alert to changes in the survival zones of products that directly and indirectly compete with them.

MANAGING THE SURVIVAL TRIPLET UNDER A CONFRONTATION STRATEGY

Under a confrontation strategy, it is not necessary or advisable to expend equal effort on all three characteristics of the survival triplet. One characteristic usually dominates the other two, and the most important characteristic of the survival triplet to the firm's customers, and hence to the firm, frequently changes over time. When the Japanese economy went into severe recession in the early 1990s, many Japanese firms changed their most important characteristic from functionality to cost. The 1992 Toyota Annual Report, for example, made the following observation:

> If Toyota does one thing better than other automakers, it is cost management. After earning a reputation for quality and fuel efficiency in the "economy models," we moved successfully into upscale models, like the Lexus line. But we still pride ourselves in the cost competitiveness of our products in every price stratum. The history of Toyota is a story of unceasing efforts to reduce costs. (Toyota Motor Corporation 1992, 5–6)

The key to success, then, lies in selecting the appropriate rate of improvement for each characteristic. In a market where the customer is demanding increased functionality and is willing to pay for it, for example, the most important characteristic is functionality. The firm that can increase the functionality of its products fastest (subject to cost-price and quality constraints) will develop a temporary competitive advantage.

Unfortunately, many Western managers have failed to understand the role of the survival triplet in confrontation strategy and have adopted a rallying call of highest quality, lowest cost, and first to market. No firm can reasonably expect to be number one in all three elements of the survival triplet. Any firm that actually achieved this distinction would dominate its competitors. Indeed, if it could sustain this advantage, it would become a monopoly because all of its competitors would be bankrupt. Western firms have adopted this "best in all three" approach because they have encountered Japanese competitors that are superior to them on all three counts. Therefore, to survive, these firms have had to improve simultaneously on all three characteristics. The resulting struggle for survival has caused many Western managers to lose sight of the critical fact that in most markets one element of the triplet is more important than the others. Once a product is inside its survival zone, the firm no longer has to improve its performance along all three elements. Instead, it has to learn to compete intelligently and to select the rate at which it increases its performance on each element of the survival triplet.

Failure to manage the survival triplet correctly risks expending too much effort on one element of the triplet and not enough on the others. At the limit, the firm will fall outside the survival zone because it is too good at one or more characteristics. A firm is too good at a characteristic of the survival triplet when its customers no longer derive benefit from the improvements. When a firm is too good at one characteristic, it will be unable to remain in the survival zone for at least one of the other characteristics. The critical point is that being too good is often as bad as being not good enough. There is evidence that many Japanese firms have fallen into this trap. Nissan, for example, is reducing its product diversity because it is not getting adequate returns from all of its products.

It is difficult to determine when a firm is too good along a characteristic of the triplet. In the camera market, for example, functionality is the critical element in the survival triplet. As part of its strategy to get its products back inside their survival zones, Olympus was increasing the number of products it produced to increase its market share. But if a firm launches so many products that the customer has trouble differentiating between them or is unwilling to pay for the costs of the extra complexity associated with product proliferation, then no competitive advantage has been derived from additional product proliferation.

To manage the survival triplet under confrontation strategy, firms must develop integrated quality, functionality, and cost management systems. These systems must be so flexible that when the most important characteristic changes, only the amount of effort placed in increasing the rate of change of the characteristics is modified, not the systems themselves. For example, when faced with both the recession and the increased value of the yen compared to the dollar, Isuzu dramatically increased the number of engineers dedicated to cost reduction but it did not change the way it managed quality or functionality.

SUMMARY

In today's business environment, many firms seek to create sustainable competitive advantages as a means of avoiding competition. There are two generic competition avoidance strategies, cost leadership and differentiation. The cost leader, by becoming the low-cost producer, creates a price barrier; the differentiator, by satisfying its customers through developing unique products, creates a satisfaction barrier. Unfortunately, both of these strategies rely on the creation of sustainable competitive advantages. When such advantages cannot be achieved, firms are forced to adopt a third generic strategy, confrontation, in which they confront competition by creating a stream of temporary competitive advantages.

Three product-related characteristics known as the survival triplet (cost-price, quality, and functionality) play a critical role in determining how firms compete. Each characteristic has maximum and minimum values, and the range between the two identifies the survival zone of a product. The survival zone, then, indicates the values of each characteristic that a product must possess if it is to succeed. Products that fall outside their survival zones simply do not sell. Few customers, for example, will accept a product with very low quality and functionality, irrespective of its price. As the level of competition increases, survival zones shrink and eventually become too small to support both cost leader and differentiator strategies. In essence, the survival zones of the cost leader and the differentiator collapse into a single survival zone in which confrontation is unavoidable.

Competition thus becomes a fight either to shift the position of the survival zones of the firm's products, thereby gaining temporary competitive advantage, or to ensure that the firm's products remain inside their survival zones, thereby avoiding giving an advantage to competitors. A firm can shift the position of a survival zone by increasing the rate at which it improves one or more characteristic of the survival triplet. If it can move the position of the survival zone quickly enough, the equivalent products of the firm's competitors will fall outside of the zone. Once outside the survival zone, the competitor's product will fail, forcing the competitor to catch up or go out of business. Given that all competing firms are trying to shift the survival zone in their own favor, the firm must remain alert to movement and try to ensure that none of its products fall outside their zones.

Firms that have adopted a confrontational strategy must determine which characteristic of the survival triplet they view as the most critical to their competitive success. It is not sufficient—it is, in fact, harmful—to try to be the best at all three. Rather, it is wise to select one characteristic at which to excel while ensuring that the other two remain inside their survival zones.

Chapter 2

Why Japanese Firms Adopted Confrontation Strategy

Two factors help to explain the early adoption of confrontation strategy in Japan: the emergence of the lean enterprise and the role that it played in shaping competition in the Japanese economy, and the existence of mechanisms for rapid technology diffusion that make it virtually impossible for firms to develop a sustainable technological advantage among competitors (see Figure 2-1).

The Emergence of the Lean Enterprise and a New Competitive Environment

The origins of the lean enterprise lie in the Japanese automobile industry, which was subjected to severe capital rationing during the early 1950s and was too small to support mass production.

Figure 2-1
Factors Leading to the Emergence of the Confrontation Strategy

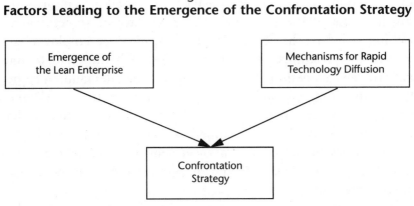

Thus, while American and European firms were well financed and produced vehicles in high volumes using a great deal of expensive equipment, the Japanese industry was forced to find ways to produce automobiles in small volumes using far less equipment. Toyota was the first to solve the capital scarcity problem by reducing set-up times from days to minutes. The reduced set-up times allowed the company to mass produce automobiles on a limited number of presses. Once set-up times could be measured in minutes, small-batch production became economically feasible. However, small-batch production created other problems, or, as it turned out, opportunities.

The small batch sizes led naturally to reduced parts inventories, which led to two additional innovations. First, while Western firms could simply scrap a defective batch and pull another one from their large parts inventories, Toyota was forced to run another batch. This frequently brought the assembly line to a halt until the part was available. As a result, there was great pressure to improve quality and reduce the number of defective parts produced. Thus, the attention to quality, a critical part of the lean enterprise, emerged naturally, culminating in the introduction of total quality management (TQM) and zero defects (ZD) programs.

Clearly, reducing defects to the required level demanded an extremely skilled and highly motivated workforce. The Japanese tradition of lifetime employment contracts made Toyota's management more than willing to invest in its workforce. This willingness coupled with a key aspect of Japanese culture—the unwillingness of the Japanese worker to "accept something for nothing"—led to the second innovation, effective employee empowerment programs. Because the unions felt they had to find ways to "give something back" to Toyota when demanding higher wages, the firm was able to tie compensation to performance evaluation through bonuses. ZD programs provided the mechanisms for employees to give something back in return for higher wages. Successful employee empowerment was crucial to the success of the TQM, ZD, and other programs that enabled the lean enterprise to emerge.

Because the new production system could not cope with either large surges or troughs in total demand or abrupt shifts in demand among products that utilized different equipment, the dealers (and eventually customers) were drawn into the organization, and the customer orientation that is a hallmark of the lean enterprise came into being. The dealers' role was expanded to include active management of sales volumes. Dealers would exert considerable additional effort to sell cars in slump periods. To reduce swings in sales demand, it became important to produce products that satisfied the customer. Thus, knowing customer preferences became critical. The important point is that setting out to satisfy customers did not lead to the lean enterprise. Rather, the pressure to satisfy the customer emerged naturally as part of the lean enterprise.

Other elements of lean production evolved either through the constraints placed on the Japanese automobile industry or through the outcome of the adoption of JIT and TQM. From start to finish, the evolution of the lean enterprise was rapid; within ten years, it had become the dominant organizational form for the Japanese automobile industry. As other manufacturers discovered that lean producers could manufacture products in lower volumes more quickly and with higher quality than mass producers and then pass the savings on to customers through lower prices, the lean enterprise spread to other sectors, including service sectors, of the Japanese economy. The gradual spread of the lean enterprise throughout the world suggests that in many sectors of the economy it is becoming the dominant organizational form and will presumably replace mass production to approximately the same extent that mass production replaced craft production.

It was the emergence of the lean enterprise that shaped the competitive environment in Japan. Instead of accepting quality levels that had defects in the parts per hundreds, firms began to compete on quality levels that were measured in the parts per thousands and then per millions. As quality and JIT programs reduced costs, prices began to fall and thus became a critical competitive issue. Customers who were used to accepting high priced, lower quality, "vanilla" functionality products were suddenly exposed to lower price products that not only were higher in quality but also had more "flavors."

Japanese customers reacted to these improvements in quality, price, and functionality by aggressively demanding more. These demands caused Japanese firms to become engaged in an intense competitive battle. The existence of four to six equivalent competitors has shifted the power to the customer. To keep their customers satisfied Japanese firms were forced to match each of their competitors' moves, making the confrontation strategy an exhausting treadmill of continuous product development.

MECHANISMS FOR RAPID TECHNOLOGY DIFFUSION

There are six mechanisms (see Figure 2-2) within the lean enterprise system and Japanese society as a whole that ensure the efficient transfer of technology between competitors and thus make it difficult, if not impossible, to create sustainable competitive advantages through technology. Some mechanisms work only when the Japanese industry is developing and foreign competition is seen as a greater threat than domestic competition. These mechanisms involve direct information sharing among Japanese

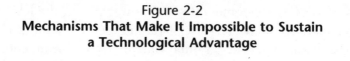

Figure 2-2
Mechanisms That Make It Impossible to Sustain
a Technological Advantage

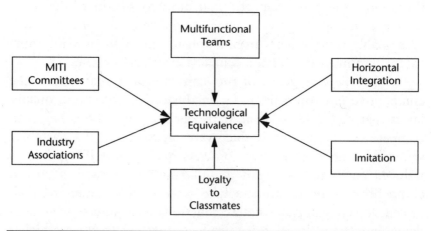

competitors, and as Japanese firms gain global dominance, they usually lose their effectiveness.

Multifunctional Teams

In the lean enterprise, new product development is undertaken by large, multifunctional teams. These teams are made up of representatives internally from engineering, production, marketing, and externally from suppliers and subcontractors. Although they play an important role in designing products that satisfy customer requirements, the teams tend to create their own barriers to extreme innovation. Before a new concept can be implemented, it must first be accepted by the design team. Natural conservatism makes it difficult for extreme innovations to be accepted, and therefore, incremental changes tend to dominate. Four forces cause these incremental changes to be similar among competitors. First, each firm in the industry is trying to satisfy the same set of customers. Second, the engineers who drive the design process have similar educational backgrounds and therefore tend to solve problems in similar ways. Third, using tear down and other value engineering techniques, teams study competitors' products and borrow ideas from them. Fourth, teams have access to the same technical sources. Consequently there is a natural tendency for firms to develop products using the same technology and hence having similar functionality.

Usually when one firm introduces a "revolutionary" product, its competitors already have equivalent products under development. By speeding up the introduction of their version of the new product, these competitors can significantly reduce the gap between the launch of a "revolutionary" product and its me-too equivalents. Only when the product can catch all of its competitors by surprise does the gap between the introduction of the new product and the appearance of its me-too equivalents become extensive. Sony's introduction of the Walkman came as such a surprise to its competitors that it took over twelve months for the first competitive product to appear on the market, a phenomenon that usually occurred within just a few short months in the Japanese consumer electronics industry.

Horizontal Integration

Japanese firms have extended relationships with their suppliers to facilitate continuous innovation and rapid adjustment to changes in demand. The interaction among firms with well-established horizontal linkages increases the diffusion of new technologies through the encouragement of cooperative arrangements that require extensive information sharing across firm boundaries.

The information sharing includes research and development and product innovation. At Nissan, for example, "parts suppliers were asked to generate cost reduction ideas. An incentive plan was used to motivate the suppliers. For example, if an idea was accepted, the supplier that suggested the cost reduction idea would be awarded a significant percentage of the contract for that component for a specified time period, say 50 percent for 12 months" (Cooper 1994i, 6). Nissan then communicates the supplier's improvements to the competitors of the innovating supplier, which would adopt the innovation and share it with their suppliers and customers. Since many of Nissan's suppliers also supply other major automobile manufacturers, innovation soon spread throughout the industry and beyond.

Imitation

The willingness of Japanese firms to imitate their suppliers and competitors also encourages the diffusion of technological innovations. In Confucian philosophy it is considered honorable to imitate and an honor to be imitated. In Japan's ancient form of teaching, the *sensei,* or master, would teach his students by demonstration, and the students would copy the master exactly until they gained the requisite skill to become master in their own right. This type of teaching still influences Japanese society, and with the availability of mass media, it is now possible for significant innovations to spread rapidly. For example, the price control system at Higashimaru Shoyu Co., Ltd., has been documented and imitated by Kirin Brewery Co., Ltd., among others. In a similar fashion, both the Taiyo system and the Isuzu (which subsequently became the Japanese) tear down approach were publicized and adopted throughout Japan.

Loyalty to Classmates

Another societal mechanism that leads to technology diffusion is the intense loyalty that engineers feel toward their classmates. Under Confucian philosophy, loyalty to classmates (like brothers) is as strong as loyalty to the company. When classmates get together after graduation (a common occurrence in Japan), they discuss freely what they are doing and the major achievements of their firms. This informal interaction makes it virtually impossible for a single firm to create and sustain a technological advantage. While the head of engineering at Olympus disputed the current importance of this mechanism in the Japanese camera industry, he agreed that it had played an important role when the Japanese industry was forming.

Industry Associations

Industry associations are an additional mechanism that helps to transfer technologies between firms. While some of these associations are funded by the Ministry of International Trade and Industry (MITI), others are made up of private groups of interested firms. One of the major purposes of these associations is to hold workshops where information is exchanged freely. Associations such as the Japan Productivity Center hold tours to other countries, including the United States, during which competitors travel together and write reports on their observations. Because competitors share information as they write their reports, these associations and tours act as technology diffusion mechanisms.

MITI Committees

Formal MITI committees constitute the final major mechanism that facilitates the diffusion of technology in Japan. Often, MITI identifies technologies that will become critical to a major industry.

If MITI believes that the effort required to develop a technology is greater than a single firm can support, it creates a committee from the major competitors in that industry. The creation of a committee signals the importance of that technology and the direction in which it should probably go. MITI committees bring together some of the best technical minds in the industry. This technological sharing ensures that even if one of the firms makes a technological breakthrough, the others will not be far behind. It was a MITI committee formed from five of Japan's six largest chipmakers that helped to design the VLSI (very large scale integration) chip (Borrus 1988, 97).

MITI committees, industry associations, and classmate loyalty have become less effective at diffusing technology as Japanese firms have begun to dominate internationally the industry in which they are competing. When this has occurred, the firms involved have become less willing to share information. Industry Associations, for example, no longer act as agents of technology transfer and training but as agents of coordination, education, and training. MITI joint development projects now provide industries with direction rather than technology. Consequently, they no longer attract the "top minds" of the participating firms. Instead, these individuals remain inside the firm, running the research projects that utilize that technology.

HOW THE TWO FACTORS AFFECTED COMPETITION

The role of the two factors that led to the adoption of the confrontation strategy can now be explored in terms of the survival zones of products. The emergence of the lean enterprise moved the minimum allowable values and the maximum achievable values for quality and functionality outward. At the same time, it decreased the minimum achievable cost, which led to a decrease in the minimum acceptable and maximum allowable selling price (see Figure 2-3). Finally, the mechanisms for technology diffusion kept the functionality of competitive products relatively similar. This similarity further narrowed the range of allowable product cost-price, functionality, and quality characteristics (see Figure 2-4).

Figure 2-3
Effects of Lean Production

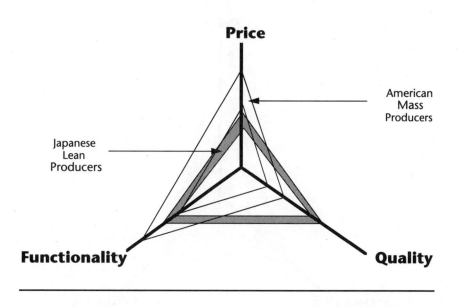

These factors affected the survival zones of various products because they affected each characteristic of the survival triplet. In many Japanese firms, successful TQM programs increased the maximum achievable levels for the quality characteristic that any additional improvements were unlikely to be considered of value to the customer. When defects are measured in parts per million, individual customers are unlikely to encounter defects, let alone detect improvements in the defect rate! At the same time, the Japanese consumer demanded such a high level of quality that even minimum acceptable levels were high. Consequently, the survival range for the quality characteristic was extremely small for most products, and quality became a hygiene factor that could be ignored as long as it was under control. This did not mean that firms abandoned TQM programs or efforts to improve quality. Quality enhancements resulted in internal benefits, including the ability to reduce additional workers from the line, faster introduction of the next generation of technology, and reduced costs.

Figure 2-4
Effect of Rapid Technology Diffusion

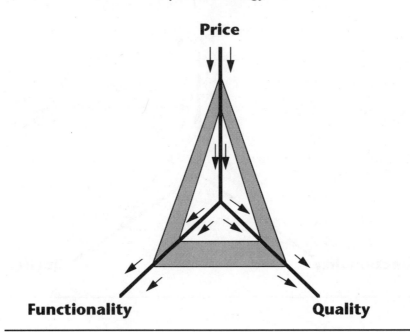

The mechanisms that diffuse technology resulted in a similar contraction in the survival range of the functionality characteristic. These mechanisms made it virtually impossible to achieve sustainable technological advantages. Therefore, the maximum achievable values for the functionality characteristics of competing firms were similar. With its ability to introduce new products rapidly, the lean enterprise made it difficult for a firm to differentiate its products based upon functionality. However, functionality remained critical. To remain profitable a firm had to keep its rate of functional innovation sufficiently rapid that its products remained inside their survival zones.

The emergence of the lean enterprise and the inability to create a sustainable technological advantage led to the contraction of the survival range for the price characteristic. While the lean enterprise structure allowed firms to become more efficient, the push toward a batch size of one and zero defects tended to make each firm use similar manufacturing technology at similar costs. The inability to achieve technological advantage made it difficult for firms to develop products with equivalent functionality at lower costs. The effect of these two factors was a reduction in the survival range for the price characteristic.

As the survival ranges for the three characteristics shrunk, the survival zone became smaller. Eventually, confrontation strategy became the dominant generic strategy for most firms, and the failure to launch products that met customer expectations (i.e., were within their survival zones) led to lost market share, as Olympus Optical, which produces and sells cameras, discovered:

> In the mid-1980s, Olympus' camera business began to lose money and by 1987 its losses were considerable. Top management ascribed these losses to a number of internal and external causes. The major internal causes were poor product planning, a lack of "hit" products, and some quality problems. (Cooper 1994j, 23)

To save its camera business, Olympus' management acted on each of the three characteristics of the survival triplet.

> Olympus' top management reacted to the losses by introducing an ambitious three-year program to "reconstruct" the camera business. At the core of this program were three objectives: first, to recapture lost market share by introducing new products; second, to dramatically improve product quality; and third, to reduce production costs via an aggressive set of cost reduction programs. (Cooper 1994j, 23)

To avoid using confrontation strategy, Japanese firms could have adopted the European model of cartels and simply split the market into segments, each owned by a separate company. If overlapping competition was unavoidable, high prices would ensure adequate profits for all. Why didn't Japanese firms adopt such an approach? The primary reasons were the existence of foreign competition when the Japanese industries matured, which made the *dango* strategy infeasible, and the way in which Japanese workers view their relationship to the firm. Japanese employees tie their self-worth to their company's success to a much greater extent than Western employees do. Japanese workers consider it important to belong to the "best" company, and the "best" company is defined as a firm that has superior products and technology as well as an impressive long-term growth record. Lifetime employment contracts further strengthen the tie between self-worth and company success. Compensation schemes that reward longevity help to reinforce the tie. Employees know that if the firm prospers, so will they. New employees are paid low salaries but know that over the years they will receive seniority raises and eventually will be well paid if the company is the "best."

In the intensely competitive Japanese market, a firm's ability to be the "best" is contingent upon launching successful products. Not being the "best" causes employees to lose face and to question the ability of the firm to provide permanent job security. The desire to be the best and to be associated with the best makes it difficult for cartels and niche competitors to develop. For cartels to form, members have to accept each other's success, but this cannot occur when every member wants to be the best. Niche players are regarded as potentially dangerous competitors because there is the risk that they will emerge from their niche at some time in the future. The intensity of the desire to be a part of the best helps to reinforce the firm's commitment to technology. Yet under confrontation, no firm is the best for long, and thus a natural tension emerges to keep improving the performance of the firm.

SUMMARY

The forces that led Japanese firms to adopt confrontation strategy are numerous but include the emergence of the lean enterprise, the existence of mechanisms for increasing technology transfer among competitors that render it almost impossible for a firm to develop and maintain sustainable competitive advantages through technology alone, and the intense loyalty that Japanese employees feel toward their firm and its success.

The fast reaction times of lean enterprises make product-related competitive advantages too fleeting to consider sustainable. Any advantages one firm achieves are so quickly matched—me-too versions can spring up in only a few months' time—that they do not differentiate the firm in the eyes of its customers. Such rapid competitive matching can dilute first-mover advantages to almost nothing.

In addition, the ability of lean enterprises to make products economically, in smaller batch sizes than can their mass-producer counterparts, opens many of the niches occupied by mass producers to attack. Thus, sustainable competitive advantages that lead to successful niche strategies are also less likely to arise when lean enterprises compete. The fast reaction times and ability to make products economically in small volumes hobble firms' abilities to develop and maintain sustainable competitive advantages.

There are also several mechanisms for rapid technology diffusion that make it almost impossible for firms to develop sustainable technological advantages. Multifunctional teams, horizontal integration, willingness to imitate, loyalty to classmates, and the existence of both industry associations and MITI committees all aid technology transfer between firms, preventing any one competitor from developing a significant technological lead. With all products being virtually equivalent technologically, firms are forced to adopt confrontation strategies.

The final key to the puzzle of why Japanese firms adopted a confrontation strategy lies in the intense loyalty of Japanese workers to their firms and the tying of self-worth to the success of those firms. This makes it difficult for Japanese firms to accept second place. Consequently, all firms strive to be the best at what they are doing, which increases the intensity of competition and forces firms into confrontation.

In terms of the survival triplet, the emergence of the lean enterprise lessened the importance of the price characteristic, which had tended to dominate the other two characteristics under mass production. The ability of the lean enterprise to produce high-quality, high-functionality products at low cost forced firms to compete more aggressively on all three characteristics of the survival triplet. Therefore, firms that adopt a confrontation strategy must carefully manage the value of each of the three characteristics of the survival triplet. Failure to satisfy the customer's requirements for product price, quality, and functionality will cause the product to fall outside its survival zone and fail. Consequently, the management of the survival triplet, the topic of the next chapter, is central to the success of a confrontation strategy.

CHAPTER 3

PRODUCT PLANNING AND STRATEGY UNDER CONFRONTATION

For a firm to be profitable, it must have enough products that are inside their survival zones and that earn sufficient returns to cover both the cost of failed products and to satisfy the firm's profit objectives. This means that managers must be able to anticipate the way in which product survival zones are changing. At most Japanese firms, consumer analysis plays a critical role in helping managers to predict the directions in which survival zones are moving. Many of these firms undertake two types of consumer analysis—short-term and long-term. The short-term analysis helps them to manage the existing product mix by helping them to understand what their customers want today and how their competition is trying to satisfy those demands. The long-term analysis focuses on the changes in customer expectation and is used to help identify potential markets and products. Armed with this information, the firm can manage the product mix of future products. It is not the acts of consumer analysis and long-term planning that differentiate a firm using a confrontation strategy from others. It is the intensity and care with which these processes are undertaken.

PRODUCT PLANNING AND THE SURVIVAL TRIPLET OVER TIME

Short-term consumer analysis allows firms to determine what their customers want now and to ensure, as much as possible, that existing products are within their survival zones. For the most part, today's consumers know the available product offerings and usually purchase only the most technologically advanced products. They are not particularly loyal to a firm and will readily switch brands if the firm does not offer a product they want or if the product is not the best available at the price they want. Therefore to keep and satisfy its customers, a firm must have a variety of products at prices acceptable to consumers. Indeed, it was this need to keep and satisfy its customers that led Olympus to offer a full product line:

> The decision to be full-line producers was based upon two strongly held beliefs: first, that Japanese consumers trade up over time, and second, that only by offering a full line could a firm obtain a balance position in the entire market. A firm trying to compete in only the low end of the market would not have access to the high-end technology that would rapidly come to define the low-end market, and a firm only selling in the high-end would not have the loyalty of consumers who were trading up. (Cooper 1994j, 6)

By designing a full product line, a firm gives its customers minimum reasons to look at competitive offerings and virtually eliminates niche competition. If a gap in the line exists, however, customers will go elsewhere and the firm will have an opportunity to win them back only if the new firm fails to keep them satisfied. Consequently, most firms believe it is unacceptable to leave a hole in the line simply because one product is unprofitable. Since everyone trading up or wishing to buy the missing product will simply switch to another firm, any estimate of profitability must include future profits from subsequent sales to customers who buy the unprofitable products.

To prevent needless product proliferation and ensure that the product line is complete, most firms break their markets into a number of segments, each of which contains a large number of customers. Each segment demands a different primary function or set of functions for the product. At Sony, for example,

> [t]he range of models . . . was designed to strike a balance between profitability and customer service. Too many models would cause production and distribution costs to be too high.

Too few models and too many sales would be lost to competitive products. . . . Walkman executives were convinced that dropping any one of the models would leave a distinct hole in the lineup of the playback category and would cost Sony market share. For example, there were 5 playback models, each of which had a very specific role in establishing the market. The two cheapest models created the market for the most popular model. The other two playback models each had specific properties that satisfied a particular segment of the market: the water-resistant model was used by sports enthusiasts and the auto-repeat model was popular with foreign language students because it allowed them to continuously listen to language tapes. (Cooper 1994l, 5–6)

The number of market segments is kept under control in two ways. First, limits are set on the top and bottom segments that the firm is willing to support. Under this strategy, the firm refuses to sell either very cheap products or very expensive ones. Olympus, for example, will not sell cameras below a given price and no longer sells high-end single lens reflex (SLR) cameras. Instead, it adds functionality to its lowest price cameras and has introduced the highly innovative LS range of SLR cameras rather than trying to compete in the high-end SLR segment. Second, the firm can redesign its products to satisfy a greater number of consumers. Under this strategy, fewer products will satisfy the same range of consumers. Great care has to be taken when a firm does this as the overall degree of customer satisfaction is usually reduced.

As market changes occur, the appropriate number of segments that the firm must support also changes. For some firms, the appropriate number of segments (and, therefore, products) may be reduced. These firms redesign their products to serve a broader segment. For example, Nissan has tried to reduce the number of products it offers while still maintaining adequate coverage by repositioning its products:

The decrease in differences among consumers in the three major markets [Japan, North America, and Europe] reduced the need to develop models specific to a single market. The increased costs associated with launching new models made it difficult to make acceptable profits if the number of new models introduced each year was too large. These trends suggested to Nissan top management that overall profitability would be increased by reducing the number of distinct models supported, while maintaining the same level of effort to design and market the remaining models. (Cooper 1994i, 2)

In contrast, Olympus has increased the number of models it sells in an attempt to gain market share. It believes that it can better satisfy its customer if it offers them an even greater choice:

Olympus' decision to introduce multiple models for some price points . . . was prompted by the observation that market share associated with some price points was considerably larger than others. For high-volume price points, it was possible to identify different clusters of consumer preferences and profitably to produce and market cameras designed specifically for those clusters. Under this new strategy, the number of models introduced at each price point was roughly proportional to the size of the market. (Cooper 1994j, 6)

Thus, Olympus uses both vertical and horizontal product differentiation to gain market share. Vertical differentiation is achieved by designing products with a much higher functionality than previously possible, for example, a compact camera with a wide-range zoom lens. This increased functionality allows the firm to create new prices. Horizontal differentiation is achieved by designing cameras with different types of functionality at the same price. The net effect of this product proliferation is to increase overall customer satisfaction through a better matching of customer preferences with product functionality. This strategy is illustrated in Figure 3-1.

The decision to change the product mix is a complex one, and there may be disagreements within the firm over the need to increase, decrease, or leave alone the product line. Too many

Figure 3-1
Olympus Camera's Vertical and Horizontal
Differentiation Strategy

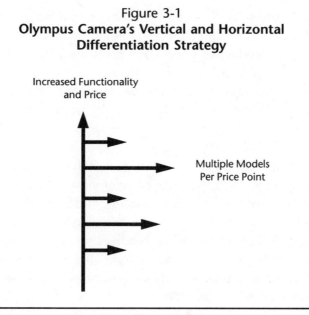

products may lead to customer dissatisfaction as customers who are faced with too many choices find it difficult to understand the range of choices and therefore to choose the "best" product. At Sony, for example,

> [in] the early 1990s, the slowdown in worldwide sales of consumer electronic products had created pressure . . . to reduce its overall product offering. In particular, Morita, Sony's chairman, had argued that Sony should reduce the number of its product variations as well as extending their life expectancies. This pressure created problems for Walkman executives because they felt that there was no way to effectively reduce the current product offering. (Cooper 1994l, 5)

It is the task of long-term product planners to anticipate changes in the way in which consumers view product offerings and to ensure that future products satisfy customers when they are launched. In other words, these planners anticipate changes in the position of the survival zones of products and design new products accordingly. Since the functionality of products must be modified as customer preferences change, the way in which customers view a product offering has a profound effect on the firm's product plan and hence on its strategy.

In the automobile industry, the way in which consumers view their cars changes every decade or so. As an executive at Nissan described it:

> [T]he US consumers in the 1950s viewed the automobile as a status symbol, using the make of automobile they owned to signal the level of their economic success. Nissan executives characterized the consumer in this era as "keeping up with the Joneses." As automobile ownership became more widespread, consumers began to view their automobiles as making a statement about who they were. Nissan executives characterized the consumer of this era as "doing his or her own thing." Consumer demand of the 1960s required more variations and a broader range of model types than in the 1950s. As the 1960s closed and individualism became less important, consumers came to view their automobiles as making statements about *what* they were. Nissan executives characterized this era as being dominated by a desire for a "consistency of lifestyle," i.e., bankers wanted automobiles that were appropriate for bankers. This shift required that more models and variations be produced to satisfy consumer demand. During the 1980s, consumers started to demand automobiles that suited multiple lifestyles. As one executive summed up the transition, "the old segmentation that assumed a single lifestyle no longer worked; we now have to design cars that allow people to be bankers by day and punk rockers at night." (Cooper 1994i, 1–2)

Until recently, these changes have caused Nissan to increase the range of its product offerings in order to keep its customers satisfied and remain competitive. In the last several years, however, the high cost of product introduction has forced Nissan to reduce the number of different models that it produces. The unavoidable outcome of this constraint is that some customers are dissatisfied with the firm's product offerings and go to other firms. Nissan's challenge, then, is to minimize the loss of market share by identifying a future product mix that will satisfy the maximum number of customers. The firm does this through careful analysis of its customers' future requirements:

> New models were conceptualized by identifying consumer "mind-sets." Mind-sets captured characteristics of the way consumers viewed themselves in relation to their cars. These mind-sets could be used to identify design attributes that consumers took into account when purchasing a new car. . . . By identifying clusters of these mind-sets, Nissan could identify niches that contained a sufficient percentage of the automobile-purchasing public to warrant introducing a model specifically tailored for that niche. . . . As a Nissan marketing executive commented, "If we believe that a sufficient market will exist in four to five years, then we will develop a model to fit it." Thus, each model and its body shape variations, such as sedan, coupe, hatchback, and wagon, was specifically designed to satisfy a different group of consumers. (Cooper 1994i, 3)

Mind-sets focus on the price and functionality dimensions of the survival triplet. For Nissan, quality levels are sufficiently high that improving them is no longer critical to the success of products. As long as Nissan's high level of quality can be maintained, then quality can be essentially ignored from a competitive perspective.

As a second step in ensuring that its future product offerings satisfy the largest number of customers possible, Nissan carefully reviews all of the vehicles that it intends to sell in the future:

> First, the designers identified the mixture of models that Nissan expected to sell over the next ten years. This mix was described in a matrix of vehicles by major market and body type (e.g., coupe or sedan). The matrix contained qualitative information about each model, such as its price range, target customers and their income levels, and the range of body types supported. (Cooper 1994i, 3)

The product matrix, which is the basis of Nissan's long-term product plan, is used to guide the development of new products. The product plan typically covers a five- to ten-year period, which includes two to three generations of products and captures the long-term product strategy of the firm.

Olympus employs a similar approach but has modified it to match the realities of its competitive environment. The firm uses a five-year (as opposed to ten-year) product plan to support the achievement of its long-term profit objective. Olympus has developed a shorter planning horizon than Nissan because the development and total product life cycles of its products are shorter (eighteen months and nine months, respectively) than those of Nissan's. Like the development of Nissan's plan, the development of Olympus' product plan involves a wide variety of information and a great deal of consumer analysis: "The information required to develop this plan came from six sources: Olympus' corporate plan, a technology review, an analysis of the general business environment, quantitative information about camera sales, qualitative information about consumer trends, and an analysis of the competitive environment" (Cooper 1994j, 3). The wide array of information sources highlights the importance that Olympus attaches to product planning (see Figure 3-2). The firm's recent turnaround has been predicated upon better product planning, and to improve its ability to plan, the firm has increased both the scope and quantity of the information that it collects and analyzes. The corporate plan plays a clearly identified central role in guiding the product plan: "The corporate plan, which was developed by Olympus' senior management, identified the future mix of business by major product line, the desired profitability of the corporation and each division, and the role of each major product line in establishing the overall image of the firm" (Cooper 1994j, 3).

Continuous innovation of technology, especially proprietary technology, is critical if Olympus is to maintain a functionality advantage. For example, developing "small in size" as a distinctive feature allowed Olympus to introduce the Stylus, a highly successful tiny compact camera. Firms, such as Olympus, locked into functionality-driven markets must compete by creating products

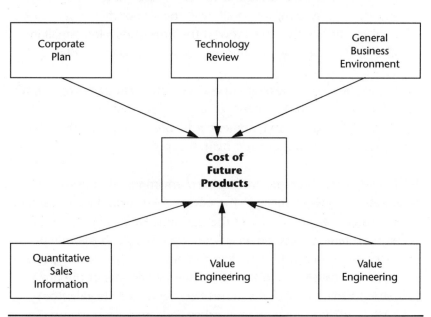

Figure 3-2
Olympus' Product Planning System

with distinctive features. While these features do not create permanently differentiated products, they do create temporary, first-mover advantages for the firm. To identify zones of technological advantage, then, Olympus spends considerable effort on technological reviews, which are fed into the product plan:

> The technology review was composed of two sections. The first consisted of a survey of how current and future technological developments were likely to affect the camera business. For example, digital image processing was reaching the stage where electronic still cameras were rapidly becoming both technically and economically feasible replacements for conventional cameras that relied upon chemical film for image capture. Olympus was in the forefront of electronic still image capture and in 1990 had introduced its first electronic camera. The second part of the review sought to determine whether Olympus had developed any proprietary technology that could be used for competi-

tive advantage. For instance, Olympus had developed an advanced electronic shutter unit that combined auto-focus control and the lens system, which allowed the size of the camera to be smaller. This shutter unit allowed the firm to develop "small in size" as a distinctive feature of its cameras. (Cooper 1994j, 3–4)

In addition to technological reviews, the firm performs sophisticated environmental reviews that are designed to capture how the general business environment and the 35mm camera market are expected to change in the near future:

The analysis of the general business environment consisted of estimates of how changes in the environment would affect camera sales and the profitability of the business. Factors included foreign exchange rates, how cameras were sold, and the role of other consumer products. How cameras were sold was especially critical, because during the 1980s the percentage of the firm's cameras sold via specialty stores had decreased steadily from 70% to 40%. . . . The role of other consumer products was important because some of them competed for the same segment of the consumer's disposable income. . . .

Quantitative information about the world's 35mm camera market was collected from three primary sources. The first was export and domestic market statistics for cameras published by Japan's Ministry of International Trade and Industry. . . . The second, published by the Japan Camera Industry Association, was statistics on camera industry shipments that captured the number of units and dollar value of each type of camera shipped from the manufacturers to each major overseas market (e.g., the United States and Europe). The third source consisted of third-party surveys, commissioned by Olympus, of retail sales by type of camera in each major market. (Cooper 1994j, 4)

The analyses of the general business and 35mm markets provide a background against which the changing tastes of consumers can be evaluated. To increase its understanding of changing consumer preferences and the impact of those changes on the survival zones of its products, Olympus undertakes several forms of consumer analyses:

> First, Olympus collected questionnaires from recent purchasers of Olympus cameras. . . . Second, group interviews were conducted by survey firms two to three times a year in each of the major markets to spot changes in consumer preferences for cameras. Third, surveys were conducted in Roppongi, the trendy fashion center of Tokyo; historically, these interviews had proven to be good predictors of future changes in the lifestyle of the Japanese population as a whole. Fourth, professional photographers were interviewed to provide insights into both the leading edge of camera design and ways to improve the ease-of-use of compact cameras. Fifth, camera dealers were interviewed by the Olympus sales force. In addition, Olympus helped pay the salaries of "special salespeople" who worked behind the counters at very large camera stores. These individuals supplied Olympus with feedback about how their cameras were being received by consumers compared to competitive offerings. Sixth, members of the product planning staff would spend some part of the year behind the counter selling cameras, thus becoming familiar with the reactions of both consumers and dealers. Finally, members of the planning staff would attend industry fairs and conventions to obtain additional feedback on industry trends. (Cooper 1994j, 4)

Figure 3-3 illustrates how this information is used to create Olympus' overall consumer analysis (see Figure 3-3). These wide-ranging qualitative analyses are critical if Olympus is to estimate changes in the positions of its products' survival zones. To survive under confrontation, Olympus must not only identify these changes before they occur but also react to them in a timely manner.

Since the products that competitors introduce have a profound effect on the shape of the survival zones of Olympus' products, the firm expends considerable effort trying to obtain information about its competitors' product plans:

Figure 3-3
Olympus' Consumer Analysis

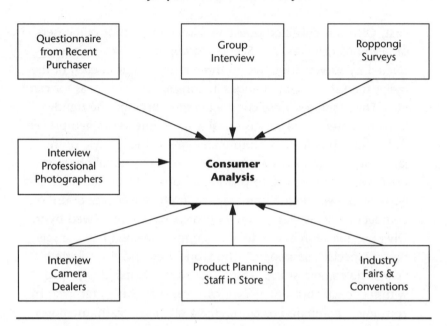

The competitive analysis was based upon any information Olympus could gather about its competitors' current and future product plans. Sources of competitive information included press and competitor announcements, patent filings, and articles in patent publications. This information was used to predict what types of products competitors would introduce in the short and long terms, and what their marketing plans were. (Cooper 1994j, 4)

To make the firm more responsive to customer demands but ensure that it does not try to satisfy its customers by relying too heavily on new technologies and not enough on modifying existing technologies, a department in sales and marketing integrates all of the collected information and creates the product plan. Overreliance on technology is one of the risks faced by firms that view functionality as the most critical dimension of the survival triplet. For these firms, the equilibrium between sales and marketing, research and development, and production is critical. Therefore, Olympus carefully reviews the product plan:

> [T]he purpose of the product plan review was to balance the demands of a consumer-oriented market with the realities of research and development and production. . . . Twice a year, the individuals in the firm responsible for worldwide marketing met with the product planners to ensure that proposed products could be successfully sold in all of the world's major markets. (Cooper 1994j, 5)

Both Nissan and Olympus, then, have developed sophisticated mechanisms to monitor how the survival triplet is evolving over time and incorporate the information from these mechanisms into their product planning.

THE IMPACT OF PLANNING ON STRATEGY

Because the product plan identifies future products, it plays a central role in tying together the firm's strategy and the survival triplet. For example, in a firm's long-term sales plan, which is a component of the product plan, expected product prices reflect the firm's efforts to manage prices. Research and development expenditures and the magnitude of the other costs associated with the rate of new product introduction reflect how aggressively a firm is managing functionality. The degree to which a firm decides to improve quality (if at all) is captured in the cost of total quality programs and in the cost of manufacturing through the reduction in defects and interruptions.

The profit planning procedures at Komatsu illustrate how long-term plans are used to provide strategic directions.

> The process of profit planning began with the development of the firm's long-term plan, which consisted of the sales, production, and product development plans. This long-term plan provided strategic direction to the corporation for the next 5 to 10 years. It was updated from time to time to reflect current condi-

tions and any changes in anticipated future conditions. (Cooper 1994f, 2)

Figures 3-4a and 3-4b illustrate Komatsu's planning process.

The creation of the long-term plan begins when Komatsu's corporate planning and control department submits a preliminary plan to the firm's board of directors, which must approve it: "The development of the long-term plan began with the preparation of a preliminary long-term plan by the corporate planning and control department. This preliminary plan was submitted to the board of directors for approval" (Cooper 1994f, 2). Once the plan is

Figure 3-4a
Komatsu's Planning System

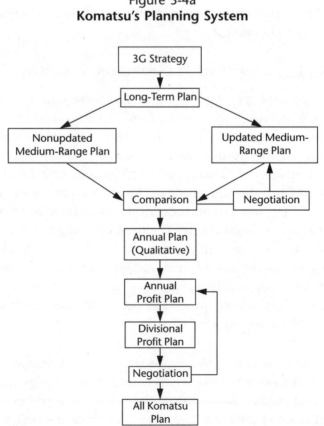

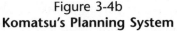

Figure 3-4b
Komatsu's Planning System

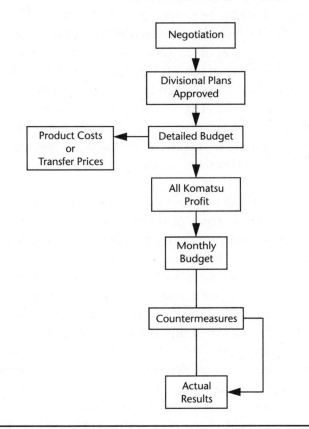

accepted, each division prepares its own long-term profit plan. The corporate planning and control department coordinates the development of divisional plans to ensure that they support the preliminary long-term plan. Negotiations between the board and the corporate planning and control department and between individual divisions and the corporate planning and control department ensure that the long-term plans reflect the corporate strategy. These negotiations are necessary to confirm the validity of the overall corporate plan and to begin the process of binding the divisions to their individual plans.

Acknowledging the difficulties associated with planning accurately for a five-to-ten-year period, firms supplemented their long-term plans with medium- and short-range plans. Komatsu, for example, has adopted a long-term strategy of growth, globalization, and group diversification, known as "the firm's 3G strategy." The growth objective requires all divisions to expand aggressively. Sales in 1995 are expected to reach ¥1.4 trillion. The globalization objective is to achieve worldwide production by the year 2000. The group diversification objective centers on aggressively developing three new business areas: electronics, plastics, and robotics. All nonconstruction products including products in these three areas are to account for 50 percent of group revenues by the year 2000.

Medium-range plans cover a period between three and five years and reflect a firm's current medium-range strategy. A medium-range strategy is a rallying device that is used to help focus the entire workforce on certain specific strategic objectives. To support its medium-range strategy, Komatsu develops two sets of medium-range plans. These plans play different, but complimentary, roles. The first set of plans captures the current medium-range strategy. This plan is not updated and does not reflect changes in the competitive environment. Instead, it acts as a benchmark against which to measure actual performance. The closer actual performance comes to the plan, the nearer the firm is to achieving its medium-range strategy. The second set of medium-range plans is updated to reflect changes in the competitive environment. The purpose of these plans is to predict as accurately as possible the future profitability of the firm and to provide achievable targets for each division. The difference between the two sets of plans captures how far the firm has strayed from its original medium-range, three-year plan. When the three years covered by the medium-range strategy are over, a new medium-range strategy is developed and two new medium-range plans are prepared and the process repeated. While medium-range strategies are usually specified over a three-year period, they are often rolled over, and the objectives are updated for the next three years.

Short-range plans are more detailed versions of the first year of the firm's medium-range plans. They are working budgets that are prepared either annually or semiannually and capture the short-term objectives of the firm. Short-range plans and medium-range plans are integrated so that achieving the short-range plan is the first step toward achieving the medium-range plan. At Komatsu, the annual company policy (strategy) is developed from the 3G strategy. The corporate planning and control department then converts the policy from qualitative to quantitative terms:

> After discussion about the implications of the annual company policy, the corporate planning and control department prepared the firm's annual profit plan. This plan identified Komatsu's profit objective for the year. The acceptance of the annual profit plan by the board of directors initiated the preparation of the annual divisional profit plans. These plans were developed using sales and cost targets prepared by the sales and production departments. (Cooper 1994f, 2)

The process is more iterative than described here. There is, for instance, a considerable amount of informal interaction between the corporate planning and control department and the various divisions in estimating the numbers put forth in the profit plan. Acceptance of the annual profit plan is the first step toward generating the final divisional profit plans. This step involves bringing the divisional preliminary plans, which were developed in response to the planning and control department's need for numbers, into line with the authorized annual profit plan for the company as a whole:

> The divisional profit plans were the basis of negotiations between headquarters and the divisions regarding production and sales volume. From these negotiations emerged the sales and production plans for each division. . . . The plans were combined to produce the preliminary divisional cost plans. The aggregation of the divisional sales and preliminary cost plans produced the all-Komatsu sales plan and a preliminary profit esti-

mate. This estimate was compared to the target profit of the annual profit plan, and after a period of negotiations, the divisional
plans were approved by the board. (Cooper 1994f, 2)

Negotiation throughout the process acts to fine-tune the profit and
other plans of both the firm as a whole and the separate divisions.
These negotiations also serve as mechanisms for strengthening the
divisional managers' commitment to the plans.

As the short-range planning process approaches completion,
the plan, or budget, becomes more detailed and deals with smaller
sections of the firm. Divisional plans shift from an annual to a
monthly basis and from a department to a product orientation:
"execution plans were monthly profit and loss plans that were
used as a benchmark against which to evaluate divisional performance" (Cooper 1994f, 2). Changes to the numbers at this stage
are small as they reflect minor corrections to the divisional plans
that have been identified by the development of more detailed
monthly plans and budgets as well as any changes in the competitive environment that have emerged since the plan was approved:

Actual sales revenue, sales quantities, and costs were compared
to their execution plan equivalents on a monthly basis. Two reports were prepared for the board. The first report identified
profit differences and the second analyzed in detail the reasons
for the difference between actual and expected performance.
Significant differences between actual and expected performance triggered the development of secondary plans, or countermeasures, as they were known. These countermeasures were
designed to ensure that profit and sales shortfalls were as small
as possible. (Cooper 1994e, 3)

The countermeasures are specific recommendations to increase
profits by stimulating sales. Their aim is to minimize both profit
and sales shortfalls. Because profits are difficult to sustain without
the underlying sales, the level of sales is considered almost as
important as profits.

SUMMARY

To remain profitable, firms must ensure that products they produce fall inside their survival zones. Given the central role of the survival zone in determining the success of a product, then, it is not surprising that firms expend considerable energy on consumer analysis. Many firms undertake two types of consumer analysis: short-term and long-term. Short-term analysis helps firms to understand what customers want today and how the competition is trying to satisfy these demands. This type of analysis helps "pull" the firm in the right direction. Long-term analysis focuses on changes in customer expectations. It is used to help firms identify potential markets and products. This type of analysis helps "push" the firm in the right direction.

The types of consumer analysis undertaken by a firm depends on the nature of the product and the rate at which consumer preferences change over time. At firms such as Nissan and Olympus, the rate of change is fast. Therefore, both firms spend considerable energy trying to guess future trends. In contrast, at Komatsu, the rate of change is slow, so less energy is spent on customer analysis and more upon internal projects.

Long-term planning is critical if the firm's overall product offerings are to be successful. The product plan, which identifies the future products of the firm, plays a central role in tying together the firm's strategy and the survival triplet. It is not the act of long-term planning, but the intensity and care with which it undertakes the long-term planning process that differentiates a firm adopting a confrontation strategy from other firms. The range of data fed into a firm's product planning process is considerable and includes information from focus groups, surveys, and assignments that enable product engineers to directly interact with customers so that they can better understand how customer preferences are changing. Competitive offerings and products that are likely to compete for the money in the customers' pockets are also considered.

Typical long-term planning horizons are often three times the life cycle of the firm's products. These plans, therefore, include existing products and their planned replacements. Because it is difficult to plan accurately over such long time periods, many firms develop medium- and short-range plans to support their long-range ones. These plans are designed to support the strategy reflected in the long-term plans.

Medium-range plans usually cover three to five years and are particularly important in conveying strategic messages that are used to shape the growth of the firm and draw attention to specific objectives. Short-range plans usually cover one year or six months and provide targets that each division and group must strive to achieve. While there is a high degree of top-down management, all plans are set through an extended negotiation process. The primary objective of the negotiations is to find ways to achieve the long-term goal and the current year's goal. To ensure that the annual plan is met, monthly analysis is undertaken. If deviations from the plan are identified and are unfavorable, considerable effort is expended to try to ensure that the plan is met. The interlocking sets of plans help firms to maintain profitability in highly competitive markets. Starting with the long-term plan and working to the short-term plan means that short-term actions can be viewed in light of a broader long-term perspective.

CHAPTER 4

CONFRONTATIONAL COMPETITION

Firms adopt the generic strategy of confrontation when they are competing in markets in which the survival zones of the products are small. Small survival zones make it impossible for the generic avoidance strategies of cost leadership and differentiation to emerge. Once a firm has adopted the generic strategy of confrontation, it must decide how to operationalize that strategy.

The way in which a firm operationalizes the strategy is determined by the way in which the survival zones of its products change over time. When customers demand products with ever-increasing functionality, for example, then the minimum allowable level for functionality increases over time. Firms competing in this market must increase the functionality of their products continuously or risk falling outside their survival zones. In contrast, if customers demand lower prices but not increased functionality, then the firm must expend considerable effort on cost reduction but not on functionality enhancement as the failure to reduce costs will cause the products, and thus the firm, to become unprofitable. By examining how firms using a confrontation strategy compete with each other, we can gain an understanding of how the changing shape of the survival zone over time affects a firm's strategy and the role that the survival triplet plays in the formation of that strategy.

OPERATIONALIZING THE STRATEGY

The exact shape of each product's survival zone is determined by the impact of the interaction of competitive pressures and customer expectations on the survival triplet. Coherent strategies emerge when the survival zones for all the products in a group are changing shape in similar ways. For Olympus, the survival zone of a given camera at any moment in time has almost no latitude on price, some latitude on functionality, and little latitude on quality (see Figure 4-1). Price has no latitude because cameras are sold at price points that are defined by the market. In 1991, for example, "the simplest compact cameras were sold in the United States at the $100 price point. The actual selling prices for a given camera varied depending upon the distribution channel (e.g., mass merchandiser versus specialty store). Thus, cameras at the $100 price point would sell for between approximately $85 and $125" (Cooper 1994j, 5). Trying to sell a camera at the wrong price point leads to virtually no sales or to losses because production costs are too high.

Some latitude on functionality is allowed throughout the de-

Figure 4-1
The Survival Zone of a Camera

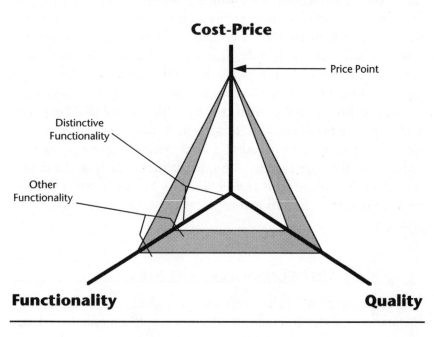

velopment cycle of a new product because the price point at which a camera is sold is determined by a single distinctive feature, such as the magnification capability of the zoom lens or the camera's small size. Therefore, other camera features can be modified if the cost of a new camera is too high for the firm to achieve its desired level of profitability (Cooper 1994j).

The firm bases its long-term strategy on the way in which product survival zones are changing over time. Because Olympus analyzes its market carefully, the firm knows that customers are demanding the same level of quality but greater functionality for their money. Thus, the change over time in product survival zones could be characterized as increasing functionality and decreasing prices (see Figure 4-2). For Olympus, then, functionality dominates the price and quality characteristics of the survival triplet, and the firm's strategy stresses continuously increasing product functionality. In 1991, to achieve this, Olympus decided to increase the number of models produced by increasing the match

Figure 4-2
The Survival Zone of a Camera over Time

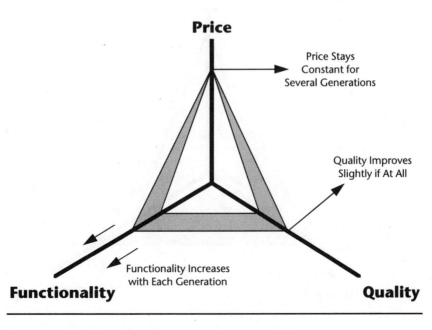

between functionality and customer requirements and to reduce the time it took to bring new products to market.

Adding more models to a firm's product line affects the range of the survival triplet's functionality characteristic and, therefore, affects the shape of the survival zone. Both the minimum acceptable functionality and the maximum achievable functionality are increased because the increased number of cameras allows each camera to be designed to satisfy a smaller number of customers. Since fewer customers are involved, the design better fits their expectations. Thus, increasing the number of camera models pushes the survival zone for each camera outward on the functionality characteristic (see Figure 4-3).

Reducing the time it takes to design a product and get it to market increases functionality because the firm is able to accelerate

Figure 4-3
**How Survival Zones Change with an Increased
Number of Products**

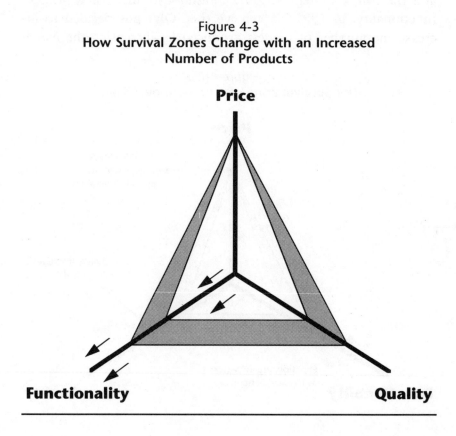

the rate at which new technologies are introduced. Shortening the time to market is also important because it reduces the risk that a firm will be left behind by its competitors. If a competitor comes out with an unexpected, highly successful innovation, then the firm can soon launch equivalent products. For Olympus in 1991, this increased ability to match competitive offerings was critical for success.

Since keeping the price point for a given distinctive feature constant for as long as possible was critical to the firm's strategy, Olympus increased the nondistinctive functionality of its products:

> Price points were typically held constant for as long as possible by adding functionality to the cameras offered. Typically, a given type of camera would be introduced at one price point, stay at that price point for several years but with increasing functionality, and then as the functionality of the next higher price point was reached, drop to the next lower price point. (Cooper 1994j, 6)

Of course, eventually increased functionality forced the firm to reduce the price point of the distinctive feature (see Figure 4-4). To avoid selling cameras at prices that were too low, Olympus decided to discontinue cameras with the least expensive distinctive features when their price point dropped. By developing new high-end features, the number of price points was kept constant or increased over time.

The joint impact of increased functionality and reduced prices placed severe pressure on the firm to reduce costs, and only by continuously taking costs out of products could the firm hope to remain profitable. Cost reduction was achieved not only through the aggressive design of products but also through improvements in the efficiency of the firm's production processes, which was sometimes anticipated when making the decision to launch a product:

> If it was not possible to increase the price or to reduce the production cost sufficiently enough to reduce the estimated cost below the target cost, then a life cycle profitability analysis was

Figure 4-4
Price and Functionality for a Camera over Time

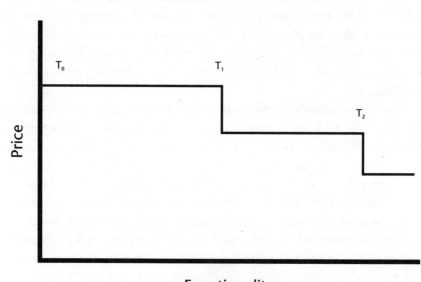

performed. In this analysis, the effect of potential cost reductions over the production life of the product was included in the financial analysis of the product's profitability. . . . The product was released if these life cycle savings were sufficient to make the product's overall profitability acceptable. (Cooper 1994j, 7)

Little latitude in quality existed because the firm had achieved levels of quality that more than satisfied its customers. Failure to maintain that level of quality would harm the firm's reputation, which the firm had discovered in the mid-1980s when new functionality caused quality problems in new products. The firm reacted to the problem by establishing a quality improvement program, which management believed would "help the firm recapture its lost market share by improving the reliability of the firm's products from the customer's perspective" (Cooper 1994j, 5). While the firm's quality levels did change at this time, the minimum acceptable level remained constant and close to the maximum achievable. Thus, while there was some latitude on quality and some benefits to be gained by improving the maximum achievable quality, these benefits were not as great as those associated with improvements in the other two characteristics of the survival triplet.

Olympus, then, competes almost solely on the functionality it offers at a given price point. Although there is some latitude, quality only becomes critical when it is unacceptable. Price is essentially a given. The allowable ranges of functionality, however, are comparatively broad, although not broad enough to allow differentiation strategies to emerge. Because Olympus must find ways to sustain the functionality race and still make a profit, the firm faces product survival zones in which cost reduction is critical. It is not sufficient for the firm to make products at the desired quality and functionality levels if product costs are too high for their price points. To survive, Olympus must find ways to continuously remove costs from its products.

For some firms, the shape of the survival zone depends upon the particular product in question. These firms face more complex competitive pressures. For example, Topcon, which competes in the ophthalmic instruments market, faces survival zones in which the allowable ranges for both price and functionality are fairly broad but the allowable range for quality is narrow:

> Topcon sold only high-technology, high-margin products that were manufactured in relatively low volumes . . . because it did not perceive that the firm had any distinctive competence to succeed in high-volume, low-margin consumer markets. Given its strategy, Topcon had to consistently release state-of-the-art products that matched its competitors' quality in order to generate the high margins required to remain profitable. . . .
>
> The two market leaders, Topcon and Nidek, competed primarily on quality and functionality. The selling price of new products was set by taking into account both customers' demands and competitors' offerings. If customers were demanding increased functionality, then prices would either remain fairly constant over time or would increase. If customers wanted lower

prices and were not overly concerned with functionality, then the price would fall over time. (Cooper 1994o, 1, 3)

Thus, the survival zones for Topcon's various products have different shapes because the customer defines either price or functionality as the most critical characteristic of the survival triplet. If the customer wants increased functionality, then the allowable range for this characteristic is wide but the allowable range for the price dimension is narrow. If the customer wants decreased prices, then the allowable range for the price dimension widens but the allowable range for functionality narrows (see Figures 4-5 and 4-6).

Figure 4-5
Topcon Product with Rapidly Increasing Functionality and Price

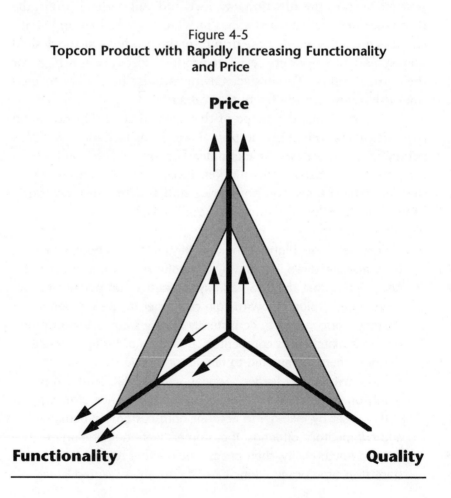

Price

Functionality   **Quality**

Figure 4-6
Topcon Product with Increasing Functionality and Decreasing Price

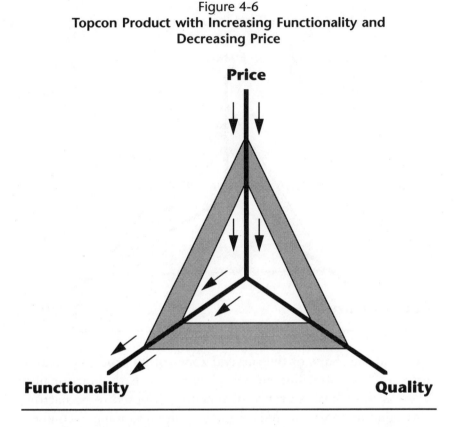

Price

Functionality   **Quality**

Unlike Olympus or Topcon, Komatsu, a heavy construction equipment manufacturer, has traditionally competed on price and quality; functionality has been more or less a given. Thus, until recently, the allowable range for product functionality was narrow but the ranges for price and quality were wide (see Figure 4-7).

Under these conditions, Komatsu's engineers have been expected to produce an alternative for each major subassembly of a new product but the alternative "was only adopted if it achieved both the desired levels of quality and cost. Frequently, one of the alternatives proposed produced a higher quality product but at a higher cost. . . . If a cost-effective way to implement the new alternative was identified, then it was adopted; otherwise, the alternative was abandoned or subject to further study for future applications" (Cooper 1994e, 4). Komatsu is currently facing a

Figure 4-7
Typical Survival Zone for a Komatsu product

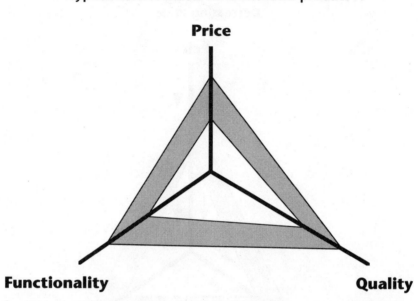

change in the shape of the survival zones of its products because customers are attaching increased importance to functionality. Whereas the allowable range of functionality used to be narrow, it is beginning to widen, and competitors are beginning to compete on the basis of the time it takes to get new products to market.

Time to market has two elements: the time it takes to get the product that customers ordered into their hands, and the time it takes to improve functionality or develop new functionality. For most Japanese firms, both elements are well under control. At Nissan, Japan's second largest automobile manufacturer, for example,

> fast delivery was considered so important that the production strategy was called by a name that translated to "deliver the car with the paint still wet." In 1990, a car ordered from a Japanese dealer and produced in the Zama plant could be delivered to the customer within 2 weeks. . . . This short delivery time de-

> spite high product diversity was achieved via aggressive use of
> just-in-time production. (Cooper 1994i, 8)

For many of the firms, the ability to develop new designs is so rapid that new products can be launched at an optimum rate. Topcon can now introduce new generations of auto-refractometers about every two years.

To achieve their other objectives within the survival triplet, firms continuously trade off functionality. Functionality is a complex set of iterations that result from product design. While time to market is important, a firm must have each aspect of functionality that is important to the firm's customers available in the product offering at the right price. During its design process, Nissan will reduce a product's functionality if the price of the end product is too high: "The first stage of value engineering and the identification of target price was an interactive process. When the allowable costs were considered to be too far below the estimated cost, the appropriate price range and functionality were reviewed until an allowable cost that was considered achievable was identified" (Cooper 1994i, 5). Olympus and Komatsu make similar trade-offs. At Olympus, for example, "first, marketing was asked if the price point could be increased sufficiently. . . . If the market price could not be increased sufficiently, then the effect of reducing the functionality of the product was explored. Reducing the product's functionality decreased its estimated cost to produce" (Cooper 1994j, 7).

No matter what the trade-off, all the firms are careful not to lose the critical window of opportunity. Sony, for example,

> believed that it was imperative to release products on a timely basis. Consequently, it did not allow product redesign to extend the launch date. The Walkman market was so competitive that failure to release a new model on a timely basis would typically result in considerable lost sales. Because the physical production facilities would still exist, the firm saw no benefit to missing a launch date. Consequently, it would launch a product even if its

profitability was below the minimum level in order to meet dead-lines. (Cooper 1994l, 8)

For Sony, then, keeping the level of product functionality in line with customer expectations sometimes overrides the firm's "sell no products at a loss" rule because a gap in the company's product line will result in lost sales. In contrast, Olympus has multiple product offerings at many price points and, therefore, is more willing to delay the release of a product.

THE DARK SIDE

When functionality is critical, firms must develop the ability to bring products to market rapidly, but the inability to sustain competitive advantages can cause firms to go too far. Stalk and Webber (1993, 94) have discussed the "dark side" of time-based competition:

> Time had become a trap, a strategic treadmill on which companies were caught, condemned to run faster and faster but always staying in the same place competitively. Companies had to commit more and more human and financial capital at an ever increasing pace to bring out more and more varieties of products, without any prospect of achieving competitive advantage, higher margins, or more attractive profits.

Stalk and Webber go on to describe how every other major camera firm introduced similar products shortly after Canon launched the first compact, fully automatic, auto-focus camera. They conclude that "Japanese managers had accomplished the unthinkable: they took a strategy based upon producing variety and made it produce commodities. They created the dark side of time-based competition" (100). Yet what were the other firms to do? The survival zone had shifted, and without equivalent products, Canon's competitors could not satisfy customer demands. While technological equivalence ensured that time-based competition would not create competitive advantage, not keeping up meant falling outside the survival zone.

According to Stalk and Webber the Japanese could have avoided the "dark side" by paying more attention to their customers. Yet many of these firms have sophisticated systems that fully monitor customer requirements. The problem does not lie in how the Japanese applied time-based competition but rather in the fact that time-based competition cannot provide any firm with a sustainable advantage. Stalk and Webber have applied the Western model of competition to the Japanese market and have concluded that the Japanese failed because they could not avoid competition by differentiating themselves. But Japanese firms were never trying to differentiate themselves in the competition avoidance sense; they were simply trying to survive.

If timed-based competition has a "dark" side, so do the other two characteristics of the survival triplet. In an environment in which price is critical, it is easy to go too far and drop prices below costs, which can result in massive losses at the industry level. The U.S. airline industry presently faces just such a problem. Airlines are unable to differentiate their products based upon quality or functionality and are therefore forced to compete on price. The massive losses posted by the major airlines in the last few years indicate that price-cutting has gone too far. The ability of the bankrupt players to continue to compete under the protection of Chapter 11 has simply compounded the problem because this protection allows companies to break contracts that nonbankrupt companies are forced to maintain. While Northwest Airlines "On time departure" strategy and Continental's "BusinessFirst" strategy are attempts to differentiate on quality and functionality respectively, they draw little attention compared to price. In contrast, Southwest airlines is succeeding because its strategy is based largely upon reducing operating costs.

Going too far on quality creates subtle problems in part because it is hard to know when a company has gone too far. There are two reasons for this. First, as long as people believe that quality is free, a firm cannot go too far because quality will attract customers. Second, customers are unlikely to volunteer that they would have accepted lower quality products. Although it is difficult to determine when quality has gone too far, there is evidence that certain Japanese firms are pulling back on quality. Such a pullback would have been unthinkable a short time ago.

Unfortunately, Western literature has not been overly helpful to firms trying to understand the critical role of the survival triplet in competition based on confrontation. It has treated each element of the triplet as if it were a separate topic to be studied and mastered. While it is possible to buy books on quality, functionality, and cost management, none of these discuss the interlocking roles of the three elements of the triplet, and most only describe quality or time to market/functionality. Stalk and Hout (1990), for example, discuss how time-based competition is reshaping global markets and note that only firms that "can provide greater varieties of products or services, at lower costs, and in less time than their pedestrian competitors" will survive (1), but they do not discuss the interaction of the elements of the survival triplet in any depth.

Christopher Meyer (1993) argues that price and quality, the other two elements of the triplet, essentially look after themselves: "FCT focuses on the time dimension and, through it, pulls cost and quality into line" (33). If this logic were true, either no cost would be too great for firms to incur to manufacture products of high quality and functionality as quickly as possible or no systems would be required to help manage costs. As we will discover, despite their ability to bring products to market rapidly, Japanese firms have sophisticated cost and quality management systems.

The confusion about the relationship between the three elements of the survival triplet has come about because some cost reduction occurs automatically when quality is improved and/or cycle time is reduced. This happens because as quality and cycle time are improved, activities that used to be required disappear. As quality is improved, for example, rework and associated activities are eliminated. When cycle time is reduced, duplicate or inefficient activities disappear. When activities disappear, costs usually decrease accordingly, but this does not mean that having the highest quality and the shortest cycle time will automatically result in the lowest costs. For this to occur, costs must be managed directly.

Many Western firms that have implemented TQM programs have not achieved the major cost savings that were expected for two reasons. First, many of the firms are giving only lip service to TQM. While the TQM and JIT programs they introduce at first produce savings, the firms fail to complete the transition to lean enterprises.

> To obtain this first round of savings (from TQM) no structural
> changes in the firm are required. The firm thus emerges onto
> the first new plateau relatively easily. To get to the next plateau
> requires making structural changes to the production process.
> The type of changes required include modifying the layout of
> the factory, shifting to vendor certification, introducing worker
> cross-training, and redesigning products (to lower the possibility
> of manufacturing and supplier error). Only after these structural
> changes are made, will the firm will be able to reap more of the
> benefits of becoming a lean enterprise. Many Western firms are
> finding this second transition more difficult to achieve than the
> first. Their JIT and TQM programs produce rapid savings in the
> early days but then these savings flatten out (the firm is on the
> next plateau). The problem faced by these firms is that they
> have not really adopted the concepts behind the lean enterprise
> and lack the confidence to make the structural changes required
> to move to the next plateau. (Cooper 1994s, 8)

Managers at firms that do not make this transition have stopped the "quality movement" before it really begins.

Second, the major savings that Western firms are expecting have never existed in the first place. At many Japanese firms, integrated cost management systems were put in place at about the same time as TQM systems. Therefore, the savings brought about by TQM and JIT programs have been confounded with those brought about by innovative cost management systems. Unraveling the source of the cost savings has been difficult because of the extended period over which the systems have evolved (and continue to evolve) and because of the integrated nature of the programs and systems.

The sophisticated cost and profit management systems in Japanese firms powerfully disprove the naive assumption that costs look after themselves. Meyer (1993) acknowledges this reality when he states, "The only way to increase product quality and reduce costs while concurrently improving product development speed is to fundamentally change the development process itself" (35). Simply improving one element of the triplet is unlikely to create the desired competitive advantage. To become fully competitive, firms must know how to manage all three elements of the survival triplet. In other words, firms must learn to view the process of managing the survival triplet as a total systems solution, not a collection of independent techniques.

SUMMARY

How a firm operationalizes confrontation strategy depends upon the way in which the survival zones of its product change over time. In particular, a firm's strategy is shaped by the characteristic of the survival triplet that is dominant at the time, and the dominant characteristic depends upon the way in which customers' perspectives are changing. In most markets, the dominant characteristic is either functionality or price. If, for example, customers want increased functionality and are willing to pay more for it, then functionality will dominate and price will be the second important characteristic. In contrast, if customers want increased functionality but are not willing to pay for it, then price will dominate and functionality will be second. Quality is not critical in most markets because firms have achieved quality levels that exceed the customers' minimum requirements. Consequently, quality matters only if it drops below acceptable levels.

To be successful, the firm must ensure that its products remain in their survival zones. This requires aggressive management of all three characteristics of the survival triplet as each characteristic plays a central role in the determination of appropriate future product mixes and the nature of the strategy that the firm adopts.

It is possible for a firm to "go too far" in one of the characteristics. Firms that push functionality too far typically introduce too many products and confuse their customers or create quality problems. If too many products are introduced, the superfluous products do not increase customer satisfaction and the cost of their development, advertising, and support is not justified. If pushing technology too hard creates quality problems, then the firm's reputation will suffer and market share will be lost.

While the management of quality and functionality has been discussed in depth in Western literature, the role of cost management has been unfortunately ignored.

PART TWO

SETTING THE STAGE

One area that has received less attention, but that I believe contributes mightily to Japanese competitiveness, is how many companies' management accounting systems reinforce top-to-bottom commitment to process and product innovation.

Toshiro Hiromoto

INTRODUCTION

Confrontation strategy is a direct outcome of the emergence of the lean enterprise. It is here to stay, and it means more intense competition and lower profits. Western managers who do not adjust their mode of competition will risk their firms. Firms that cling to the concept of sustainable competitive advantages and only invest resources in businesses that they believe have sustainable advantages will discover investment opportunities decreasing over time. Firms that cling to the traditional strategies of cost leadership and differentiation will discover that their ability to maintain these strategies is eroding. They will be forced to retreat from their markets as lean competitors outmaneuver them. Niche players may find themselves maneuvered into nongrowth niches as lean competitors launch products directly into their niches. A similar fate awaits firms that try to cling to their historical profit margins. Competition between lean enterprises is more fierce than competition between mass producers, and overall profit margins are smaller. Retreating from products that have lower profit margins will be successful only if higher margin profits can be identified, and often the products associated with these profits will not be available. If the products are available, there is the risk that chasing these products will lead to niches that will eventually turn into technological dead ends.

While this may not be an attractive picture of the new world of competition, it is realistic. Consequently, as more firms become lean, managers need to accept a confrontation strategy and learn how to use it. Firms that adopt confrontation strategy face three challenges. First once a firm has achieved near parity with its competitors and its products are within their survival zones, it must choose how much energy to invest in improving each characteristic of the survival triplet. Rallying cries of being the best at all three will distract the firm from choosing an appropriate strategy. To choose the appropriate strategy, cost management, quality, and time-to-market systems will have to be blended together so that the survival triplet is managed as efficiently as possible and managers will have to be aware of changes in the dominancy of any of the three characteristics of the survival triplet.

Second, while the shift to multifunctional design teams improves a firm's ability to integrate the three dimensions of the survival triplet, it risks a "sameness" in design. Therefore, managers will have to be creative in findings ways to take advantage of multifunctional groups without paying a price in terms of innovation. Furthermore, managers will have to learn to control the way in which technology diffuses through supplier chains and committees. The technology sharing that occurs so freely in Japanese supplier chains does allow firms to innovate more rapidly but it also tends to lead to technological equivalence and hence confrontation.

Third, firms that adopt the confrontation strategy must learn to manage costs as aggressively as possible. Cost management has played an important role in the success of many Japanese firms. It is only by understanding its importance that Western firms can manage the survival triplet correctly and succeed in using the confrontation strategy.

CHAPTER 5

THE ROLE OF COST MANAGEMENT

As Western firms have adopted Japanese lean enterprise practices and begun to reach parity in terms of quality and functionality, the failure to reach cost parity has caused them to suspect that there is a missing piece to the puzzle of Japanese superiority. The missing piece is the role of the cost management systems that the Japanese have developed. Japanese cost management systems are designed to affect all aspects of the economics of manufacture. They influence the supply of purchased parts, the design of the products, and the manufacture of these products. At each stage of the production and delivery process, there are techniques to reduce costs. Unfortunately, these techniques have never been fully analyzed in Western literature. While both Hiromoto (1988) and Worthy (1991) agree that Japanese cost management practices are virtually unknown in the West, they ascribe different reasons to the lack of Western understanding. Hiromoto believes that Westerners simply have not paid enough attention to how "management accounting systems reinforce top-to-bottom commitment to process and product innovation" (Hiromoto 1985, 4).

In contrast, Worthy argues that Japanese managers have deliberately hidden their cost management techniques from Westerners:

> Heading home empty-handed after an intelligence-gathering mission in Japan, the German consultants were thoroughly angered. They had hoped to learn how Japanese auto manufacturers accounted for costs, but instead sat through session after blood-boiling session with smiling factory managers who kept

explaining: Sorry, we don't keep track of what you're looking for. After a frustrating week the Germans gave up, convinced that they had run smack into another case of Japanese stonewalling. (Worthy 1991, 72)

According to Worthy, Japanese managers are keeping their cost management systems hidden because these systems provide a strategic advantage. However, this seems unlikely since the Japanese have consistently demonstrated an amazing openness in sharing their other innovations. Because there is a strong culture of sharing innovations in Japan, this openness is neither accidental nor transitory. Given this, why should Japanese managers suddenly choose to hide their cost management practices? A simpler and more compelling explanation is that the Western managers and academics who visited Japanese firms simply did not know what questions to ask or how to ask them.

WHY THE ROLE REMAINED HIDDEN

The questions that Westerners are most likely to ask first about Japanese cost management practice naturally reflect their own experiences, which have been shaped by Western cost management practices. Unfortunately, the forces that have shaped Western practices are different from the forces that have shaped Japanese practices. Consequently, the areas of interest to students of Western cost management are not necessarily the same as the areas of interest to students of Japanese cost management. This difference makes it difficult for the two groups to communicate effectively.

Western cost management is dominated by financial accounting. Consequently, cost accounting systems (as opposed to cost management systems) are the primary source of cost information. Cost accounting systems have different objectives from cost management systems. Cost accounting systems support the financial accounting process by determining the cost of goods sold and inventory values. These systems report distorted product costs and do not provide powerful mechanisms for cost management or control. In contrast, cost management systems are designed to help the firm manage costs. Their objectives include accurate product costs and the creation of pressures to reduce and control costs.

The competitive environment that arose from the lean enterprise and confrontation strategy demanded the development of sophisticated cost management practices to keep costs down, and from early on, the Japanese recognized that the most efficient way to keep costs down was to design them out of products, not to try to reduce costs after products entered production. This orientation makes sense given the high degree of costs that are essentially designed into products. By adopting a feedforward approach in which costs are designed out of products before production, the focus of Japanese cost management systems shifted from feedback techniques of cost accounting systems (such as product costing and operational control) to feedforward techniques (such as target costing and value engineering). It was the development of these innovative feedforward techniques that led to **cost down** programs. Little innovation was applied to feedback techniques. Consequently, Japanese product costing and control systems are structurally identical to those encountered in the West, but they are not used as intensively. Thus, Western managers and academics looking at Japanese cost accounting systems may not see anything that is structurally unusual or innovative. The way in which those systems are used is innovative, but this usage would be difficult to identify in early interviews because questions would focus on structure, not application and, without knowing about the feedforward role, the difference in application is easy to miss. Furthermore, given their cost accounting orientation, Western managers and academics may expect to find innovative product costing systems that were highly accurate, but it is only recently that Japanese firms have begun to explore the application of activity-based costing (ABC) principles.

Thus, Western managers and researchers who are trying to understand Japanese cost management practices by asking questions about cost accounting systems will find little of interest. While subtle differences caused by a feedforward, as opposed to a feedback, orientation may be detected, they may not be understood. The structural similarities of the product costing and cost control systems can only add to the confusion, making it appear that the Japanese are achieving the impossible from systems virtually identical to those in Western companies.

The way in which Japanese managers answer questions when interviewed can only contribute to further confusion of Western managers and analysts since Japanese managers tend to answer the questions they are asked, not the questions they should have been asked. A Japanese manager will not say, as a Western manager might, "That's not the right question, let me tell you about. . . ." Instead, he will do his best to answer the question he was asked, even if he does not consider it relevant because he does not wish to embarrass the questioner by pointing out that he or she is asking the wrong question. The effect of this effort to avoid embarrassing someone was brought home to me during an extended interview at one research site. I encountered a system that could not report individual product costs although it could report product line costs. As I found it difficult to believe that the firm could function without knowledge of individual product costs, I asked, "How does the system report individual product costs?" The answer I received each time I asked the question was, "It does not." Only when I asked "How do you determine individual product costs if you need them?" was I told about the way in which company engineers used equivalent units to determine individual product costs. Since the determination of individual product costs occurred *outside* the formal cost system, the correct answer to my original question was the one given. To keep me from "losing face," the manager I was interviewing did not point out the error in my question.

Questions that require explanations dealing with multiple causality run into similar cultural problems. While a Westerner may describe all or most of the factors that need to be considered, a Japanese usually will only suggest the most important one. Other factors will not be mentioned unless the manager is questioned further. Western researchers and managers who are unaware of this trait will often walk away with only a partial understanding of Japanese practice.

Language differences only compound these problems. By

Western standards, the Japanese language lacks precision. Frequently the subject of the sentence is omitted in Japanese, making it sometimes difficult for Westerners to follow. Furthermore, communication between Japanese individuals relies heavily upon a common frame of reference. This frame of reference permits discussions to take place on two levels. On the surface, the spoken language is vague and its meaning unclear; at a deeper level, the common frame of reference allows the real meaning to be understood. This mode of communication often interferes with conversations with Westerners even when everyone is speaking in English.

In addition, many Japanese managers have developed stock answers to questions asked by Western visitors. These stock answers are simplified descriptions of reality. At one firm I visited, a senior manager refused to accept a paragraph in one of the cases because it reflected his stock answer. He agreed that the paragraph accurately captured what he had said, but upon reading it in light of the rest of the material, he said he could not accept its oversimplifications. He then told me that the original text reflected an answer that he had developed to enable Western visitors to understand how his system operated. It was not that the answer was wrong but that it was too simplified to capture the complexity of practice.

There are at least two other factors that help to explain why Japanese cost management systems have not been fully analyzed. First, because the lean enterprise allows Japanese firms to make higher quality and functionality products at a lower cost without recourse to innovative cost management practices, Western managers and academics may assume that any cost advantage comes through the increased efficiency of the enterprise. This assumption allows any indication of superior production efficiency on the part of Japanese firms to be accepted without having to explore their cost management systems. The higher quality and functionality of Japanese products has distracted attention from costs. While consumers can easily detect the quality and functionality of products, they cannot observe production costs.

Second, while the lean enterprise can produce higher quality and functionality products at lower costs than mass producers, it does not show superior profitability. Theoretically, if all else is held constant, improved cost management must show up in one of two ways: increased profitability or reduced selling prices without decreased profitability. Unfortunately, not everything else is constant. Japanese firms consistently report lower profits than their Western counterparts. As Kagono, Nonaka, Sakakibara, and Okumura have commented:

> Clearly, the U.S. outperforms Japan in most industries in terms of profitability, implying that the basic assumption of Japanese success may be an illusion. Of course, profitability is only one of many criteria of success. It is, however, difficult to conclude that Japanese companies have generally been more successful than American firms. (Kagono et al. 1985, 2)

These lower profits reflect two underlying differences between Japan and the West. First, the inability to create a sustainable competitive advantage and the adoption of confrontation strategies lead to reduced profits. Second, Japanese and Western firms have different objectives. In Japan, the shareholder is less powerful than shareholders in the West and, therefore, generating high profits (hence, dividends) is less critical. In Japanese firms, the shareholder comes after the employees, customers, and creditors. Therefore, the primary objective of Japanese firms is to achieve stability and long-term reliability by creating and reporting continuously improving financial results, particularly growth. As Carl Kester (1991) has stated, "[C]orporate growth tends to emerge as the common denominator among the stakeholder groups—the one objective that nearly everyone can agree on as having a potential benefit" (77). By achieving this objective, Japanese firms send strong signals to their employees and future employees that the firms are good places to work and will provide the permanent security implied by lifetime employment contracts. Thus, lifetime employment creates a feedback loop that supports the firm's achievement of its growth objective.

When the higher profits that indicate superior economic performance do not appear, the inability to observe underlying cost structures makes it easy for some to argue that the Japanese are buying market share or dumping products. Analysts who do not accept these arguments claim that higher quality and faster time to market have led to better controlled production processes that can make products in smaller volumes at lower costs:

> [V]ertical integration may have made General Motors and Ford more efficient when they competed between themselves or with smaller American or European producers. But this strategy offered no advantage over the Japanese in the 1970s and 1980s, once they perfected production systems characterized by worker productivity that was twice as high as in the United States. (Cusumano 1985, 213)

However, both of these arguments overlook the importance of cost management systems.

COST MANAGEMENT IN ACTION

To lower its costs, a firm must manage the mix of products (both present and future) that it sells. While the type of products, cameras or cans, for example, is set by the strategy of the firm, the mix of models the firm sells or intends to sell is determined by a number of factors. Three factors appear to be dominant: the competitive environment (in particular, how the firm competes using the survival triplet), the maturity of the product's technology, and the length of the product's life cycle (see Figure 5-1).

The nature of the competitive environment is critical because it determines, among other things, how aggressively costs have to be managed. With the downturn in the Japanese economy and the rapid increase in value of the yen compared to other major currencies, many firms have shifted their dominant characteristic of the survival triplet from functionality to cost. At Isuzu, for example, a manager noted:

Figure 5-1
The Forces Shaping the Role of Cost Management

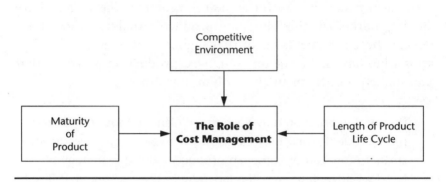

[W]e have increased the size of our cost creation teams significantly. The original team contained seven highly trained members. They were called the "brain team": they came up with the
ideas and others implemented them. In December 1992, we
added 23 new members to the cost creation team. In October
of 1993, we added another 22 members to this second team.
The two teams have been very active finding ways to reduce
costs. In the first two months the team identified savings worth
¥2.2 billion. Their target for next year is ¥8.4 billion. (Cooper
and Yoshikawa 1994a, 11)

The maturity of the technology is critical because it determines
the rate of introduction of new products and the degree to which
they differ from their predecessors. The maturity of high technology makes it difficult for costs to be removed from the production
process. In contrast, managing the costs of future products is
important in firms where the technology is still developing. At
Olympus, for example, new products are constantly refined. Parts
are reduced, materials are replaced, and expensive adjustment
processes are eliminated whenever possible (Cooper 1994j, 6–7).

The product's life cycle is important because it determines how
much time the firm has to reduce the costs of existing products.
If a product has a short life cycle, there may not be enough time
to reduce costs significantly. At Nissan, for example, the four-year

life of the automobile makes it difficult to justify product design changes once a product has entered production.

Managing the Product Mix

Once the type of product the firm sells has been established, managing the product mix primarily consists of ensuring that only profitable products are sold. Because profit is revenue minus costs, product costs reported by the firm's cost accounting system play a critical role in helping a firm to manage its product mix (see Figure 5-2). The determination of inventory values for financial accounting purposes is not a demanding role for a cost system, and every cost accounting system studied performs this role. Frequently, however, the constraints of Japanese financial accounting conventions force firms to select accounting methods that are not appropriate for product-related decisions. Sometimes these methods, which try to satisfy both financial and managerial functions, create conflicts, but many firms resolve the conflicts by correcting for them before using reported product costs to make decisions. For example, depreciation charges are usually set to maximize the cash flow associated with tax deductions rather than to reflect the economic life of the equipment. However, Nissan modifies its

Figure 5-2
Managing Product Mix

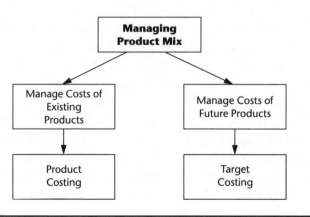

depreciation calculations when it does a "life cycle contribution study" to estimate the overall profitability of a proposed model:

> The depreciation charge used for the life cycle contribution analysis was not the one used for financial reporting purposes. Nissan reported depreciation using a declining balance approach for both tax and financial reporting purposes. However, for the life cycle contribution calculation it used a straight-line approach. Management modified the depreciation calculation because it felt that the straight-line approach better captured the relationship between asset use and models produced than the declining balance approach. (Cooper 1994i, 4)

Similar types of modifications were undertaken at other companies. For example, at Shionogi, a pharmaceutical manufacturer,

> [t]he National Health Insurance (NHI) reimbursement prices of new pharmaceutical drugs in Japan was set by the Ministry of Health and Welfare (MHW) using two different approaches. If other drugs that performed the same pharmaceutical function already existed, then the price of the new drug was set based upon their prices. If the drug was unique, then the price was based upon Shionogi's total cost. Total cost includes Shionogi's development, manufacturing, and sales, general, and administrative expenses, the costs of distribution, and an allowance for profits for Shionogi and its wholesalers.
>
> It was to Shionogi's advantage to negotiate its highest reimbursement prices possible for its drugs since the higher the NHI price the higher the manufacturer's selling price to its wholesalers. In contrast, it was to MHW's advantage to keep the NHI reimbursement prices at a reasonable level.
>
> The cost reported by the firm's standard cost systems required two major adjustments before they could be used to price a new drug. The first adjustment reduced the amount of depreciation charged to the drug during its first few years of production. The cost system, in accordance with Japanese financial accounting practices, used an accelerated depreciation charge.

Consequently, in the first few years of a product's life, very high depreciation charges were allocated to it. This high depreciation charge was further compounded by the low volume of sales that most new drugs achieved in their first few years. Therefore, a second adjustment for more realistic long-term production volumes was required to generate an adjusted cost that could be used for cost-plus pricing and price negotiation in general.

If a drug was unprofitable, Shionogi would negotiate with the MHW to try to increase the NHI reimbursement price sufficiently to make the drug profitable. Shionogi took its social responsibility to provide drugs seriously and would only withdraw drugs as a last resort. (Cooper 1995a, 17–18)

Product costs (before or after correction) are used in at least six ways to help manage the product mix. In the first way, product costs are used to set selling prices. In the second, they are used to refuse to launch unprofitable products. In the third, they are used to refuse to sell unprofitable products. The final three ways involve product-related decisions, such as redesigning, outsourcing, and discontinuing (see Figure 5-3).

Figure 5-3
Managing the Product Mix through Product Costs

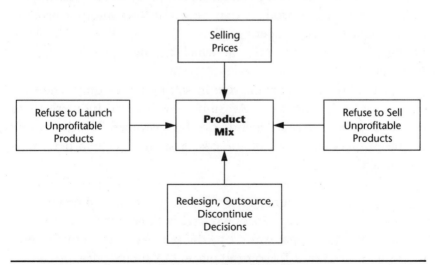

Setting Selling Prices. Under confrontation strategy, prices are usually set by the market; thus reported product costs are used to determine the profitability of products, not to set prices. Even the most revolutionary product usually has a counterpart that can be identified and used to establish a price for a new product. Therefore, cost-plus pricing is almost unheard of. At Citizen,

> [c]ost-plus pricing was rarely used . . . because most products were sold into competitive markets where the competitors had similar product offerings. Occasionally, Citizen would bring out a watch or movement for which there was no direct competitive offering. In these cases, where there was no market price, the selling price was determined using a "to be accepted" market price. This price was determined by market studies and analysis that consisted of an evaluation of the attractiveness of the product and a comparison with other watches and other consumer products. (Cooper 1994a, 5)

At Olympus, "consumer research had shown that many consumers were trying to choose between buying a compact disc player or a compact camera. Therefore, Olympus viewed compact disc players as competitive products" (Cooper 1994j, 4). When such a wide view of competitive products is adopted, it is almost impossible to introduce a product that does not have another product against which it is competing. Under these conditions, the competing product sets the price at which the new product must be introduced.

Costs play an important role in setting prices only when the product is truly "unique." At Sumitomo Electric Industries, the length of wire ordered depends on the customer. Therefore, one of the primary purposes of the cost system is to help determine the "price" of products.

> One of the major purposes of the cost system was to determine the price of products. Prices were set in three steps. First, the annual price for copper was set by the purchasing department, located at the firm's Tokyo head office. (An annual price, not a

current price, was established because copper prices fluctuated daily, and since there was no mechanism for SEI to track actual material costs, a standard was required. An annual standard was chosen because it allowed the firm to monitor price changes across the year via the calculation of monthly price variances.) The purchasing department also set the annual price of all of the other metals used in SEI products. Second, the cost of the bare wire was set by the bare wire division, located in the Osaka Works. It was determined by adding the direct and indirect production costs to the scrap-adjusted cost of the copper. And third, the cost of the assembled products was determined by adjusting the material costs by the standard loss ratio to allow for material losses. (Cooper 1994m, 8)

Refusing to Launch Unprofitable Products. To ensure that new products are profitable, many firms have rules to prevent the introduction of unprofitable products. These systems, which are discussed in part 3, focus on managing the costs of future products and involve target costing, value engineering, and interorganizational cost management. They are heavily oriented toward product design and are the critical point at which the survival triplet is managed. A variety of mechanisms exist to reinforce these rules. At Citizen, for example, "products would be introduced only if they could be sold at a profit. . . . If the watch was profitable it was introduced and orders accepted from Citizen Trading Company and other customers. If the watch was unprofitable, then the selling price, production cost, and design were reviewed. If there was no way for the product to be made profitable it was never introduced" (Cooper 1994a, 5–6).

Yokohama has a similar policy against introducing unprofitable products, but because of the power customers exert over the firm, the policy had not been applied consistently in the past, which had reduced the firm's profitability. As part of its strategy to return profits to their previous levels, the firm developed a new strategy that included a more disciplined application of the "no unprofitable product rule." While it identified new products that could be produced at competitively low costs and then aggressively bid for contracts, "Yokohama resolved that any new product that was not going to generate an adequate profit margin across its life would not be introduced" (Cooper 1994d, 3). Sony's rule, like Yokohama's, includes a minimum acceptable profit: "As a matter of policy, Sony would not sell products at a loss and, under most conditions, would not sell them below the minimum profit margin established by the appropriate business group's manager" (Cooper 1994l, 7).

For most companies, the only major exception to the "no unprofitable launches" rule occurs when not introducing a product will have serious deleterious effects or when the product is considered strategically important. At Citizen, the need to maintain the corporate image can override the "no unprofitable launches" rule: "If there was no way for the product to be made profitable, it was never introduced. The only exceptions to this rule were products that were considered strategically important to Citizen's corporate image, such as the perpetual calendar watch" (Cooper 1994a, 6). At Olympus, "If the estimated costs were still too high, the product was abandoned unless some strategic reason for keeping the product could be identified. Such considerations typically focused on maintaining a full product line or creating a "flagship" product that demonstrated technological leadership.

Refusing to Sell Unprofitable Products. Many firms apply the same "no unprofitable products" rule to existing products. These firms have systems designed to create pressures to reduce the costs of existing products. The systems, which are discussed in part 4, focus primarily on the production process, as opposed to the products, and involve product costing, operational control, and *kaizen* costing. There are two primary determinants of how much energy is placed into ensuring existing products are profitable. The first is the duration of the market life of the product, and the second is the rate at which selling prices are decreasing. For Olympus, short product lives and an intensive cost reduction effort make it unusual for a product to become unprofitable before it is replaced by a new model. For Topcon, the typical decrease in price across the life of its products is about 15 percent, which is insufficient to make them unprofitable. However, for firms with products that are relatively long lived, there is always the risk that an existing product will become unprofitable. At Citizen, where some product lives are measured in decades, existing products are continuously checked to ensure that they do not become unprofitable:

> When the selling price of a product was expected to fall below its cost in the near future, the product was subjected to an intense specific cost reduction analysis. . . . If the cost reductions identified by the analysis were insufficient to reduce costs so that the product would remain profitable, then complete product redesign was explored. If even complete redesign was unable to make the product profitable, it was usually discontinued. (Cooper 1994a, 6)

Not all firms have such strict rules against selling unprofitable products. Some firms will sell unprofitable products as long as they make a positive contribution. For example, at Mitsubishi Kasei, Japan's largest integrated chemical company,

> individual product costs were compared to selling prices when there was a risk that they were being sold below variable cost. Export sales were often made at prices that were much lower than domestic prices. . . . Mitsubishi Kasei accepted these low prices to keep plants busy. However, accepting such business only made sense if the variable costs of the products sold did not exceed their selling prices. (Cooper 1994h, 6)

Selling positive contribution but negative profit products makes sense in the short term but not in the long term, and it is not necessarily the sensible thing to do when there is a high degree of communication among the customers. For example,

> [i]f Yokohama sold that product to another customer below its effective market price, there was a substantial risk that once the new price leaked out that it would rapidly become the market price for that product. If the revenue gained by selling the prod-

uct at the reduced price to the new customer was less than the revenue lost by the decreased selling price to existing products, Yokohama would be worse off by accepting the new customer's price. (Cooper and Yoshikawa 1994d, 5)

Mitsubishi Kasei is not concerned about such an occurrence because there is less communication between the firm's export customers than there is between Yokohama's domestic customers (therefore, the risk of setting a new market price is less) and because it is extremely capital intensive (therefore, a typical product's profit and contribution are different).

Capital intensity affects the "no unprofitable products" rule because in a highly capital intensive business, an unprofitable product is quite likely to have a positive contribution. In contrast, in less capital intensive firms, a product with a positive contribution often generates a profit. Therefore, in a low capital intensity business, shifting the "only sell" rule from positive profit products to positive contribution products probably makes little difference to the number of products identified by the rule. At Sumitomo Electric Industries, however, this change in the rule is significant:

Top management believed that it was more important to maintain or gain market share than it was to be profitable. However, products were expected to at least cover their direct costs. The criteria for accepting a bid was that it should at least cover its direct, depreciation, and finance charges. If a product could not cover these charges, and it was a mature product with little opportunity for additional cost reduction, it became a candidate for cost reduction. (Cooper 1994m, 9)

Firms using a confrontation strategy face intense pressure to reduce selling prices. Profit levels can be maintained only by implementing rules that can be used to say no to a customer who is pressuring the firm to accept unprofitable business.

Redesigning, Outsourcing, and Discontinuing Products. Once a product is identified as unprofitable or at risk of becoming unprofitable in the near future, it is redesigned to reduce costs, outsourced, or discontinued. The action taken depends upon the exact conditions faced. For instance, at Topcon,

> the TOV system was used to identify products that were rapidly losing profitability and required more focused cost reduction efforts. . . . Although some cost reduction was possible across the life of the product, the short life cycles coupled with high material content made it extremely difficult for Topcon to reduce costs as rapidly as prices fell. (Cooper 1994o, 7)

Nippon Kayaku, a pharmaceuticals and fine chemicals manufacturer, also uses reported product costs to identify candidates for redesign. Unlike Topcon, however, Nippon Kayaku's cost reduction programs focus on product replacement. The high direct costs of the firm's products (particularly material) makes it difficult to reduce costs without redesigning products and their material content:

> The savings that could be achieved by replacing an expensive product with a less expensive one were much higher than could be achieved via cost reduction of existing products. The greater cost savings could be achieved from product redesign because of the high percentage of total product cost that was represented by material and equipment-related expenses. Consequently, only by changing either the raw materials or equipment required to produce a product, or both, could cost be significantly reduced. (Cooper and Yoshikawa 1994c, 1)

Many firms use product cost information to help determine which products are candidates for outsourcing. Usually products are outsourced only when they can be acquired for less outside the organization. Most firms have mature outsourcing programs and are not actively involved in outsourcing major portions of their businesses. However, Yamanouchi Pharmaceutical, which wants to reduce its dependence on internal manufacturing, is actively involved in outsourcing products. To keep the size of its manufacturing operations constant, it outsources production of mature products to make room for the production of new products:

> The reported product costs . . . played a critical role in determining which processes and products were candidates for outsourcing. Products were only outsourced when Yamanouchi was convinced that overall costs would fall. Labor costs were not included in this determination because lifetime contracts meant that labor was essentially a fixed cost. Therefore, outsourcing was only considered when another product was ready to be manufactured internally. (Cooper 1994q, 6)

Harnessing the Entrepreneurial Spirit

There is at least one other way a firm can lower the costs of its products, by harnessing the entrepreneurial spirit of its workforce. This method focuses on the workforce, not the products or production processes. There are two techniques for accomplishing this. The first technique creates pseudomicroprofit centers from cost centers and the second technique converts the firm into many real microprofit centers (see Figure 5-4).

Pseudomicroprofit Center. Firms that use the first technique convert cost centers into profit centers and change work group leaders from cost center managers to business managers. The development of this technique was motivated by the belief that the way in which individuals view their responsibilities can sometimes be as important as the responsibilities themselves. There are four primary

Figure 5-4
Harnessing the Entrepreneurial Spirit

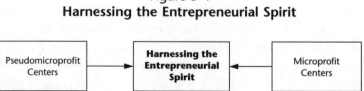

reasons for using the technique. First, by using profit as the performance metric, work groups can get a better feel for the impact of their contributions on company performance. Second, the creation of profit centers provides management with a mechanism to reward publicly, thus reinforce, behaviors that lead to increased profits. Third, because profits are a universal metric, each work group can evaluate its own performance and compare it to that of other groups. Finally, the creation of profit centers can revitalize the firm's cost management systems.

Treating work groups as profit centers as opposed to cost centers affects how workers view themselves and the pressure they place on themselves to perform. Evaluating the groups based upon profitability has the effect of including revenues in the evaluation process. Since a profit center manager is interested in both increasing revenues and decreasing costs, he or she is willing to take actions that could increase both costs and revenues or decrease costs and revenues if the overall effect is to increase profits. A cost center manager, however, will try to reduce costs, often to the detriment of revenues. This shift in mind-set from reducing costs to increasing profits encourages workers to identify new ways to reduce costs and thus revitalizes cost management systems.

The profit center systems created at Higashimaru Shoyu, Kirin Breweries, and Olympus Optical break production processes into pseudoprofit centers because there are no available market prices for their outputs and the creation of a real profit center requires the ability to determine arm's length selling prices. The inability to create real profit centers stopped these firms from taking advantage of the second technique in which the firm is broken into a number of smaller entities.

Real Microprofit Centers. Kyocera Corporation and The Taiyo Group employ the second technique and break themselves into a collection of autonomous small enterprises that must be profitable to survive. Under the approach used by Kyocera a large number of profit centers, called amoeba, are created. These are not independent firms but highly independent pseudofirms that are responsible for selling products both internally and externally. In contrast, the approach used by the Taiyo Group creates separate legal entities. Each entity is responsible for several products. At the heart of both approaches is the fundamental assumption that small firms are inherently more efficient and effective than large firms; they do not require an expensive and ineffective bureaucracy and they can react quickly to changes in competitive conditions. Both firms believe the ability to reduce or control the growth of bureaucracy is a major mechanism to control costs.

Since the creation of many autonomous profit centers risks having each center optimize its profits at the expense of the firm's profits, both firms put into place mechanisms that ensure the individual profit centers operate in ways that are beneficial for the group as a whole. At Kyocera, the managerial reporting systems and the philosophy of the firm's founder ensure the welfare of the firm. At the Taiyo Group, the welfare of the firm is ensured by group presidents who acted as consultants to each other.

SUMMARY

The role of cost management in the success of many Japanese firms has remained hidden for numerous reasons. First, Western academics and managers tend to ask questions about Japanese cost accounting systems and not cost management systems. Second, Japanese managers do not answer questions in the way most Westerners expect. The Japanese have a cultural tendency to answer the question asked, not the one that should have been asked. This tendency keeps them from redirecting the attention of Westerners to the innovative practices that have been developed. The somewhat vague nature of the Japanese language plays a smaller but critical role in increasing the confusion. The Japanese language with its subtle shadings and tendency to omit the subjects of sentences can make it difficult for Japanese managers to explain sophisticated concepts. Reacting to this difficulty, many Japanese managers have developed simplified stock answers to questions frequently asked by Westerners. These answers are not incorrect, but oversimplifications. Westerners, unaware of this practice, often walk away thinking they have understood Japanese practice when, in fact, they have not.

The effectiveness of Japanese cost management techniques remained hidden because they were obfuscated by the superiority of Japanese products (in terms of their quality and functionality) and by the lack of extra profits that appear when there is a sustainable competitive advantage.

When firms use a confrontation strategy, highly effective cost management systems are a necessity. Many Japanese firms have developed cost management systems that create a discipline throughout the firm to reduce costs across the entire life cycle of the firm's products.

Firms manage costs in three ways. First, they manage the mix (both present and future) of products that the firm sells. To do this, they must also manage the costs of future products and the costs of existing products. Three factors play a dominant role in determining the effectiveness of the three methods of cost reduction. These factors are the competitive environment (in particular how the firm competes using the survival triplet), the maturity of the product, and the length of the product's life cycle.

Managing the product mix primarily consists of ensuring that only profitable products are sold. Since profit is simply revenue minus costs, reported product costs play a critical role in helping the firm manage its product mix. For existing products, reported product costs are generated by the firm's cost system. For future products, costs are generated by the firm's target costing system. Reported product cost information is used in several ways to help manage the product mix. The first way deals with setting selling prices. The second way concerns refusing to launch unprofitable products. Because managing the cost of future products is the only way to ensure that the products will be profitable when launched, firms have developed three specific cost management techniques: target costing, value engineering, and interorganizational cost management systems. The third way deals with refusing to sell unprofitable products. To ensure that unprofitable products are not sold, firms must manage the cost of existing products. There are three cost management techniques used to help reduce the costs of existing products. These are product costing systems, operational control, and kaizen. There is at least one other way to manage costs. That way involves harnessing the entrepreneurial spirit. There are two techniques for doing this. The first is to create pseudomicroprofit centers, and the second is to create real micro-profit centers. The final three deal with product-related decisions such as redesigning, outsourcing, and discontinuing products.

Together, the first six techniques create a continuous down-ward pressure on costs. The techniques are applied by self-directed small groups that are managed by group leaders with well-developed managerial skills. The importance of these groups cannot be underestimated, and they are the focus of the next chapter.

CHAPTER 6

CREATING THE RIGHT
ORGANIZATIONAL CONTEXT

The key to successful cost management lies in the existence of a committed, motivated, and managerially aware workforce. It is not sufficient to simply launch cost reduction programs. Without the right organizational context, these programs will not work. In Japanese firms, the workforce is usually organized into self-guided teams, or groups, and it is these teams that actually achieve the firms' cost reduction objectives. Consequently, the way in which these teams are motivated helps to determine the success of the firms' cost reduction programs.

At most firms, the team leaders (typically high-school graduates) function like managers and act with a high degree of autonomy. Team members are often drawn from different parts of the firm. Since successful cost reduction must trade off all three characteristics of the survival triplet, multifunctionality is critical. At Topcon,

> [t]he MAST [management activity by small team] program consisted of cross-functional, self-directed teams that were formed to achieve a specific objective. A typical objective for an accounting MAST team would be to find ways to improve the accuracy of the inventory records. . . . MAST teams operated at the division manager level. The leader of the team would form a cross-functional team typically from manufacturing, production, accounting, marketing, and in particular, the TQC and VA departments. Typically, each manager would be a leader of one team and a member of several others. This interlocking member-

ship allowed the teams to be aware of the actions of other teams, thereby avoiding duplication of effort. (Cooper 1994o, 8)

At Nissan, "[The allowable] cost was set by teams derived from almost every functional area of the firm, including product design, engineering, purchasing, production engineering, manufacturing, and parts supply" (Cooper 1994i, 5).

Every team is involved in cost management because every team has a cost reduction target. In most firms, the procedure for setting team cost reduction targets is part of a hierarchical target-setting process. The process begins with corporatewide cost reduction targets that are set during the annual planning process (see chapter 3). The corporatewide cost reduction target is distributed among the divisions. At this stage, negotiations over the targets are between the corporate planning department and the divisional managers. In the next stage, the divisional cost reduction targets are distributed among production facilities in the divisions and then to the teams. At Sumitomo Electric Industries, for example,

the division managers were responsible for setting the cost reduction targets at both the division and group levels. The critical player in setting these targets was the plant manager, who had access to detailed information about what was happening on the factory floor and at the division level. The plant manager would act as the conduit between the factory floor and the divisional manager, helping him or her identify realistic stretch targets for each group. Once the informal targets were established, the groups entered formal negotiations to fine-tune the targets and commit to them. (Cooper 1994m, 6)

In companies using a bottom-up approach, team leaders are responsible for setting their own targets; in companies using a top-down approach, upper management sets the targets.

At Olympus, for example, "cost reduction targets were identified for each product produced by the group. . . . The group leaders recommended their cost reduction targets and then these recommendations were reviewed by divisional management. . . .

If the overall savings were insufficient, the targets were renegotiated until the savings were acceptable to divisional management" (Cooper 1994j, 8).

At Citizen,

> Group leaders were responsible for labor content reduction. Each of the 59 group leaders was required to set cost reduction targets every three months. These targets were submitted to the administration department, which consolidated the targeted reductions and, if they were sufficient firm-wide, accepted them. If the overall reductions were not satisfactory, they were sent back to the group leaders for more aggressive targets. (Cooper 1994a, 7)

The top-down approach does not always create commitment, as Olympus discovered:

> Over the years, the groups' initial cost reduction targets had become biased downward to create "slack" that could be used to help the groups achieve their negotiated targets. To the extent possible, when divisional management became aware of this practice it would take this into consideration when establishing new targets. (Cooper 1994k, 6)

While team leaders have considerable autonomy, it is conditional on their success. If a team fails to achieve its target, a series of steps are taken to correct the problem. At Olympus the workforce was split into teams and groups. When a team or group failed to meet its target,

> the team leader and foreman in each group met daily to discuss their progress. . . . Weekly meetings were held by group and team leaders to report on progress. If a group did not meet its weekly objectives, the group leader was expected to explain why the group had failed and what corrective actions were going to be taken. . . . Occasionally, if a group consistently failed to meet its objectives, engineering would be sent in by manage-

ment. Such an action was viewed as a serious blow to the reputation of the group. (Cooper 1994j, 9)

Thus, the role that these small teams play in achieving the cost management objectives is critical. Without them, the grassroots commitment to cost reduction would not occur.

THE HIGASHIMARU SHOYU EXPERIENCE*

At most firms multifunctional teams have been in operation for so long that it is almost impossible for management to recapture how the groups were formed and motivated initially. However, at Higashimaru Shoyu, a soy sauce manufacturer, the process of developing self-motivated teams did not begin until 1974 and, therefore, is still remembered.

The Higashimaru factory was organized around five sections. Each section was then broken into groups and there were seventeen groups, or teams, in all. The five sections responsible for the major production processes were fermentation, production, inspection, machinery maintenance, and distribution. The fermentation section contained five groups, the highest number of any section. Of these five groups, two were devoted to koji preparation, two to moromi pressing, and one to wastewater treatment. The machinery maintenance section only contained one group, appropriately called machinery maintenance. A complete organization chart is shown in Figure 6-1.

The seventeen groups were run by group leaders. The average group leader was a junior high school graduate who had been with the firm for over twenty years. While not highly educated, the group leaders were proud of their achievements and highly motivated. Within the factory, they were considered self-made men. Unfortunately, they were not well enough educated to help manage the modernization program that was to be introduced. This pro-

---

* A version of this section was published as "Human Reengineering" by R. Cooper and M. Lynne Markus in *Sloan Management Review* (Summer 1995).

Figure 6-1
Higashimaru Shoyu Organization Chart

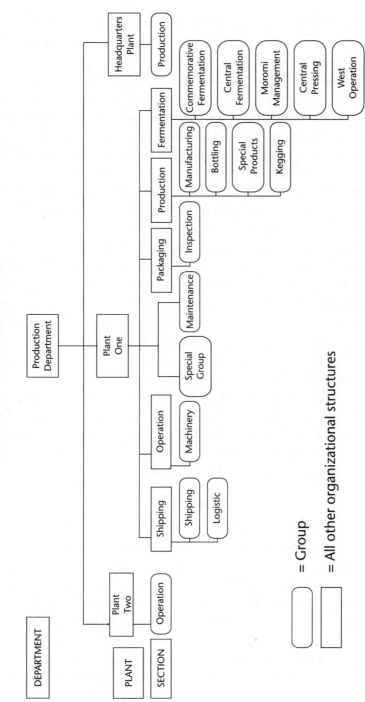

Source: R. Cooper, "Higashimaru Shoyu Company, Ltd. (B): Revitalizing the Organization," case study 9-195-051 (Boston: Harvard Business School, 1994), 12.

gram included plant automation, increased cost awareness, and development of more modern production control procedures, such as temperature monitoring.

Recognizing that the managerial skills of the group leaders needed to be improved, the firm appointed Toshio Okuno, who had been the assistant manager of the research center, plant manager and gave him the task of revitalizing the factory. His task was to find ways to increase the managerial skills of the group leaders so they could perform their tasks more efficiently. To achieve this objective, Okuno had to find ways of converting a reluctant workforce into one that was willing to both accept and initiate change. He did so by introducing five new programs designed to increase the managerial skill of the group leaders.

Okuno started by organizing a study group for the group leaders to improve their overall education level. Unfortunately, reaction to the study group was universally negative. As one group leader put it, "The reason that I joined Higashimaru was to avoid studying. If I liked studying, I would have stayed at school." Okuno listened to the reactions of the group leaders to the first meeting, accepted the inevitable, and canceled all future study meetings. After some thought, he developed a strategy designed to revitalize the organization. At the heart of this strategy were five programs that were introduced over a four-year period: monthly group leader meetings; a price control system; a draft system; a *tatsumaki* program; and the *hangen* game.

Monthly Team Leader Meetings

After canceling the study sessions, Okuno coined the phrase *sagyo-shigoto* to create pressure for continuous improvement. *Sagyo-shigoto*, literally meaning "job-work," does not translate easily into English. Within the phrase, *sagyo* means performing a job without any improvement and *shigoto* means performing the work in an improved way. The phrase became very popular with the workers, who would say to each other, "You are just doing *sagyo*, I am doing *shigoto*." The phrase became a symbol of the new attitude of the workers, who began to think about what they were doing, how they were doing it, and how to improve the way in which they did it.

Sagyo-shigoto alone was unable to create the magnitude of change in worker behavior that Okuno desired. The core problem, he believed, was the group's natural resistance to change. As he put it, "The typical group has a 20:20:60 reaction mix to change. That is, 20 percent of the group will support the change, another 20 percent will resist the change, and the remaining 60 percent will be neutral or hesitant towards the change." In Okuno's eyes, teams with the 20:20:60 structure were inherently too cautious to make significant changes continuously. Consequently, one of Okuno's early objectives was to change the reaction mix from 20:20:60 to either 30:20:50, or 20:10:70, thus reducing the number that opposed change. To accomplish this, Okuno held monthly meetings with the group leaders. Since Okuno wanted to get all levels of the organization used to communicating effectively with each other—a critical step in introducing a continuous improvement program—the primary purpose of these meetings was to confirm that his instructions were communicated to the lowest levels of the firm.

To test how well communications were occurring at the lowest levels of the firm, Okuno would visit the production floor and talk to employees. If he found that employees did not know his instructions even when they were posted on the notice boards, he would bring the problem to the attention of the group leader, and every time he encountered a group that was communicating particularly well, he would praise that group at the monthly meeting. It took about two years of holding group leader meetings before the reaction mix in most of the groups had shifted to the desired level. One group that was particularly innovative had followed Okuno's example and initiated its own meetings.

In Okuno's mind, his interaction with the group leaders at the meetings was one of the keys to achieving the desired change in the reaction mix. His aim in these interactions was to teach the group leaders to think for themselves. Therefore, whenever one of his group leaders asked, "What should I do?" Okuno would not answer the question but rather ask the leader for his ideas. If the leader did not have any ideas, Okuno would suggest that he first think through the problem and come up with ideas. If the leader had an idea but Okuno thought it was wrong, he would discuss the solution and drop hints about how to think about the problem more productively. He would not tell his solution to the leader. If the leader's original or redeveloped solution was the same as Okuno's, he would praise the leader and tell him that it was a great idea without mentioning that he had already thought of it.

As communication levels within the groups increased, Okuno began to work on the level of communication among groups. Group leaders typically met only when they had problems to resolve. While Okuno supported this type of meeting, he wanted to encourage a more positive approach to communication. Consequently, he suggested that the group leaders should think about "visiting their customers," that is, a group that either was next in the production process or was one of the groups supported by the group. At one point, for example, Okuno encouraged the leader of the moromi management group to visit the sterilizing group to find out how the members of the group were doing and what they thought of the quality of the raw soy sauce they were receiving. Okuno thought these informal meetings would give group leaders a chance to discuss ways in which they could help each other before problems emerged. He also hoped that the leaders would begin to discuss topics of general interest, such as new projects or ideas that they had. To impress upon the group leaders the importance of these meetings, at each monthly group leader meeting, a group leader was asked to present the results of one of his "visits with his customer." Okuno hoped these presentations would create an environment in which employees could talk to each other productively.

After two years of encouraging and supporting improved communications and increased decision autonomy, Okuno felt that the group leaders were ready to attend study meetings:

> The primary purpose of the group leader meetings was to develop the managerial skills of the group leaders. The majority of

participants were keen to take part in these meetings: they were highly motivated to succeed. We didn't use commercial text-books or manuals. Instead, we discussed their views about their work and their roles at work. Over time, we extended the discussion beyond just Higashimaru. For example, at one meeting we discussed how to save a local railway line that was threatened with closure because of its losses. The group came up with a number of innovative but practical solutions. These suggestions proved to me that the group leaders were now thinking like managers. (Cooper 1994c, 9)

This time, there was no resistance to the meetings, and the formal education of the group leaders began. Among the topics covered at the study meetings were the concepts of fixed and variable costs and breakeven analysis. These concepts were critical to the success of the price control system.

Price Control System

Okuno introduced the price control system (PCS), which is described in depth in chapter 13, in 1980. The objective of the PCS was to install a profit-making attitude in the groups. Under the system, groups were treated as profit centers. They were expected to buy the resources they consumed from the previous group in the production process and to sell their products to the next group. Group leaders were expected to act like presidents of small firms. They were not expected to act like entrepreneurs because, as Okuno noted, "It was too difficult to get them to act like entrepreneurs, that was asking too much."

Okuno commented on the success of the Price Control Program as follows:

I was prepared to face a strong negative reaction to the price control system because it would give the employees extra clerical work in addition to their normal work loads. However, in real-

ity the system worked more smoothly than expected and did
not add much extra to their work load.

I believe the PCS was successful because, first, I did not give
any significant weighing to the profit or loss figures of the
groups, but instead attached more importance to their efforts towards improving their performance. Second, I believe that making money is of common interest to all human beings and the
price control system enabled all of the workers to join in the
money-making process at Higashimaru. Finally, I think it was successful because it introduced a sense of fun into the workplace.
In my opinion, people should feel that, "It is tough to do but
fun," if they are to be highly motivated to succeed. (Cooper
1994c, 9–10)

Indeed, the PCS so motivated groups to maintain their profitability that it sometimes got in the way of other plans that Okuno
had for the facility, including his plan to introduce a job rotation
system. To avoid decreased profitability, the groups usually were
unwilling to rotate their best members. Okuno overcame this
resistance by introducing the draft system.

The Draft System

In Okuno's view, the problem with his first job rotation program
was that it lacked clear rules to determine who was going to be
rotated and why. To correct these problems, Okuno created the
draft system. Under this system, any individual who had been in
the same group for at least five years and was ranked in the top
three of his group became a candidate for rotation. Every year one
person from each group that had a qualifying candidate was
rotated. Groups that did not have qualifying candidates dropped
out of the draft system for that year. The qualifying candidates
were reassigned, using a system based upon the system used by
the Japanese professional baseball league. The names of the qualifying candidates were written on a blackboard, and a lottery was
held. The lottery identified the order in which the participating
group leaders could select the individuals they wanted. Under these

rules, individuals viewed rotation as an indication of superior performance, and group leaders knew their new employees were among the best in the factory.

After selecting the "draftee," the group leader had to meet with the individual and try to convince him to join the group. Group leaders were expected to be persuasive and to prove to the selected individual that he was wanted and could be beneficial to the group. Apparently, the group leaders were very persuasive. In the first five years of the draft system, no group leader was turned down by a selected individual.

When coupled with the PCS, the draft system created significant pressure on both the groups and the rotated individuals to reduce any dislocation caused by the rotations as quickly as possible. In the past, it had taken about six months for a group's performance to recover from a rotation. Under the draft system, the recovery time decreased to less than three months. Three factors drove this reduction. First, the rotated individual was highly motivated and one of the firm's top performers. Second, knowing that the new member was a top performer and that group performance and PCS profitability were best served by helping the rotated individual learn his new job as quickly as possible, the other members of the group were motivated to make the rotation a success. Third, the groups knew ahead of time which individual was going to be rotated. This gave them time to prepare for the rotation. They could, for example, cross-train remaining members and develop training materials for the new individual.

The draft system was well received by all participants and ran for five consecutive years before being halted. However, it placed far greater pressure on the rotated individuals than had been anticipated. Two of the rotated individuals had nervous breakdowns because they worked too hard in the first few months after their transfers. Fortunately, both individuals recovered. Okuno halted the system after five years because all of the firm's best employees had been rotated and halting the rotations gave everyone a break. Four years later, the program was reinstated. Okuno expected future group leaders to be chosen from individuals who had been rotated twice and, therefore, had been highly rated members of three groups.

In discussing the purpose of the draft system, Okuno noted,

> I believe that in order to find life worth living, individuals require more than just money; they have to be recognized by others as being a valuable person. The draft system achieved this objective by increasing the number of people that felt valued, and by increasing the number of people who thought they were valuable from just one group to many groups. (Cooper 1994c, 10)

Although group leader meetings, the PCS, and the draft system did increase the managerial skills of the group leaders, Okuno introduced two additional programs designed to improve communication between groups leaders and their employees and to encourage creativity within the groups.

The Tatsumaki Program

The *tatsumaki* (or tornado) *program* served two purposes. First, it further increased the managerial skills of the group leaders, and second, it reduced the dependence of group members on those leaders. Under the *tatsumaki* program, all seventeen group leaders were intercepted as they were about to enter the plant one day and told they could not enter the plant or communicate with their employees for the next three days. The group leaders were initially surprised by the program, and some were apprehensive about the ability of the factory to operate without them. Their apprehension led Okuno to ask them to discuss among themselves their roles as leaders in the hope that they would learn to differentiate between leaders who made themselves indispensable and leaders who "worked themselves out of a job."

For the first *tatsumaki*, Okuno arranged a three-day program for the leaders. On the first day, they were to visit local supermarkets and other stores to see how their products were advertised and sold. On the second day, they were told to visit some local factories to see how they solved problems of interest to Higashi-maru. On the third day, they attended meetings with the firm's sales personnel so that they could discuss the interaction between the factory and the sales department. Okuno hoped this meeting would expand their awareness of the issues and problems faced by the entire firm, not just manufacturing.

By 1991, three *tatsumaki* programs had been held. The second was held about eighteen months after the first, and the third, about a year later. In the later programs no schedule of activities was given to the group leaders. Instead, they were told that they could do anything they liked with the next three days. Both times, the leaders met in a local coffee shop to decide how they could productively spend the three days, and both times, the activities undertaken by them were somewhat similar to those associated with the first *tatsumaki*. For the second program, for example, they visited a number of supermarkets and two firms, a local truck company and a Toshiba facility. They picked the truck company because they wanted to learn how to manage the firm's truck fleet more efficiently. They visited the Toshiba facility because it used conveyor systems similar to the ones in Higashi-maru's bottling area. Since the firms visited were not in competition with Higashimaru, information sharing on both sides was extensive.

Although the primary purpose of the program was to give group leaders a chance to review how they worked and to broaden their horizons, it also increased communication between group leaders, subordinates, and other members of the group.

> They [subordinates] had no choice about taking responsibility because their leaders were gone. This forced responsibility led to increased communication between the group leaders, their direct subordinates, and other group members. . . . In hindsight, the program was risky because it could have caused problems or accidents. Fortunately, it didn't and was viewed by all as a great success. (Cooper 1994c, 10)

The *Hangen* Game

The *hangen* (or "reduce by half") game was designed to reduce head count and encourage creative approaches to problems. According to Okuno,

> [i]t is very easy for people to become comfortable with the status quo. People tend to think that their job is particularly difficult. However, to become more efficient it is necessary to continuously review one's job to ensure that every task is absolutely necessary. Unfortunately, it is impossible to do so under normal conditions. There simply isn't enough pressure to allow creative thinking to occur. In the typical cost reduction program, work content is reviewed and unnecessary tasks are eliminated and the size of the work force reduced accordingly. This approach is typically only marginally successful.
>
> The Hangen game was successful because it forced people to think creatively. . . . Instead of marginal, they identify fundamental reductions. I experienced the power of this approach personally as I listened to the workers review their jobs and come up with unique solutions that reduced their work load. I called it a game because I wanted them to enjoy the creative process. We proved that people really do become more creative when they are placed in a tight corner. Just as importantly, we proved that it can be fun to be creative. (Cooper 1994c, 10–11)

The game was based on Okuno's observation that it is often more difficult to remove one person from a group than several. According to Okuno, this strange result comes about because "if 10 people perform 10 tasks, then getting rid of one person requires that 9 people perform 10 tasks, a difficult situation to manage. In contrast, if 5 people are removed, then 5 people are required to perform 10 tasks. While this situation looks impossible, it forces the group to reconsider every task it performs and ask whether each task is necessary." Thus, according to Okuno, cutting a group in half may lead to more creative thinking than downsizing by one. Even so, Okuno did not expect to be able to cut a group in half permanently, and once the group had completed the exercise, he would return several members to it. In the long run, however, the overall result was a significant reduction in the number of group members.

The bottling group was the most successful of the groups in this program. This group originally consisted of twenty-five members. Okuno split the group into two parts. The first part, made up of thirteen members, was asked to run the bottling area while the other part, made up of twelve members, watched. The twelve watching members were told not to interfere even if something went wrong. As a result of this exercise, the entire group discovered that it was possible to run the line for about an hour with only thirteen people before control was totally lost over the process. Once the group realized it was possible, they were more open to change.

The exercise was repeated several times. Each time, the length of time the group of thirteen could run the line increased. Once it became clear to the group that a smaller number of people could run the line, Okuno suggested adding three people to the thirteen to act as troubleshooters, helping out whenever needed. Once the sixteen individuals had run the bottling line without interruption for several days, the other nine individuals were reassigned to other groups. This improvement in efficiency attracted a lot of attention. The bottling group won the firm's President's Award for Improvement and a similar award from the governor of Hyogo prefecture.

The *hangen* game was not always successful; in particular, it was not well suited to reducing the size of small groups. If applied to a group of four, for instance, adding back one member means that only one person has been replaced. Thus, applying the *hangen* game to small groups is identical to asking a group to identify ways to replace one member. At one point, Higashimaru introduced a bottling line operated by only two workers. Analysis showed that the only way to reduce the number of workers in small groups was to introduce a robot.

It is difficult to objectively measure the success of Okuno's strategy. Certainly, my meeting with one of the groups and several of the group leaders suggested a highly motivated and committed workforce. As one of the group leaders talked about the improvements in the process his group had achieved, his pride was apparent. The group members were equally enthusiastic and appeared to have a good grasp of the group's profit and loss statement and balance sheet (see Figure 6-2).

SUMMARY

The success of Japanese cost management programs is highly dependent upon the right organizational context. A committed, motivated, and managerially aware workforce is critical for success. Because the typical Japanese organizational context consists of self-guided teams that are responsible for achieving the firms' cost reduction objectives, the way in which these teams are motivated determines the success of the cost reduction programs.

Nearly all of the companies studied had established an appropriate organizational context long ago. Their groups were highly motivated, semi-autonomous, and had leaders with well-established managerial skills. The only marked exception was Higashimaru Shoyu, where the workers were reluctant to change. The objective of Toshio Okuno's strategy was to convert a reluctant workforce into a workforce that was ready to accept and initiate change. This shift in their perspective was necessary if plant modernization was to be successful and the firm was to continue to become more efficient. The only other firm that acknowledged similar problems was Olympus, where the shift from cost to profit centers was seen to offer several advantages, including "a change in the mind-sets of the factory workers from a passive wait for instructions approach to a more pro-active approach as they pursued their group's profit target" (Cooper 1994k, 5).

What is impressive about Okuno's strategy is the creativity he applied to the problem of changing a reluctant workforce into an effective one. Each one of Okuno's five programs was designed to teach additional managerial skills and to create a positive attitude toward change.

The group meetings had three primary objectives. The first was

Figure 6-2
Fermentation Group Profit and Loss Report

Revenues

Sales of mold	¥985,607	97.1%
Bonus for quality	27,000	2.9
Support revenue for lending out personnel	31	0.0
TOTAL REVENUES	¥922,638	100.0%

Variable expenses

Material cost	¥687,450	74.7%
Wheat-roasting cost	13,309	1.4
Energy cost	63,791	6.9
Electricity	29,791	3.2
Wastewater charge	8,972	1.0
Support expenses for borrowing personnel	465	0.0
TOTAL VARIABLE EXPENSES	¥803,641	87.3%

Fixed expenses

Personnel	¥51,711	5.6%
Depreciation—machines	41,520	4.5
Machine costs—maintenance	10,231	1.1
Machine costs—repair	7,349	0.8
Machine costs—parts	3,793	0.3
Factory maintenance	847	0.1
Miscellaneous consumables	1,565	0.2
TOTAL FIXED EXPENSES	¥117,641	13.7%

Total expenses	¥920,717	100.0%

Summary

Revenues	¥922,638	100.0%
Variable expenses	803,641	87.1
Contribution	¥118,997	12.9%
Fixed expenses	117,076	12.7
Profit	¥1,921	0.2%
Breakeven point	¥907,875	98.4%

Source: R. Cooper, "Higashimaru Shoyu Company, Ltd. (B): Price Control System," case study 9-195-050 (Boston: Harvard Business School, 1994), 11.

to change the attitude of the workforce toward *its work*. Through the use of "*sagyo-shigoto*," Okuno made group members think about what they were doing, how they were doing it, and how it could be improved. The fun that characterized the interactions among workers was the key to transforming change from a threat into a game. The second primary objective of the monthly group meetings was to increase the level of communication among the members of the groups. Okuno achieved this objective by rewarding groups that were communicating well and by talking directly to group members to see how well his communications were being spread to group members. The third objective was to increase communication among the groups. Okuno's "visiting the customer" approach changed the way in which groups perceived each other. By rewarding significant intergroup communication, Okuno managed to change the way group leaders viewed their roles and the roles of other groups.

Through PCS, Okuno instilled a profit-making attitude into the groups and extended the managerial abilities of the group leaders. However, the ability of the firm to modernize also required a future generation of group leaders. Using the draft system to rotate the best workers rather than the worst, Okuno created a set of workers with broad exposure to the production process, a positive attitude to change, and significant managerial skill—all prerequisites of a good group leader.

The *tatsumaki* program continued the push toward change. Its primary objective was to make group leaders realize that they should not make themselves indispensable to their groups but rather strive to "work themselves out of a job." Such a change in perspective is necessary if the next generation of group leaders is to emerge. Okuno also used the *tatsumaki* program to broaden the experiences of the group leaders by exposing them to the firm's retailers, other supporting companies, and representatives of the sales department.

Finally, the *hangen* game was designed to force the groups to engage in creative thinking. At the heart of this game is the assumption that if the number of employees available to perform a given operation is halved, the only way the remaining group members can succeed is by completely changing the way in which they operate. The success of the *hangen* game is best illustrated by the bottling group, which was reduced from twenty-five to sixteen workers.

Through the skillful use of different programs designed to

make learning and adapting to change challenging and fun, Okuno changed his reluctant workforce into a highly motivated one that first accepted and then initiated change. It was within this organizational context that effective cost management could be undertaken.

PART THREE

MANAGING THE COSTS OF FUTURE PRODUCTS

Just as you cannot inspect quality into a product,
You cannot account costs out of it.

INTRODUCTION

Under confrontation strategy, the objective of cost management is to instill in everyone in the firm a disciplined approach to cost reduction. This discipline must begin when products or services are first conceived, continue throughout the manufacturing process, and end only when the product or service is discontinued. Successful cost management cannot be limited to the four walls of the factory or even to the boundaries of the firm. It must spread across the entire supplier chain and the customer chain. It must cover all of the value chain for the products or services that the firm sells, and it must create significant pressures on individuals throughout the firm to reduce costs.

Given this, effective cost management must start at the design stage of a product's life because once a product is designed the majority of its costs are fixed. After all, the way in which the product is designed determines the number of components, the different types of materials used, and the time it takes to assemble the product. Some authorities estimate that as much as 90 to 95 percent of a product's costs are designed in; that is, they cannot be avoided without redesigning the product (see Figure III-1). Consequently, effective cost control programs must focus on the design phase as well as the manufacturing phase.

The primary cost management techniques used by many Japanese firms during the product design stage are target costing and value engineering. These two techniques are extended across the supplier chain through the use of interorganizational cost management systems (see Figure III-2). Target costing has two primary objectives. The first is to identify the cost at which the product

Figure III-1
Life Cycle Costs

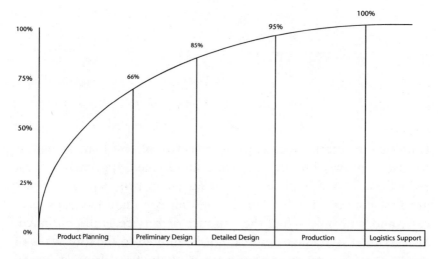

Source: Adapted from B. S. Blanchard, *Design and Manage to Life-Cycle Cost* (Portland, Ore.: M/A Press, 1978).

Figure III-2
The Systems Used to Manage the Costs of Future Products

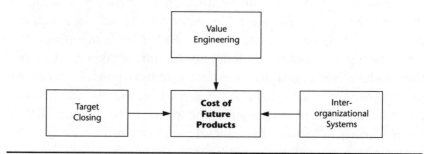

must be manufactured if it is to earn its target profit margin at its target, or expected, selling price. The target margin is the margin the firm must earn on a product if the firm is to achieve its profit objectives. The target price is the price at which the product will be sold when it is launched. Determining the target price requires careful analysis of the quality, functionality, and price the customer wants. Once the expected selling price is determined and the target margin is established, the **target cost,** the cost at which the product must be manufactured, can be calculated.

The second objective of target costing is to set the purchase prices of externally acquired items. This is achieved by breaking the target cost down to the component level. By predicting the rate at which the costs of components are falling, the firm can develop a target purchase price for each component. These prices are set so that the sum of all of the components when added to the manufacturing and assembly costs equals the target cost of the product. The firm's suppliers are then expected to find ways to deliver the components at their target prices and still make adequate returns.

Value engineering (VE) is a series of procedures that firms use to help design products so that they can be manufactured at their target costs. There are four major ways to apply VE principles to product design. These ways are zeroth, first look, second look, and teardown. Zeroth look VE is the application of VE principles at the concept proposal stage, the earliest stage in the design process. Its objective is to introduce new forms of functionality that have not existed previously. First look VE, which is defined as developing new products from concepts, focuses on the major elements of the product design. The objective is to create enhanced functionality by improving the capability of the existing functions. Second look VE is applied during the last half of the planning stage and the first half of the development and product preparation stage. The objective of second look VE is to improve the value and functionality of existing components. The objective of teardown is to analyze competitive products in terms of materials they contain, parts they use, the way in which they function, the way in which they are manufactured, and the way in which they are coated, and the types of coating used.

The final technique to manage the cost of future products consists of developing systems that cross organizational boundaries. These interorganizational cost management systems are designed to achieve three objectives. First, they create conduits that transmit to suppliers the competitive pressures faced by the end producers. Second, they permit the product engineers at all the firms in the supplier chain to design products jointly that can be manufactured more cost efficiently than if the firms acted independently. Finally, through trade-offs in the survival triplet, these cost management systems create a way for the end producer's parts specifications to be modified. These modifications allow the product to be sold at its target price while still generating an adequate return for all firms in the supplier chain.

CHAPTER 7

TARGET COSTING

Most firms use target costing to ensure that new products are profitable. Target costing is a **structured approach to determining the cost at which a proposed product with specified functionality and quality must be produced in order to generate the desired level of profitability at the product's anticipated selling price.** Discussing target costing in terms of the survival triplet is important because it links product price and quality with functionality. Since target costing uses price information, it is necessary to consider the customers' quality and functionality requirements. Without this link, there are no constraints on the target costing process, and it is possible to set a target cost that is too low to enable the product to be manufactured with acceptable levels of quality and functionality. Thus, target costing must take into account the constraints of product quality and functionality. This definition also differentiates between target costing and *kaizen* costing, which is discussed in chapter 12. Unlike *kaizen* costing, which focuses on reducing a product's cost through increased efficiency in the production process, target costing focuses on reducing the cost of a product through changes in its design. Therefore, target costing is applied during the design phase of a product's life cycle.[1] Combining *kaizen* costing and target costing under a single name is not beneficial because each relies upon different cost reduction techniques. There are two major steps in target costing. The first

---

[1] The existing literature is ambivalent toward restricting target costing to the product design phase. Some authors agree with this limitation, while others define target costing as encompassing the entire product life cycle.

is to determine a product's target price and target margin in order to determine its target cost. The second is to break the target cost down to the component and raw material level so that the purchase prices of items acquired externally can be determined. A product's target cost is determined by subtracting its target profit margin from its target selling price. That is:

$$\text{Target Cost} = \text{Target Price} - \text{Target Margin}$$

The target price of a new product is determined primarily from the analyses done for product planning (see chapter 3). The target margin is determined by corporate profit expectations, historical results, competitive analysis, and, sometimes, computer simulations.

Once the product's target margin and target price have been determined, they are used as the basis for determining the purchase price of externally acquired components and raw materials. At Isuzu, for example,

> the target cost for an entire vehicle in the concept proposal stage was distributed among the vehicle's 8,000–10,000 components at the major function or group component levels. . . . Group components were the major subassemblies purchased from the firm's suppliers and subcontractors. There were only about 100 such components, and yet they amounted to as much as 70%–80% of the manufacturing cost. (Cooper and Yoshikawa 1994a, 5)

Target costing differs from the conventional Western (Worthy 1991) and cost-plus approaches found in many firms in that the desired cost to manufacture is specified. Under the conventional Western approach, the product's expected profit margin, not its cost, is the dependent variable. It is determined by subtracting the product's expected cost from its target selling price:

$$\text{Expected Profit Margin} = \text{Target Selling Price} - \text{Expected Cost}$$

The product's cost is expected, not target, because the product is designed to achieve its functionality and then its cost is determined.

Under the cost-plus approach, the product's anticipated selling price becomes the dependent variable. It is determined by adding an expected profit margin to the expected product cost.

Target Selling Price = Expected Cost + Expected Margin

Under this approach, price is simply a calculated figure. When these two approaches are used, product designers have no specified cost objective to achieve. Instead, they are expected to minimize the cost of the product as they design it. In theory, these approaches should outperform target costing because they set out to minimize a product's cost rather than reduce it to a prespecified level. If, however, the target cost is also the product's minimum cost, then the numerical objectives (the product's cost) for the three techniques are identical.

In practice, target costing appears to lead to products with lower costs than the other two approaches. The most likely explanation for this is that designing to a *specified* low cost appears to create more intense pressure to reduce costs than designing to an *unspecified* minimum cost. This explanation is in keeping with Locke and White's (1981) research on goal setting, which finds that better performance emerges from setting specific, challenging goals than from setting the more general goal of doing one's best. Later research by Locke and Latham (1984) corroborates that specificity in goals results in more reliably directed action.

While it is possible to imagine modified versions of the three techniques in which estimated costs can be exceeded "if necessary" or the target cost can be exceeded without penalty, what distinguishes target costing from modified forms of the other two techniques is the intensity with which the product is designed to its target cost. Japanese target costing systems rely heavily upon this rule: "The target cost can never be exceeded." Without this rule, target costing systems lose their effectiveness.

Of course, in practice, the "never exceeded" rule is broken at times, but conditions must justify it and specified procedures must be followed to authorize it (see chapter 8). In other words, decisions to break the rule are not based on design engineers saying, "If we just add this feature, the product will be so much better (and only cost a little more)."

FACTORS AFFECTING THE DESIGN OF TARGET-COSTING SYSTEMS

Nissan, Komatsu, Olympus, and Topcon, among others, have developed sophisticated target-costing systems that form only one part of their cost management systems. These target-costing systems differ in several important ways, including their structures and objectives, because of the way in which each firm competes using the survival triplet. Three factors—the type of product manufactured, the type of customer serviced, and the degree of influence over part suppliers and subcontractors—affect the role of the survival triplet and thus the structure of a target-costing system (see Figure 7-1).

The Role of the Nature of the Product

The type of product manufactured plays a critical role because as the cost, complexity, and duration of product design increases, the target-costing system appears to become more important and more complex. This increase in importance and complexity makes

Figure 7-1
Factors Affecting the Structure of a Target-Costing System

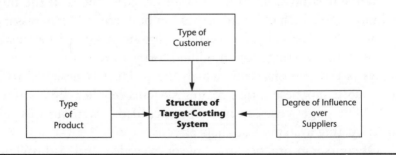

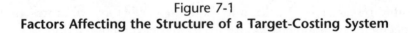

sense because the potential savings are greater, and formal systems are likely to have a bigger payoff.

Nissan and Komatsu, for example, manufacture large, complex products that are highly capital intensive. Product development cycles at these two firms are longer than those at Olympus and Topcon—approximately four years and eighteen months, respectively. Longer and more complex product development cycles result in target-costing systems that are tied closely to the firms' value engineering programs (see chapter 8). Longer development cycles also mean that the earliest target costs established are fairly uncertain. Nissan specifically excludes its earliest (price − margin = cost) estimates from its formal target-costing system by calling them allowable costs. Komatsu calls its early cost estimates "target values" to differentiate them from target costs. Furthermore, both firms have developed intermediate target costs; at Nissan, these are called "draft target costs."

At Olympus and Topcon, short development cycles lead to less sophisticated target-costing systems that interact less intensely with their value engineering programs. Consequently, initial or intermediate target costs are not broken out from their formal target-costing systems. Short development cycles allow these two firms to increase the functionality of their products rapidly. Because competition for them is based upon product functionality, these firms must shorten their product development cycles, and thus, reduce the time available for target costing and value engineering. Sony's target-costing system reflects this influence:

> Because capital investments were small, Sony could afford to experiment with different models; the failure of a single model did not adversely affect profitability. Short development cycles meant that when Sony was estimating the sales volume, selling price, and production cost of a new product it usually had information about last year's model to act as a starting point for its estimates. Because the new product was usually designed to replace the previous year's product and was quite similar in nature, the previous product's sales volumes and selling prices were good predictors of the success of the new model. Conse-

quently, Sony product planners were relatively confident about most of their estimates. (Cooper 1994l, 7)

The Role of the Type of Customer Serviced

The type of customers serviced plays a critical role because it is the customers who decide the relative importance of each characteristic of the survival triplet and the rate at which each should be improved. If the customer is the general public and the product is subject to changing tastes, keeping track of those tastes becomes important and designing them into the product cost effectively becomes critical. The target-costing systems of firms producing goods for the general public have a heavy consumer analysis orientation. In contrast, if the customer is a commercial buyer looking for quality over functionality, durability may be critical and increased functionality less important. Target-costing systems in these cases focus on cost reduction more than consumer analysis.

At Nissan and Olympus, the target-costing systems are used primarily to link marketing and design. These firms view the general public as their customer; thus, one of the keys to their survival is keeping ahead of changes in consumers' tastes. The same is true at Isuzu, where the customer plays a critical role in setting target costs:

> The target costs of these major functions and group components were determined using monetary values or ratios. The monetary values were determined by using market research that asked customers to estimate how much they would pay for a given function. Ratios were developed by asking customers to estimate the relative importance of each function using a 100-point scale. The monetary values and ratios were used to prorate a product's target cost to the major functions. . . . [I]f the prorated target cost for a component was too low to allow a safe version to be produced, the component's target cost was increased and the target cost of the other components was decreased. (Cooper 1994a, 5)

In contrast, Komatsu and Topcon sell to commercial enterprises, and the desired functionality of the product is more stable and less prone to changing tastes. This difference does not mean that functionality is unimportant, rather that it is more predictable. The primary difference between Komatsu and Topcon is the customers' degree of willingness to pay more for increased functionality; Komatsu's customers are less willing.

The target-costing systems at Nissan and Olympus contain numerous interactions with marketing and frequent monitoring of consumer trends. At Komatsu and Topcon, some market analysis is performed, but the number of such analyses, their intensity, and the degree of interaction with the target-costing system are reduced. Consequently, the target-costing systems at Komatsu and Topcon focus more on cost and less on functionality, reflecting the critical characteristic of their survival triplets.

Role of Degree of Influence over Parts Suppliers and Subcontractors

Power over suppliers is important because one of the outputs of a target-costing system is the price at which the firm is willing to buy components from its suppliers. Determining these prices is valuable only if the firm has some degree of control over its suppliers. One of the primary objectives of Nissan's and Komatsu's target-costing systems is the development of target costs (i.e., purchase prices) for purchased parts. This is important because both firms rely heavily upon outside suppliers for purchased components. At Nissan, the cost of an existing functional equivalent of a product's major components coupled with historical cost reduction trends, is used to determine the cost reduction targets for each of the new model's major components. These cost reduction targets are decomposed to the part level to set the target selling prices for the firm's suppliers and subcontractors. At Komatsu, functional and productivity analyses are used to estimate target costs. Both techniques determine feasible target costs for purchased components and create a strong downward pressure on supplier prices.

At Olympus and Topcon, the role that target costing plays in influencing suppliers and subcontractors is less well developed. At Olympus, this situation reflects the firm's high degree of vertical integration. The firm produces most of its own components and, therefore, has less need to create systems to indirectly influence its suppliers. At Topcon, the low volume of production means that the firm has less control over its suppliers and subcontractors and therefore cannot take advantage of this target-costing role.

THE TARGET-COSTING SYSTEMS

Nissan Motors has a mature, sophisticated target-costing system that has two objectives: first, to manage product functionality and ensure that the product can be manufactured at its target cost; second, to create a downward price pressure on the firm's suppliers and subcontractors.

Nissan competes in a market in which prices are declining slightly or staying the same while functionality is increasing rapidly. When coupled to changing customer tastes, the complex nature of the product makes it necessary for the firm to determine the functionality that the consumer requires for each type of automobile designed. The selling price is determined primarily by the functionality of the product and customer expectations. That is:

$$\text{Customer Expectations} \rightarrow \text{Functionality} \rightarrow \text{Price}$$

Functionality depends on many different attributes such as engine size, audio system sophistication, and degree of sound proofing. Because the product's desired functionality alters as the role of the automobile in the customer's life changes, the interaction between price and functionality is complex and becomes the central focus of Nissan's target-costing system. The large number of variants of a single model could create a problem, but the firm simplifies the task of generating target costs for all of its product variants by establishing the target cost of the variant that will sell the highest number of units. If this variant can earn its target margin, then the model from which it is derived should also earn its margin: "The financial analysis consisted of a rough profitability study in which the profitability of the highest volume variant of the new model was estimated using historical cost estimates and the latest estimate of that variant's target price" (Cooper 1994i, 4).

The target margin is determined by a careful consideration of available information on the consumer, the firm's anticipated future product mix, and the firm's long-term profit objectives. Each new model's target margin is established by running simulations of the firm's overall profitability for the next ten years. These simulations are based on the assumptions that the models identified in the future product matrix are selling at their expected sales volumes. The simulations start by plotting the actual profit margins of existing products. The desired profitability of planned models is then added, and the firm's overall profitability is determined over the years at various sales levels. This predicted overall profitability is compared to the firm's long-term profitability objectives, which have been set by senior management. Once a satisfactory future product offering that achieves the firm's profit objective is established, the target margins for each new model are set (see Figure 7-2).

Target prices cannot be established in a vacuum. They are determined by market factors, in particular, the strength of the firm's products compared to competitive offerings and market prices for comparable products:

> This target price was determined by taking into account a number of internal and external factors. The internal factors included the position of the model in the matrix and the strategic and profitability objectives of top management for that model. The external factors considered included the corporation's image and level of customer loyalty in the model's niche, the expected quality level and functionality of the model compared to competitive offerings, the model's expected market share, and finally, the expected price of competitive models. (Cooper 1994i, 4)

Figure 7-2
Identifying the Target Margin at Nissan

Source: R. Cooper, "Nissan Motor Company, Ltd.: Target Costing System," case study 9-194-040 (Boston: Harvard Business School, 1994), 13.

The six-year development cycle makes it impossible for the firm to set a target cost at the beginning of the design process and guarantee to meet it without the ability to modify products later in the design process. This ability provides necessary slack to ensure that the firm achieves its target cost. By making what was to be a standard feature an optional feature, for example, the firm can reduce the cost of the standard variant and thus achieve the target cost objective.

The firm's second objective—to create a downward price pressure on suppliers and thus pass cost reduction pressures on to them—begins by developing an order sheet that details the characteristics of the twenty to thirty major functions of the proposed model, such as the engine, air conditioner, transmission, and sound system. The characteristics of each major function are chosen to satisfy the consumers for which the model is designed. The

Figure 7-3
Establishing the Target Cost of the Major Functions
of an Automobile

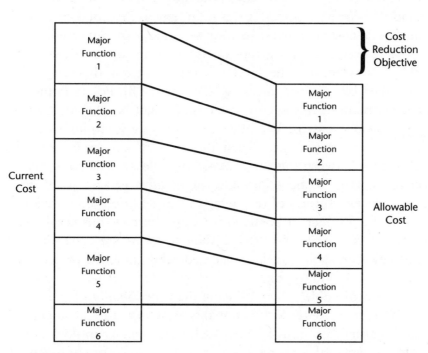

Source: R. Cooper, "Nissan Motor Company, Ltd.: Target Costing System," case study 9-194-040 (Boston: Harvard Business School, 1994), 16.

current cost of the model is determined by summing the current manufacturing cost of each major function (see Figure 7-3).

The next step is to identify the allowable cost of each major function. The **allowable cost,** an early estimate of the target cost, is determined by subtracting the target profit margin from the target price. The allowable cost is set by teams derived from almost every functional area of the firm including product design, engineering, purchasing, production engineering, manufacturing, and parts supply. While usually the allowable cost is lower than the current cost, sometimes it is higher because the product specifications demand higher performance and functionality than the performance and functionality specified in existing designs. **In total, the sum of the cost reductions for each major function must be equal to the level of cost reduction required to achieve the model's allowable cost.** It is this requirement that total cost equals allowable cost that gives the target-costing system its teeth.

The excess of the current manufacturing cost over the allowable cost identifies the level of cost reduction that has to be identified by value engineering (see chapter 8). For example, the current manufacturing cost of a model might be ¥1,500,000 with an allowable cost of ¥1,350,000, identifying a required cost reduction of 10 percent. When the level of cost reduction (the difference between the current cost and allowable cost) is considered too large to be achievable, an iterative process is initiated. This process consists of reviewing the target price and functionality of the product. If possible, the target price is increased and a new target margin and, hence, allowable cost are determined. If this new allowable cost is considered achievable, the project continues. If it is still too high (or marketing does not believe a higher price is achievable), then reducing the functionality of the model is considered. Reduced functionality is achieved by changing the technical specifications of the model. For example, antilock brakes may be replaced with disc brakes. Before they are approved, all such reductions in functionality are reviewed by marketing to ensure that they do not invalidate the product's target price. An iterative process is required because the changes in functionality may lead to a change in the target price.

Once the allowable cost of each major subcomponent is identified, the expected cost of manufacture, the **draft target cost,** can be computed. The draft target cost is an updated allowable cost. This cost is computed for each variant, rather than just the highest volume variant. After the first round of cost cutting is completed, a major review of the model is undertaken. The review compares the expected profitability of the model (given by the target price minus its draft target cost) to the latest estimates of the capital investment and remaining research and development expenditures required to complete the design and begin production. If the financial analysis is acceptable, the project is authorized, and the model shifts from the conceptual design stage to the product development stage.

The first step in the product development stage is the preparation of a detailed order sheet that lists all of the components the model requires. Value engineering is used at this stage to determine the allowable costs for each component. The order sheet is analyzed to see which components should be sourced internally and which components should be sourced externally. Suppliers, both internal and external, are provided with a description of each component and its potential production volumes. Suppliers are expected to provide price and delivery timing estimates for these components: "The target costs for each component were compared to the prices quoted by the suppliers. If the quoted prices were acceptable, the quote was accepted. If the initial quote was too high, then further negotiations were undertaken until an agreement could be reached" (Cooper 1994i, 7).

The process used to generate the target costs for each component of every major function is essentially the same as the process used to generate the allowable costs of the major functions (see Figure 7-4). Because the number of target values that need to be developed can be overwhelming, most firms have developed specific procedures. At Nissan, for example,

> To avoid having to develop target costs for all 20,000 components in a typical new model line, the engineers only performed detailed target costing on two or three representative variations. Each variation contained approximately 3,500 components, and typically 80% of the components were common across variations. Therefore, about 5,000 components were subjected to detailed target costing. The target costs of the other 15,000 components were estimated by comparing them to similar components in the 5,000 already target-costed. (Cooper 1994i, 6)

The magnitude of determining so many target values, even after reducing the pool of items as Nissan did, should not be underestimated. It takes considerable effort to develop and maintain such a system.

Figure 7-4
**Establishing the Target Cost of the Components
of an Automobile**

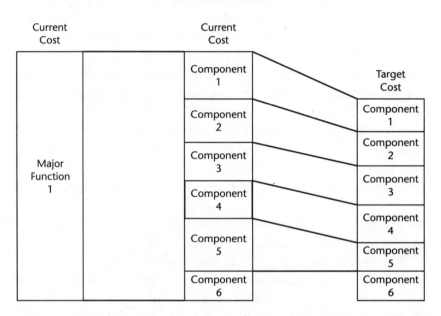

Source: R. Cooper, "Nissan Motor Company, Ltd.: Target Costing System," case study 9-194-040 (Boston: Harvard Business School, 1994), 17.

By comparing the allowable cost of the subcomponent and the sum of the expected cost of the components in that subcomponent after cost reduction, it is possible to determine whether or not the major subcomponent can be produced at its allowable cost. When the sum of the component costs are too high, additional cost reduction objectives are identified until the total target cost of the representative variation is acceptable. This is a critical step. It reinforces the requirement to produce the product to its target cost.

The next phase in product development is to construct two or three prototype vehicles. Since assembly times can be estimated quite accurately from these prototypes, assembly target costs are identified and included in the product's target cost. Unlike draft target costs, target costs include indirect manufacturing costs.

As the vehicle enters production, accounting monitors all component and assembly costs, and if these are not in line with the target costs, cost, design, and engineering groups are notified and value engineering is performed to reduce costs to the target levels.

Komatsu, like Nissan, has a mature and sophisticated target-costing system that is used to ensure that the product will be profitable when released for mass production and to identify when cost reduction techniques are required. In contrast to Nissan, however, Komatsu competes in an environment where functionality changes more slowly and customer preferences are more obvious. The primary pressure on Komatsu is to reduce its prices and, therefore, its costs. Because the rate of change of functionality is slower for Komatsu than for Nissan, it is easier for Komatsu to determine the target prices of its new products. Consequently, Komatsu's target-costing system is primarily designed to determine the cost of components, not to make trade-offs between cost and functionality. Since price is more important than functionality in Komatsu's environment, the firm first identifies the target price of a new product and then tries to maximize its functionality. That is:

Customer Requirements → Price → Functionality

Reflecting this approach, the Komatsu target-costing system adopts a more internal perspective than Nissan's and is heavily focused on managing costs.

Because the degree of design changes from one model to the next are smaller for Komatsu than for Nissan, Komatsu relies more heavily upon using existing component costs to estimate the future cost of products than Nissan does. However, this reliance does not mean that Komatsu uses either a conventional Western approach or a cost-plus approach. Instead, the firm uses market analysis to predict the selling price of the new model and its target cost.

While Nissan identifies the difference between the current cost and the target cost and then distributes the cost reduction objectives among the components based upon expected savings, Komatsu takes the current costs of the major components and adjusts them by their expected cost reductions. This number, the *target value,* is compared to the product's target cost. It is this determination of target values that is different from the process at Nissan. By comparing the target values to the target cost of the new model, Komatsu can identify areas that require aggressive cost reduction techniques.

Three different cost reduction techniques are used at Komatsu to identify when cost reduction techniques are required. Design analysis is used to identify the approximate structure of the major subassemblies in new products. Functional analysis and productivity analysis are used to identify the target costs of the major subassemblies. It is the way in which these techniques are applied that illustrates the strength of Komatsu's target-costing system.

Design analysis is the process of identifying alternate designs for major subassemblies and selecting the most appropriate of the alternate designs. Two major factors are taken into account when choosing among alternatives: functionality and cost. A new design alternative is adopted only if it achieves the desired level of functionality and cost. Frequently, one alternative may produce higher functionality but at a higher cost. When this happens, product engineers explore ways to manufacture the higher functionality alternative at the original cost. If such a way cannot be found, then the engineers look for offsetting cost reductions elsewhere in the product. If sufficient additional savings can be identified to allow the new product to be manufactured for its target cost, then the new alternative is implemented.

It is this second step of finding an alternative way of making the savings that illustrates the application of target costing in the design analysis phase. Improvements that increase product cost are allowed only if additional savings that will maintain the product's ability to be manufactured at its target cost can be identified. For example, in Komatsu's larger bulldozers, the engine and torque converter, transmission, and steering clutch and brakes were physically separate modules, but customers had complained about the length of time required to mount and dismount the modules during maintenance. Komatsu wanted to reduce this time below its current level of eighty-six hours.

Design analysis identified two different ways to position the three components. The first approach integrated the three modules into two, one consisting of the engine and torque converter and the other the transmission and steering clutch and brake modules. The integration of the transmission and steering clutch and brake modules into a single module reduced the mount/ dismount time to 44 hours. The second approach also integrated the three modules into two, but this time the torque converter, transmission, steering clutch and brakes were integrated into a single module. This approach had the advantage of removing the need to change the oil, thereby reducing the mount/dismount time to 33 hours [see Figure 7-5]. Unfortunately, both of the new design alternatives were more expensive

Figure 7-5
Komatsu Ltd.: Target-Costing System, Design Analysis Example

Design	Mount/ Dismount Time	Modules		
Existing Approach	86 Hours	Engine and Torque Converter	Transmission	Steering Clutch and Brake
First Proposed Approach	44 Hours	Engine and Torque Converter	Transmission, Steering Clutch, and Brakes	
Second Proposed Approach	33 Hours	Engine	Torque Converter, Transmission, Steering Clutch, and Brake	

Source: R. Cooper, "Komatsu, Ltd. (A): Target Costing System," case study 9-194-037 (Boston: Harvard Business School, 1994), 9.

than the old design; the fastest design was also the most expensive.

> This conflict between quality and cost was resolved by changing the way the ripper mounting bracket was attached to the bulldozer. . . . The new approach allowed the mounting bracket to be welded, as opposed to bolted, to the mainframe. Welding was cheaper than bolting and the savings equaled the additional cost of adopting the alternative design of the engine, transmission, and torque convertor. (Cooper 1994e, 4–5)

This example illustrates two critical aspects of the interaction between Komatsu's target costing and value engineering systems. First, if a functionality improvement that increases costs is to be allowed, the target cost must be maintained by finding offsetting savings elsewhere. This discipline of forcing the target cost to be achieved halts a steady increase in the new product's cost as the design engineers enhance its quality and functionality. Second, the objective is to achieve a target cost, not a minimum cost. If the objective were to achieve a minimum cost, then the engineers would continuously search for cost reduction opportunities rather than only when the target cost is exceeded.

Once the design approach for the major subassemblies is identified, their target costs are determined using either a functional analysis or a productivity analysis. The choice of technique depends upon who is responsible for designing the subassembly. Functional analysis, which does not require in-depth knowledge of the production process, is utilized for parts designed and produced by Komatsu's suppliers. Productivity analysis, which does require such knowledge, is used for parts designed by Komatsu and then produced by the firm or a subcontractor.

Functional analysis attempts to identify the lowest feasible cost, given aggressive cost reduction applied to existing technology, for a major subcomponent. The analysis relies upon two databases, functional tables, and cost tables. A functional table contains information about the physical characteristics of each existing component and its functionality. It is used to determine the firm's most efficient existing components. A cost table contains information about the physical characteristics of each existing component and its cost. It is used to determine the most cost effective components. By combining the information from a functional table with the information from a cost table, the firm can identify the target cost of the "most efficient" and "most cost effective" component. This target cost is used to set the purchase price of the component. For example, to develop the target cost of an excavator cooling system, Komatsu began its functional analysis with an analysis of the functions of the cooling system and how they were achieved. The primary function was identified as the system's cooling capacity. Secondary functions included the speed with which the system started cooling after the engine was first switched on and the stability of the temperature maintained by the system.

The determinants of the system's cooling capacity were then identified in order of importance. Because analysis had shown that the most important determinant was the surface area of the radiator,

> the functional analysis began by plotting the cooling capacity versus the radiator surface area for all existing products that used the same type of cooling system. This information was maintained in functional tables. From this plot the average and minimum lines for existing equipment were determined [see Figure 7-6]. The average line was determined using linear regression and the minimum line was drawn so that it passed through the most efficient cooling systems. The required cooling capacity for the new model was used to identify the minimum cooling area required according to the best designs. The minimum cooling area was that which generated the desired cooling capacity on the minimum line. . . .
>
> The target cost for the cooling system was determined by a similar process, using surface area versus cost information for existing products. This information was maintained in functional cost tables. A graph of the cost of cooling systems against their surface area was plotted for all existing models using the same cooling technology. The average cost per surface area was deter-

Figure 7-6
Determining Target Radiator Size Using Functional Analysis

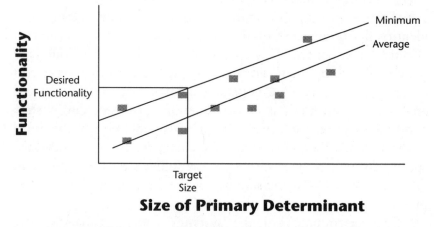

Size of Primary Determinant

Source: R. Cooper, "Komatsu, Ltd. (A): Target Costing System," case study 9-194-037 (Boston: Harvard Business School, 1994), 10.

---

mined using linear regression. The minimum cost line was again drawn passing through the most cost efficient designs [see Figure 7-7]. The minimum surface area identified from the cooling capacity/radiator surface area analysis was used to identify the minimum cost of the new cooling system. This minimum cost for the minimum radiator surface area became the target cost for the radiator. . . . (Cooper 1994e, 5–6)

The double minimum approach (minimum surface area and minimum cost) creates more intense pressure than a single minimum approach that takes into account both size and cost as the new design must achieve both minimum size and minimum cost, not just minimum cost. Consequently, suppliers must continually push the frontiers of technology to achieve more efficient designs.

When Komatsu's engineers design the component or it is manufactured internally, more information is available to the firm and a productivity analysis is undertaken. At the heart of the productivity analysis is a set of cost tables that identify the cost of each production step as a function of its physical characteristics.

Figure 7-7
Determining Radiator Target Cost Using Functional Analysis

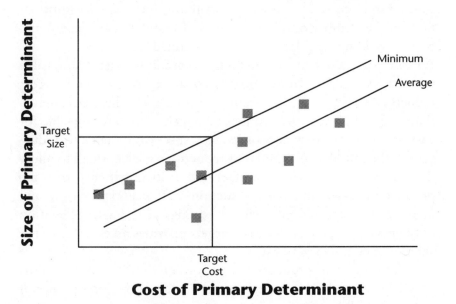

Source: R. Cooper, "Komatsu, Ltd. (A): Target Costing System," case study 9-194-037 (Boston: Harvard Business School, 1994), 11.

Figure 7-8
Productivity Analysis Table

	Current	Target
# of Different Materials		
Cost of Materials per Kilogram		
Weld Length		
Weld Cost		

In the analysis, the major steps in the new subassembly's production process are analyzed and the sum of their costs is compared to the target cost. The cost tables contain, for example, information on the number of different types of material used, length and cost of welding, and labor times maintained (see Figure 7-8).

When the expected cost is too high, the section leaders responsible for each step in the production process are asked to identify a cost reduction target. The ultimate responsibility for these cost reduction targets lies with the product manager, who is responsible for ensuring that the new subcomponent successfully enters production. If the initial aggregated cost reductions are too small to allow the subcomponent to be manufactured at its target cost, then the product manager and the production staff negotiate to try and increase the expected productivity savings. The final aggregation of the negotiated cost reduction targets provides an estimate of the subcomponent's target cost.

The process of productivity analysis at Komatsu can be illustrated by the redesign of a mounting socket in the mainframes of the firm's bulldozers:

> In the old design, the mounting socket consisted of a hole drilled through the body of the mainframe. This design was simple to manufacture but had the drawback of creating a stress zone around the hole. To ensure that the mounting socket was strong enough, that section of the mainframe had to be manufactured out of expensive, high-grade materials. Productivity analysis had identified the reduction of the level of high-grade material in the mainframe as one way to reduce costs. The new design consisted of welding to the vehicle mainframe a mounting bracket that contained the mounting socket hole. The new mounting unit was designed to reduce the strain imposed on the mainframe so that normal-grade steel could be used. (Cooper 1994e, 6)

Komatsu's target-costing system allows the firm to maximize the functionality of its products (subject to the constraints of price and quality) and to develop aggressive purchase prices for needed subcomponents. Unlike Nissan, where functionality (to a certain extent) can be added and subtracted at will, Komatsu must design in functionality. Consequently, product functionality and cost are deeply intertwined, and Komatsu's target-costing system is more heavily focused on cost control than Nissan's system.

Olympus also has a well-developed target-costing system that it uses to set the prices of its cameras:

> The first step in setting target costs was to identify the price point at which a new camera model would sell. For most new products, the price point was already established. . . . The appropriate price point for a camera was determined by its distinctive feature. . . . The relationship between distinctive features and price points was determined from the competitive analysis and technology review used in the development of the product plan. (Cooper 1994j, 5–6)

As noted in chapter 4, Olympus competes in an environment in which prices are given and functionality is increasing even more rapidly than it is for Nissan. Usually, subsequent generations of a product are sold at the same price point as the previous model and have the same distinctive primary functionality, such as a zoom lens or given focal length range. When it is no longer possible to add functionality to a product, the selling price of the following generation falls to the next lower price point and the process is repeated. As a result, Olympus' target-costing system focuses on managing functionality more than either Nissan's or Komatsu's. Like Nissan, the functionality of the camera determines its price point or target price. That is:

Customer Preferences → Distinctive Functionality → Price →
Supporting Functionality

Although second-order functionality plays a role similar to its role at Nissan, it is less significant because Olympus cannot delete a particular function, such as a flash unit, from the base cost of a camera as the camera would not sell. Because of the shorter design cycle, Olympus also lacks the ability to vary the design of its products other than by changing functionality. Hence the firm must "get it right the first time," which means the interaction between cost and functionality is monitored closely during the design process.

Once the price point of a new camera is identified, the revenue per unit is determined. For a camera that will be sold in the United States, the revenue per unit is the free-on-board (FOB) price. This price is calculated by subtracting the appropriate margin of the dealers and Olympus' U.S. subsidiary as well as any import costs such as freight and import duty. To determine its expected margin, the price is divided by the product's estimated manufacturing cost (its current cost). Guidelines for acceptable target margins are set by the divisional manager every six months. These guidelines are developed in tandem with the division's six-month profit plans. By comparing the new product's expected cost ratio to its target-cost ratio, the firm can identify the degree of cost or functionality reduction required.

Although a product's target cost is based upon the price point for its distinctive feature, a research and development design review is responsible for identifying the other features of the camera (for example, the type of flash and shutter units). Feature identification is an iterative process in which the cost of each new design is estimated and compared to the product's target cost. Approximately 20 percent of the time, the estimated cost is equal to or less than the target cost and the product design can be released for further analysis by manufacturing. The other 80 percent of the time, the research and development group must do further analysis. When this happens, marketing is asked if the price point can be increased so that the target cost will equal the estimated cost. If the price can be increased, the product is released to production. If the market price cannot be increased, the effect of reducing the product's functionality is explored. Reducing the nondistinctive functionality of the product decreases its estimated production cost. If these cost reductions are sufficient and the product can still be sold at its target price point, then the product is released to production (see Figure 7-9).

Figure 7-9
The Target-Costing Process at Olympus

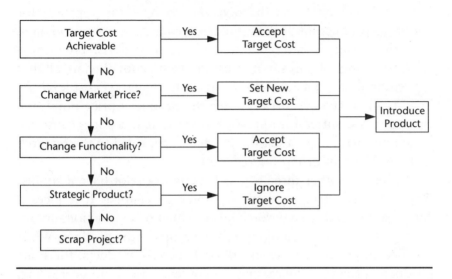

If it is neither possible to increase the price nor reduce the cost enough to bring the estimated cost below the target cost, then a life-cycle profitability analysis is performed. In this analysis, the effect of potential cost reductions over the production life of the product are included in the financial analysis of the product's profitability. Currently, Olympus expects to reduce production costs by about 35 percent across the production life of its products. If these life-cycle savings are sufficient to make the product's overall profitability acceptable, the product is released. If the estimated costs are still too high, the product is abandoned unless there is a strategic reason, such as maintaining a full product line or creating a "flagship" product, for keeping the product.

Once the new product is released to manufacturing, it undergoes a manufacturing design review. This review determines where and how the new product will be produced. To do so, a detailed production blueprint that identifies the technology required to produce the camera and the components the camera contains is developed. Using this blueprint and the cost estimates from suppliers and subsidiary plants, the production cost of the product is reestimated. If this cost is less than or equal to the target cost, the product is submitted to the division manager for approval for release to production. If the estimated production cost is too high, then the design is subjected to additional analysis. Frequently, relatively minor changes in nondistinctive functionality are all that are required to reduce the cost estimate to the target cost level. As long as these changes do not alter the product's price point, the product is submitted for approval. If the design changes cause the price point to change, then the product is returned to the research and development group for redesign.

Unlike the other three firms, Topcon does not have a sophisticated target-costing system. As noted in chapter 4, it faces a complex competitive environment in which price-functionality relationships vary depending upon the nature of the product. While functionality is increasing for all of Topcon's products, for some products, prices are increasing, for others, prices are decreasing, and for the remainder, prices are staying the same. To add to the complexity, while the functionality of Topcon's products is increasing rapidly, it is doing so in ways that make costs difficult to estimate. This more complex price-functionality competition reduces the benefits of a target-costing system because the selling price is heavily dependent upon the product's functionality. While for the other three firms, the selling price of a product can be established somewhat independently of its final functionality, this is not the case for Topcon. At Topcon, the exact functionality of the product determines its selling price. That is:

$$\text{Functionality} \leftrightarrow \text{Price}$$

Since the focus of competition is on functionality, the firm is often better served by increasing the selling price and maintaining the level of the new product's functionality than by reducing the functionality of the new product to enable the target cost to be met. This interaction delays the point in the design cycle at which the product target price can be set. In Topcon's case, the determination of the target price occurs late in the design cycle, when most of the costs are committed. For this reason, target costing is less effective and important to Topcon than it is to Nissan, Komatsu, and Olympus. Topcon uses its target-costing system primarily to determine the profit margin that the firm is likely to earn on a new product, not its selling price. Thus, the system is much closer to the systems used by many Western firms selling products in highly competitive markets.

At Topcon, the target margins for products are determined by competitive conditions. Company strategy sets the average profit margin for the entire business line. For example, the Medical and Ophthalmic Business Unit is treated as a single business line and is expected to generate a certain percentage profit each year. The target profit margin of a new product, such as an auto-refractometer, is set by the Medical and Ophthalmic Business Unit Planning Group, which is responsible for managing the product mix so that the overall profit equals the target profit margin of the unit.

While the target profit margin for a given product depends upon a number of factors, three factors are dominant. The first is the relative strength of the competitive offerings, the second is the strength of the Topcon offering, and the third is the historical profit margins for that type of product. The allowable range of market prices is determined by competitive forces. For example, although Topcon will introduce a new auto-refractometer and price it around the prices of competitors, if the firm believes that its product has greater functionality than the competitive products, then its price will be higher. If the functionality is perceived to be lower, then the price will be set correspondingly low:

> Typically over the life of an auto-refractometer, the price would fall slightly, usually somewhere between 5–10%. This price reduction reflected the increased competition that the product faced from newer products introduced by competitors. Since the most technologically advanced product was usually the last one introduced, the price reductions were used to offset the increased functionality of competitive offerings. (Cooper 1994o, 3)

If the Topcon product is appropriately priced, it will capture the expected share of the market. If it is overpriced, then market share will be lost. If a product is determined to be overpriced, Topcon will lower its price to regain market share. Following standard business practice in Japan, no price adjustment is made when a new product's price is found to be too low even if the product is extremely successful and doing so is likely to increase the overall profits of the firm.

THE BENEFITS OF TARGET COSTING

Japanese managers have argued that target costing outperforms the conventional Western approach and the cost-plus approach because it provides a specified cost reduction target for everyone in the firm to work toward. Once cost reduction negotiations are complete, the target cost becomes the common focal point that all the departments must work together to achieve. While Japanese budgets are set to be achievable, doing so requires some "stretching" on the part of the work team, which is in keeping with the literature on goal setting. For goals to be successful, according to current literature, there must be commitment to their achievement. As these budgets are the result of extensive negotiations among all levels of management and workers, the commitment to them is firm. In most Japanese firms, final short-term budgets are similar to binding contracts. At Topcon, for example, the expression, "The budget is God," captures the intensity with which Japanese workers and managers strive to achieve their target profits.

By providing numeral objectives and tying into the high motivation level of the workforce (see chapter 2), target costing creates tremendous pressure for cost reduction. For this pressure to be effective over the long-term, management must correctly estimate the maximum cost reduction reasonably achievable by both the workforce and the firm's suppliers and subcontractors. A fine line is drawn between the product's minimum cost and its achievable minimum cost. As long as target costs are set so that they can be achieved most of the time, the target-costing system will create a sustainable downward cost pressure. As long as this pressure is greater than the pressures created by the fuzzy minimum cost objectives of the conventional Western and cost-plus approaches, target costing will be superior.

SUMMARY

Target costing is not a single technique but a collection of techniques that provide a vital communications link between marketing, engineering, purchasing, and manufacturing.

Three factors appear to have a significant impact on the survival triplet and the design of target-costing systems. These factors are the nature of the product, the type of customer serviced, and the degree of influence over the firm's parts suppliers and subcontractors. The nature of the product is important because, as products become more capital intensive and complex, the product development cycle becomes longer and the need to control that cycle becomes more intense. Nissan and Komatsu have developed target-costing systems that are also extensive value engineering programs. At Olympus and Topcon, where the capital investment is lower and development cycles shorter, the target-costing systems are less comprehensive.

The customer serviced influences the degree of involvement of marketing and customer analysis in the target-costing procedure. At Nissan and Olympus, where the customers are the general public, the target-costing system interacts more heavily with marketing than it does at Komatsu and Topcon, where customers are commercial enterprises.

The influence the firm has over its suppliers and subcontractors is critical for cost management. Nissan and Komatsu rely heavily upon outside firms for parts, therefore their target-costing systems work to discipline suppliers. At Olympus, which is more vertically integrated, the ability to discipline suppliers is less well developed, and at Topcon it is virtually nonexistent due to the firm's low-volume production and small degree of influence over suppliers.

The primary purpose of Nissan's target-costing system is to achieve the target cost by creating downward pressure on suppliers' selling prices and by modifying the functionality of the product. In contrast, Komatsu sets the product's target price and then determines the functionality that can be supported at that price. Consequently, Komatsu's target-costing system focuses primarily on cost control, not functionality management.

Olympus determines the distinctive functionality of its products first and then sets target prices. In subsequent steps, the firm determines the other functional characteristics that the target prices can support. Unlike Nissan, which can reduce functionality right up to the launch date by simply omitting features, Olympus must set product functionality before manufacturing commences. Consequently, setting the functionality of the product is central to the focus of Olympus' target-costing system.

Finally, the selling prices of Topcon's products are determined in part by their overall functionality. The sensitivity of the target price to the product's functionality makes it difficult for Topcon to set a target price until the functionality of the product is known. This late determination means that early stages of product development are managed using more of a conventional Western approach than target costing. Late in the development process, however, target costing is utilized to ensure that the product achieves its target profit.

The type of competition these firms face plays a role in determining when the selling price of a product can be determined in the development cycle. At Nissan, Olympus, and Komatsu, competition is based primarily upon keeping prices constant and increasing product functionality with each new generation. Therefore, selling prices can be determined fairly early in the development cycle. At Topcon, however, a product's price is more influenced by its functionality than prices are at the other three firms. Therefore, the target selling price cannot be estimated accurately until late in the design process. Thus, target costing is less important at Topcon than the other three firms.

CHAPTER 8

VALUE ENGINEERING

In Japanese firms, value engineering (VE) is an organized effort to analyze the functions of goods and services in order to find ways to achieve those functions in a manner that allows the firm to meet its target costs. VE helps to manage the trade-off between functionality and cost, the two dominant characteristics of the survival triplet. The objective of most Japanese VE programs is not to *minimize* the cost of products but to achieve a *specified* level of cost reduction that has been established by the firm's target-costing systems. This objective differs from the objective of VE in Western firms, as the definition of VE in British Standard 3138 illustrates: "A systematic inter-disciplinary examination of factors affecting the cost of a product in order to devise means of achieving the specified purpose *most economically* at the required standard of quality and reliability [emphasis added]" (Yoshikawa et al. 1993, 57). J. Kaufman's (1990, 1) definition of VE as "an organized effort directed at analyzing the functions of goods and services to achieve those necessary functions and essential characteristics *in the most profitable manner* [emphasis added]" highlights the tendency of many Western firms to minimize the costs of products without setting a specific target. However, as chapter 7 noted, a prespecified target is more powerful than an unspecified minimum because it is tied into intense profit planning processes, while fuzzy minimums are difficult to formalize and include in the "negotiated-effective contract" discussions.

At the heart of VE lie two deceptively simple equations. These equations are:

$$\text{Value} = \text{Function/Cost} \qquad (1)$$

and

$$\text{Perceived Value} = \text{Perceived Benefits/Price} \qquad (2)$$

Equation (1) reflects the perspective of the producer; equation (2) reflects that of the customer. Cost and price play the same role in these equations that they do in the survival triplet. While in equation (1) functionality captures what the product can do, in equation (2) perceived functionality (or perceived benefits) captures the value the customer attaches to the product's functionality. For firms using the confrontation strategy, the management of perceived value is critical, and the task of VE is to help a firm maintain the perceived value of its products by helping the firm's product engineers make appropriate trade-offs between functionality and cost. Consequently, VE practices are heavily integrated with consumer analysis and other techniques designed to ensure customer satisfaction. Often, VE programs are as concerned with the product's final quality and functionality as they are with its cost.

Since cost down techniques must not be undertaken without taking into account both the quality and functionality of the product, each product's basic and secondary functions must be identified and the value of these functions must be analyzed. A basic function is the principal reason for the existence of the product. For example, a camera's basic function is to take pictures and an automobile's basic function is to provide transportation. The secondary functions are outcomes of the ways the designers choose to achieve the basic functions. For example, the secondary functions of an automobile include the heat and pollution generated by the engine. While it is difficult to identify the secondary functions of a camera, I recently used a camera to fend off an aggressive (and large) trigger fish, thereby discovering that its secondary function could be identified as a club.

Like target costing, VE is applied during the design phase of product development and involves a multidisciplinary, team-based approach.[1] Teams are typically drawn from multiple functional areas, including design engineering, applications engineering, manufacturing, purchasing, and, sometimes, the firm's suppliers and subcontractors. In practice, it is extremely difficult to draw a line between VE and target costing, and the techniques are so intertwined that it does not always make sense to make such a distinction. At Nissan, for example,

> The first stage of value engineering and the identification of target price was an interactive process. When the allowable costs were considered to be too far below the estimated cost, the appropriate price range and functionality were reviewed until an allowable cost that was considered achievable was identified. (Cooper 1994i, 5)

This interactive process makes it difficult to determine if an activity is being performed to establish a target cost or to determine if VE can find a way to achieve the target cost. An iterative process is necessary because, in theory, target costing does not pay attention to the feasibility of the target cost. Therefore, VE is required to determine whether or not the target cost is achievable. Since, however, the fundamental purpose of target costing is to set an achievable target, the two techniques must be intertwined. At Olympus, the target costing and VE programs are effectively a single program:

> As part of the program to design low-cost products, target costs were set assuming aggressive cost reduction and high quality levels. . . . Aggressive cost reduction was achieved by applying three rationalization objectives. First, the number of parts in each unit was targeted for reduction. For example, the shutter unit for one class of compact camera was reduced from 105 to 56 pieces, a 47% reduction that led to a 58% decrease in production costs. Second, expensive, labor-intensive, and mechanical adjustment processes were eliminated wherever possible.

---

[1] In contrast, value analysis, like *kaizen*, is applied during the manufacturing phase.

Finally, metal and glass components were replaced with cheaper plastic ones. For instance, by replacing metal components that required milling in an SLR body with plastic ones that could be molded, the SLR body costs were reduced by 28%. Similarly, replacing three of the glass elements with plastic ones in an eight-element compact camera lens reduced the lens cost by 29%. (Cooper 1994j, 6–7)

Because the trade-off that is inherent to competition using the survival triplet must always be considered as the product development cycle unfolds, marketing continuously explores changes in characteristics of the survival triplet that will alter the quality, functionality, and price-cost economics of the products. At Nissan, for example,

After the first value engineering stage was completed, a major review of the new model was conducted. This review included an updated profitability study and an analysis of the performance characteristics of the model. In the profitability study, the expected profitability of the model given by the target price minus the target cost was compared to the latest estimates of the capital investment and remaining research and development expenditures required to complete the design of the product and allow production to commence. In the performance analysis, factors such as the quality of the hardware, engine capacity, exhaust emissions, and safety were considered. If both the financial and performance analyses were considered acceptable, the project to introduce the new vehicle was authorized and the model shifted from the conceptual design to the product development stage. (Cooper 1994i, 6)

Sometimes, the decisions made during the first VE stage affect the functionality of the products introduced. For instance, at Nissan,

several critical decisions about the model were made during this stage of the conceptual design process, including the number of body variations, the number of engine types, and the basic technology used in the vehicle. For example, the original concept for the model might include a five-door variant. However, if during this stage of the analysis it was determined that developing such a variant would be too costly or take an excessive amount of time, plans for a five-door variant would be postponed to the next version of that automobile. (Cooper 1994i, 5)

VE AT ISUZU

VE has two major objectives: to ensure that products are designed to have the highest value possible; and to ensure that the prices paid for purchased parts are low enough to achieve the product's target cost.

To explore the range of VE processes firms use to accomplish these objectives, we will examine in depth Isuzu's VE practices. Isuzu was chosen because it is a pioneer in VE. Its adaptation of General Motor's teardown methods was initially known as the Isuzu teardown approach and only later came to be known as the Japanese teardown approach. At Isuzu, VE has been developed to cover all stages of product design and manufacture. Indeed, three different stages of VE—zeroth, first, and second "looks"—are used in the design phase to increase the functionality of new products and eight teardown methods as well as four other VE techniques are used throughout product development to reduce costs or functionality.

Isuzu uses two different techniques to help guide its VE program—a cost deployment flowchart and a cost strategy map.

To help achieve its cost reduction objectives and thus ensure that a product meets its target cost, Isuzu relies heavily upon the cost deployment flowchart (see Figure 8-1), which was first developed to ensure that cost reduction activities were applied to a product as early as possible in its development. The chart came about because Isuzu's management realized no significant analysis was performed during the product planning stage to ensure that the target cost could be achieved. Thus, when it became clear that the product could not be manufactured for its target cost, it was

Figure 8-1
Portion of Cost Deployment Flowchart

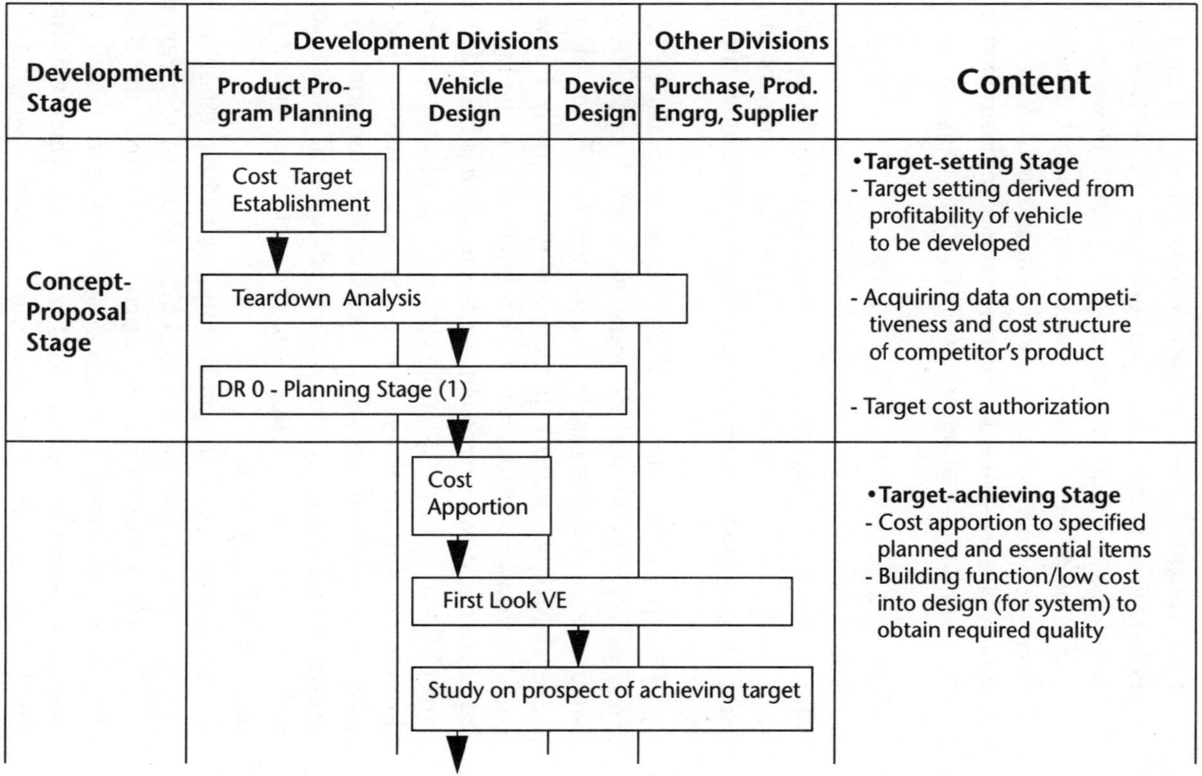

Development Stage	Development Divisions				Other Divisions	Content
	Product Program Planning	Vehicle Design	Device Design	Purchase, Prod. Engrg, Supplier		
Concept-Proposal Stage	Cost Target Establishment					• **Target-setting Stage** - Target setting derived from profitability of vehicle to be developed - Acquiring data on competitiveness and cost structure of competitor's product - Target cost authorization • **Target-achieving Stage** - Cost apportion to specified planned and essential items - Building function/low cost into design (for system) to obtain required quality
	Teardown Analysis					
	DR 0 - Planning Stage (1)					
		Cost Apportion				
		First Look VE				
		Study on prospect of achieving target				

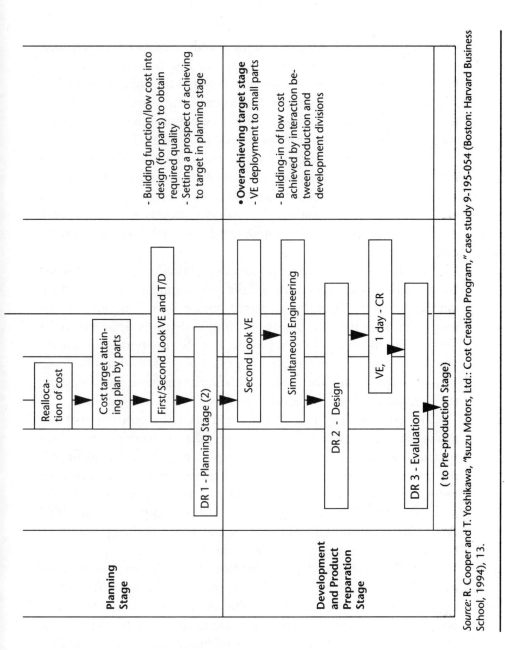

Source: R. Cooper and T. Yoshikawa, "Isuzu Motors, Ltd.: Cost Creation Program," case study 9-195-054 (Boston: Harvard Business School, 1994), 13.

too late in the development process to reduce costs effectively and economically to achieve the target cost. The flowchart identifies five development stages in a vehicle's design: the concept proposal stage, the planning stage, the development and product preparation stage, the development and production-sales preparation stage, and the production-sales preparation stage.

It also indicates the type of cost reduction activities required, the steps involved in each activity, the division responsible for the activity, and development stages at which each activity should occur. For instance, during the concept proposal stage, a new vehicle's target cost is determined, teardown analysis is performed, and a design review is held.

To ensure that the appropriate cost reduction techniques were considered at the right time in the development process, Isuzu developed a cost strategy map (see Figure 8-2). This map is required because the appropriate technique depends upon not only the stage of the development process but also the part in question. Some cost reduction techniques, for example, first and second look VE, are suitable only for making drastic changes to a part's design; they are unsuitable for slightly modifying an existing design.

The cost strategy map is prepared after the cost deployment flowchart. For each development stage, the applicable cost reduction techniques are identified. In the planning stage, for example, the cost deployment flowchart identifies two major blocks of cost reduction, first look VE and a mixture of first and second look VE and teardown. The corresponding cost strategy map identifies twelve techniques. Eight of these are teardown methods; the other four are types of first and second look VE.

Together, the cost deployment flowchart and the cost strategy map are used to ensure that the appropriate cost reduction techniques are used as soon as possible in the development of new products. To maximize cost reduction, the firm has created a comprehensive program consisting of many different cost reduction techniques. Some of these have been developed by Isuzu, others have been adopted from systems developed by other firms.

Zeroth Look VE

Zeroth look VE is a recent introduction and represents the logical extension of VE into the earliest stage of the design process, the concept proposal stage when the basic concept of the product is developed and its preliminary quality, cost, and investment targets are established. Unlike first look VE, which acts to enhance the functionality of a product by improving the capability of existing functions, the role of zeroth look VE is to introduce some form of functionality that has not previously existed. While the underlying concept of designing revolutionary products has always existed as a part of VE, codifying the VE process as zeroth look at this stage makes it an integral part of product design and increases the likelihood of it occurring.

Zeroth look VE was applied in the development of Isuzu's NAVI-5 transmission system, which combines the higher fuel efficiency and performance of a manual transmission with the convenience of an automatic transmission. In simplified terms, NAVI-5 is a computer-controlled manual transmission that is capable of changing gears automatically. It was zeroth look VE that first identified the basic concept behind the new system:

> The objective of zeroth look value engineering was to find ways to add value to products from the consumer's perspective while simultaneously increasing the firm's portion of the value-added to the product. The NAVI-5 system achieved both objectives, based upon market studies that showed that consumers liked the performance provided by a manual transmission but found the process of changing gears in Japan's crowded cities too tiring. . . . The new product increased the portion of Isuzu's value-added because Isuzu manufactured its manual transmissions (and purchased automatic ones from a supplier). Without the discipline of zeroth look value engineering, the firm probably would not have identified the NAVI-5 as a new product. (Cooper and Yoshikawa 1994a, 6)

Figure 8-2
Portion of Cost Strategy Map

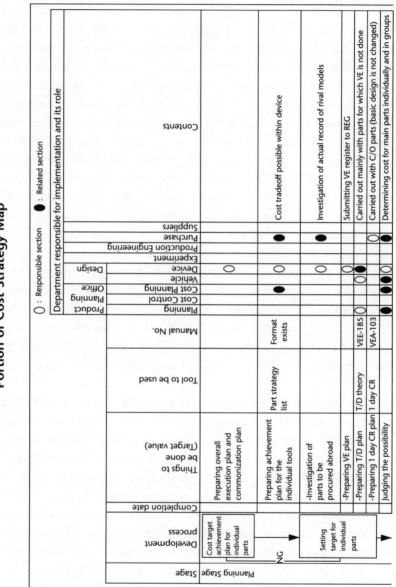

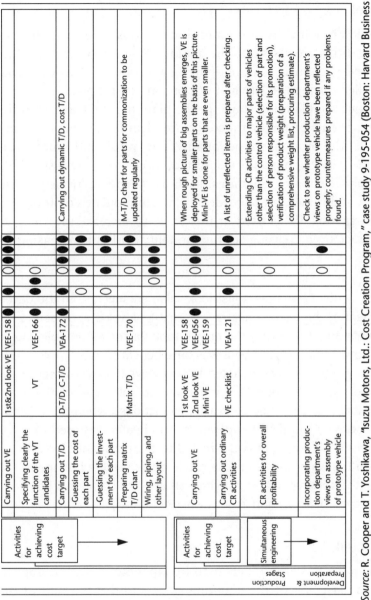

Source: R. Cooper and T. Yoshikawa, "Isuzu Motors, Ltd.: Cost Creation Program," case study 9-195-054 (Boston: Harvard Business School, 1994), 14.

First Look VE

First look VE, which is more traditional and is used by numerous Japanese firms, focuses on the major elements of the product design and is defined as developing new products from concepts. It is applied during the last half of the concept-proposal stage and throughout the planning stage. In the planning stage at Isuzu, the key components or major functions are identified, the commodity value (i.e., the product's type, quality, size, price, and function) is determined, a design plan is submitted, target costs are distributed to the vehicle's major functions, such as its engine, transmission, and air conditioner, and the degree of component commonality is set. First look VE is used at this stage to increase the value of the product by increasing its functionality without increasing its cost:

> Isuzu's engineers applied first look value engineering to the development of the Gemini heater. . . . First look value engineering identified that reducing the time it took for the automobile interior to warm up would be a welcome benefit for users. Consequently, a project was initiated to find ways to heat the car interior before the engine warmed up. The ultimate solution was to install a ceramic heater that only functioned when the engine was below a specified temperature. This heater was used to warm the air flow that was directed to the occupants' feet. When the water in the engine reached the specified temperature, the ceramic heater switched off and the traditional heater took over. (Cooper and Yoshikawa 1994a, 6–7)

Second Look VE

Second look VE is also widely used by Japanese firms. It is applied during the last half of the planning stage and the first half of the development and product preparation stage. In the development and product preparation stage, the components of the main functions are identified and handmade prototypes are assembled. At this stage, VE works to improve the value and functionality of existing components, not to create new ones. Consequently, the scale of changes is much smaller than it is for zeroth and first look VE.

> Second look value engineering was applied . . . on the ELF, a light-duty truck. Experience with earlier models had shown that the gear level, which was positioned between the two front seats, sometimes got in the way of the occupants. The vehicle's functionality and hence its value would be improved if the gear lever was repositioned so that it was out of the way. The solution was to develop a gear lever that could fold down while the vehicle was stationary but would not collapse while the vehicle was in motion. (Cooper and Yoshikawa 1994a, 7)

The Eight Teardown Approaches

Isuzu's approach to teardown indicates the large range of cost reduction activities that are included in VE at the firm. Teardown methods are used to analyze competitive products in terms of materials they contain, parts they use, ways they function, ways they are manufactured, and ways they are coated and the types of coating used. Isuzu defines its teardown method as "a comparative VE method through visual observation of disassembled equipment, parts, and data that are arranged in a manner convenient for such observation" (Cooper and Yoshikawa 1994a, 8).

Teardown methods were first introduced in 1972, a year after General Motors purchased a 37 percent share of the firm. The GM, or static teardown, method, as it was known in Isuzu, was modified over a three-year period to fit Isuzu's needs and then allowed to proliferate throughout the company. The primary difference between the GM approach and the Isuzu method is the scope of the application of teardown principles. At Isuzu, teardown methods are used in all stages of product development. The firm has eight different teardown methods: dynamic, cost, material, static, process, matrix, unit-kilogram, and group estimate. The first three methods are designed to reduce a vehicle's direct manufacturing cost. The next three are designed to reduce the investment required to produce vehicles through increased productivity. The last two are integrations of teardown and VE techniques (see Exhibit 8-1).

Other VE Techniques

In addition to zeroth, first, and second look VE and the eight teardown approaches, Isuzu uses four other cost reduction tech-

Exhibit 8-1
The Eight Tear-Down Methods at Isuzu

Tear-Down Methods for Reducing Direct Manufacturing Costs

Dynamic Tear-Down

The objective of dynamic tear-down was to identify ways to reduce either the number of assembly operations required to manufacture a vehicle or the time it took to perform them. The method consisted of taking apart competitors' products, analyzing their assembly processes, and comparing them with Isuzu's to see if their application to Isuzu's products would be beneficial.

Cost Tear-Down

The objective of the cost tear-down method is to reduce the cost of the components used in a vehicle. The method consisted of performing a cost comparison of the components used by Isuzu and its competitors. If the Isuzu component was more expensive, its functionality was analyzed to see if the extra cost provided increased functionality. If the functionality was the same, the component was subjected to cost reduction activities. Types of actions taken from the cost tear-down method included functional improvement, weight reduction, set-up time reduction, and process elimination.

Material Tear-Down

The material tear-down approach consists of comparing the materials and surface treatments of the components used by Isuzu and its competitors. Competitive products would be purchased and torn down so that any innovations introduced by competitors could be identified and, if thought advantageous, adopted by Isuzu for future products. To be effective, the analysis was restricted to parts with the same work function. For example, in a given subassembly, Isuzu might be using metal parts while its competitors are using less expensive plastic ones.

Tear-Down Methods to Increase Productivity

Static Tear-Down

The static tear-down approach was the most basic of all the tear-down approaches. It consisted of taking a competitor's product and disassembling it into its components and then laying them out on a table or the floor so that the design engineers could see the difference between their products and their competitors'.

Process Tear-Down

Process tear-down consisted of comparing the manufacturing processes for similar parts and reducing the difference between them, with the long-term objective of producing multiple products or components on the same production line. Achieving this objective was particularly important to Isuzu because its relatively small production volumes required mixed production if the firm was to be profitable. Reflecting this objective, Isuzu was the only automobile manufacturer that could produce mixed products (such as four-door, two-door and left- and right-hand drive cars) on the same assembly line.

Matrix Tear-Down

In the matrix tear-down method, a matrix of all components used in Isuzu products was developed. This matrix identified the volume of each component used per month by each model and the total usage across all models. The matrix was not a regular report; it was prepared on an as-needed basis. Any low-volume components were flagged and actively designed out of existing products and banned from future products.

Integrated Tear-Down and VE Methods

Unit-Kilogram Tear-Down Method

In the unit-kilogram method, parts produced using similar manufacturing processes were treated as a product group and analyzed for possible cost savings opportunities. In this approach, the efficiency of the product or component was expressed in terms of its cost per kilogram. A product's cost per kilogram was determined by dividing its cost by its weight. The cost per kilogram for each product in the same product group was plotted against its weight. The resulting scatter diagram was used to identify the outliers that had much higher costs per kilogram than the majority of products. These outliers were analyzed to determine what was causing them to have such a high cost per kilogram and methods to reduce their material cost identified. The targeted savings were identified as the difference between these products' current costs and what their costs would be if their cost per kilogram was the same as the group's average cost per kilogram.

Group Estimate by Tear-Down Method

The group estimate by tear-down (GET) method was a combination of basic VE and tear-down procedures. It was a modified version of the kilogram-unit price method and consisted of treating parts that had similar functions as a group and analyzing them for possible cost savings. For example, the windshield washer tank and the radiator surge tank both performed the same fundamental function: holding liquids. Since the two tanks performed essentially the same function, they were compared under the GET method to see if there were ways to produce them more efficiently. The result was that in some vehicles, the two tanks were combined into a single combined tank with two compartments.

A scatter diagram of the cost of the parts in each group against their functionality was constructed to help identify outliers with abnormally high costs. The typical causes for the abnormalities were differences in either the part's design, production methods utilized, production volumes (as identified by the tear-down matrix), and degree of external purchases. In this comparison, the reasons behind these differences were analyzed and appropriate cost reduction actions taken. For instance, if the high costs were caused by the use of special materials, the part was redesigned to allow for more conventional materials to be used. Similarly, if the cost differential was related to low production volume then ways to standardize the manufacture of that part were identified so that production volumes could be increased.

Source: Cooper and Yoshikawa 1994a, 7–8.

niques: the checklist method, the one-day cost reduction meeting, mini-VE, and the VE reliability program.

Checklist Method. The checklist method is used to identify a product's cost factors and to suggest ways to reduce costs. The checklist consists of a number of questions that are designed to guide the firm's cost reduction activities through the identification of cost reduction opportunities (see Exhibit 8-2). Checklists help to ensure that all possible avenues for cost reduction are explored.

One-Day Cost Reduction Meeting. One-day cost reduction meetings are used to improve the efficiency of the entire cost reduction process including VE and teardown methods. Participants from engineering, production, cost, and sales are expected to come up with ideas about new cost reduction possibilities. The meetings are designed to overcome limitations in the approval process that is used for most cost reduction proposals. Most cost reduction proposals are written proposals (known as RINGI) circulated to all involved parties, who indicate acceptance by signing off on them. Unfortunately, this approach severely reduces the exchange of information and modification of ideas. At the one-day meetings, the results of various teardown programs are used to help initiate discussion.

Mini-VE. Mini-VE is a simplified approach to second look VE. It is applied to specific areas of a part or to small, inexpensive parts. Isuzu applies this process to the design of mirrors, doors, and door locks. For example, as a result of mini-VE, mirrors may be redesigned to be more ergonomical. Mini-VE is applied during the development and product preparation stages, the development and production-sales preparation stage, and the production-sales preparation stage.

VE Reliability Program. The VE reliability program—essentially a "quality of VE" program—is designed to ensure that the most appropriate form of VE is applied to each problem. If, for example, a completely new product design is required, then applying

Exhibit 8-2
A Typical Checklist

1. Number of parts.
   a. Can you reduce number of parts?
   b. Could you reduce costs by increasing the number of parts?
2. Shape.
   a. Can you make it smaller?
   b. Can you make it lighter?
   c. Can you make it simpler and more standardized?
   d. Is there any different shape that makes it easy to process?
   e. Is it suitable for the next process to produce?
   f. Is it a suitable shape to increase yield ratio?
3. Materials.
   a. Can you change quality of materials?
   b. Can you use less expensive materials?
   c. Is it easy to process?
4. Surface treatment.
   a. Is it a suitable surface treatment?
   b. Is the surface suitable for heat treatment?
5. Tolerance.
   a. Is it easy to achieve specified tolerance?
   b. Are the specified tolerances higher than expected?
6. Processing and assembling.
   a. Can you run more machines simultaneously?
   b. Can you integrate production processes?
   c. Can you save more production time?
   d. Can you reduce number of *Kosuu* (direct labor hours)?
   e. Can you save set-up time?
   f. Are you producing in optimal lot sizes?
   g. Can you speed up more?
7. Equipment.
   a. Can you use less expensive equipment?
   b. Can you automate?
8. Models.
   a. Can you make it smaller?
   b. Can you make it simpler?
   c. Is the quality of materials adequate?
   d. Do they take advantage of designs from old models?
9. Workers.
   a. Are all movements necessary?
   b. Is the work force optimal?
   c. Is the work process standardized?
10. Inspection and shipping.
    a. Can the defect rate be reduced?
    b. Do you have excessive returns?
    c. Are the shipping methods and equipment suitable?
    d. Is the shipping lot size too big?

Source: Cooper and Yoshikawa 1994a, 13.

second look VE is not appropriate. Like mini-VE, the program is applied during the development and product preparation stages, the development and production-sales preparation stage, and the production-sales preparation stage.

SUMMARY

VE, which plays a critical role in tying together the cost and functionality dimensions of the survival triplet, is used at many Japanese firms to help them achieve their target-costing objectives. Its primary objective is to increase the value of the firm's products, when value is defined as the functionality of a product divided by its cost. VE, which, like target costing is an adaptive, not mono-lithic approach, is a multifunctional discipline that analyzes products in terms of their basic and secondary functions. A product's basic function is the principal reason for the existence of a product. Secondary functions are outcomes of the way the designers chose to achieve the basic function. When VE is integrated with a target-costing system, which holds the cost of each product constant, its objective is to increase the functionality of a product, while maintaining target cost. A deep understanding of perceived value is critical if the firm's VE programs are to increase the value of products and keep those products within their survival zones.

The ways in which firms increase the value of their products using VE can be quite complex, and Japanese firms have developed numerous variations of VE techniques. Isuzu, for instance, uses three stages of VE (zeroth, first look, and second look) as well as eight different teardown approaches and four other cost reduction techniques to improve the value of its models. The three VE looks focus on different phases of the design process. The zeroth look focuses on the earliest phase of product design. Its objective is to introduce new forms of functionality. First look VE focuses on the conceptual phase of product design and works to enhance the functionality of new products. Second look VE focuses on the last phases of product planning and attempts to find ways to improve the functionality of existing components. Although each of the eight teardown methods focuses on a different objective, they all, to some extent, rely upon the knowledge gained when a product (either Isuzu's or a competitor's) is taken apart.

In addition to the three stages or looks of VE and the eight teardown methods, Isuzu uses other VE programs to reduce a new product's cost or functionality. These programs are the checklist, one-day cost reduction meetings, mini-VE, and the VE reliability program. Finally, to help guide the entire VE process, Isuzu uses a cost deployment flowchart and a cost strategy map. These two documents provided guidelines on which VE techniques to use at each phase of product design.

CHAPTER 9

INTERORGANIZATIONAL COST MANAGEMENT SYSTEMS

The pressure to become more efficient has caused many firms to try to increase the efficiency of supplier firms through interorganizational cost management systems. These systems have emerged because it is no longer sufficient to be the most efficient firm; it is necessary to be part of the most efficient supplier chain. To achieve this, many Japanese firms blur their organizational boundaries. Organizational blurring occurs when information that is critical to one firm is possessed by another firm either further up or down the supplier chain. The two or more firms then create relationships that share organizational resources, including information that helps improve the efficiency of the interfirm activities. Mechanisms for information sharing include joint research and development projects, placing employees of one firm in others, and establishing interorganizational cost management systems.

As functionality becomes the dominant element of the survival triplet, requiring constant innovation on the part of the firm, the time it takes to get new products to market becomes more important. The blurring of organizational boundaries becomes critical as competition intensifies because it not only reduces the time it takes the entire supplier chain to bring out new products with increased functionality but also allows quality to be improved while reducing costs. Komatsu, which is facing a competitive environ-

Note: A version of this chapter was published as "Interorganizational Cost Management Systems: The Case of the Tokyo-Yokohama-Kamakura Supplier Chain," by R. Cooper and Takeo Yoshikawa, *International Journal of Production Economics* 37, no. 1 (1994).

ment that is beginning to shift towards functionality, has reacted
by increasing the level of communication with its suppliers:

> Part of Komatsu's plan to improve its design for manufacturing
> was to change its relationship with its suppliers. In 1993,
> Komatsu manufactured about 30% of its products, designed and
> subcontracted another 50%, and purchased from outside suppli-
> ers the remaining 20%.
>
> The firm set target costs for the subcomponents manufac-
> tured by its suppliers and expected its suppliers to find ways to
> achieve these targets. Though target costs were supposed to be
> negotiated with suppliers, Komatsu management was concerned
> that in reality these negotiations were relatively one-sided. Addi-
> tionally, management felt that the suppliers were brought into
> the negotiations too late in the design process.
>
> To allow the suppliers to have greater input into the design
> process, Komatsu initiated periodic meetings between the suppli-
> ers' research and development staff and its own. The aim of
> these meetings was to integrate the research and development
> efforts of the two groups, allow suppliers to provide input much
> earlier in the design process, and help ensure that target cost ne-
> gotiations were more substantive. (Cooper 1994j, 3)

Komatsu sees organizational blurring as increasing its suppliers' power, because the more that suppliers are asked to do, the
more important they become and the more equal the relationship
must become. In contrast to Komatsu, which only recently began
blurring organizational boundaries, some other Japanese firms had
been engaged in this trend for some time. At Citizen, for example,

> [t]he cost reduction program . . . encompassed the entire pro-
> duction chain, including subsidiaries and outside suppliers. For
> subsidiaries, the firm knew the material, labor, and overhead con-
> tent of the purchased parts or subcomponents. The corporate
> technical staff would provide engineering support to help the
> subsidiaries find ways to become more efficient. The technical
> staff would visit the subsidiaries to observe the production pro-

cess and make suggestions on how it might be improved. For external suppliers, the process focused on steady cost reduction. Citizen's current target was 3% per annum. All external suppliers were expected to deliver at least this level of annual cost reduction. If a supplier was able to exceed the 3% target, then it retained the surplus. If a supplier was unable to achieve the 3% target, there was no punishment, but Citizen's engineers would assist it in achieving the 3% the following year. (Cooper 1994a, 6)

THE TOKYO-YOKOHAMA-KAMAKURA SUPPLIER CHAIN[1]

As the birthplace of the lean enterprise, the automobile industry probably has the most advanced interorganizational cost management systems. The degree of sophistication of such systems is well illustrated by the practices encountered in the Tokyo-Yokohama-Kamakura (TYK) supplier chain. This chain consists of Tokyo (an automotive manufacturer), Yokohama (a first tier supplier to Tokyo and several other automobile manufacturers), and Kamakura

Figure 9-1
Structure of the Tokyo-Yokohama-Kamakura Supplier Chain

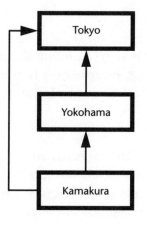

---

[1]All company names have been disguised in this section at the request of the firms involved.

(a family-owned, second tier supplier to Yokohama, other first tier suppliers, and several automobile man- ufacturers). The TYK supplier chain is illustrated in Figure 9-1.

With the exception of a minor shareholding position of Yokohama by one major customer, the three firms are independent entities that enter into arm's-length transactions. Consequently, their major ties are based upon their customer-supplier relationships. Yokohama's customers, for example, Tokyo Motors, are much larger than it is, and Yokohama is much larger than Kamakura. Both Yokohama and Tokyo Motors have taken advantage of their sizes to develop cost management systems that spread across their organizational boundaries. In contrast, Kamakura is too small to develop such systems but does try to use the interorganizational systems that have been created to its advantage. The relationships described in this section are not unique to these firms. Tokyo Motors treats Yokohama in the same way that it treats other first tier suppliers of equivalent size, and Yokohama treats Kamakura in the same way that it treats other small suppliers.

The complex interactions among the firms show considerable innovation in cost management. In particular, four interorganizational techniques can be identified: information sharing, target costing, price-quality-functionality trade-offs, and minimum cost investigations.

Information Sharing

A great deal of information is shared among the organizations in the TYK supplier chain. This information is used primarily by Tokyo Motors to create an environment of continuous downward cost pressure:

> Most of the time, it was up to Yokohama engineers to continuously innovate and find ways to manufacture its products so that they could be sold at the target prices and make adequate returns. In theory, the customer was not interested in the level of Yokohama's profit margins, only its ability to provide products

at the target price. Thus, if Yokohama found a way to significantly reduce the cost of one of its products it could make a
high return on that product. However, since there was considerable sharing of production information between Yokohama and
its customers, it did not take long for the target price to reflect
the new production cost. In addition, Yokohama's customers
would share information about the innovation with their other
suppliers, who typically were Yokohama's competitors. This sharing allowed the competitors to match Yokohama's costs. Once
the competitor's costs were reduced, the target selling price rapidly fell to match the underlying production costs. (Cooper and
Yoshikawa 1994d, 4)

To ensure that its suppliers continue to share information,
Tokyo creates incentives:

[T]he parts suppliers were asked to generate cost reduction
ideas. An incentive plan was used to motivate the suppliers. For
example, if an idea was accepted, the supplier that suggested
the cost reduction idea would be awarded a significant percentage of the contract for that component for a specified time period, say 50% for 12 months. This incentive scheme was viewed
as particularly important because even if a cost reduction could
not be achieved for this model, it signalled to the suppliers that
when the next model was developed this component would be
subject to cost reduction pressures. (Cooper 1995b)

Thus, an equilibrium is created. Tokyo rewards the innovative
supplier but ensures that the innovation spreads to all suppliers.
This helps keep the pressure on the suppliers to reduce costs.
Isuzu uses almost exactly the same approach in managing its
suppliers:

The nature of the bidding process depended upon the strength
of a supplier's relationship with the firm. For some suppliers,
Isuzu would provide capital and design support to enable them

to produce the advanced components required for the next generation of products. For other firms, the relationship was less important and the supplier offering the greatest value was chosen; for these types of bids, three suppliers were contracted for each component and asked to develop prototypes. The suppliers were told the target quality, functionality, and price of the component and were expected to produce prototypes that satisfied all three requirements. . . . The product with the highest perceived value was selected and the component's supplier was typically awarded the total contract.

The primary benefit of this "maximize value" approach was its ability to bring out the strengths of each supplier. Where ethical, Isuzu would share innovations made at one supplier with other suppliers to help them achieve target costs and make an adequate return. Originality also played a role in the selection of the winning design. If one of the suppliers identified a way to add additional functionality to the component that increased its value, Isuzu engineers would incorporate this functionality into the part's specifications. Typically, the creative supplier would achieve a higher value than the other suppliers because its component already contained the extra functionality. In this way, suppliers were encouraged to act as ancillary research and development laboratories for Isuzu. Incorporating the additional functionality spread the innovation to other suppliers, thus increasing their abilities to provide higher-value-added components in the future. (Cooper and Yoshikawa 1994a, 5)

While paying too much attention to transitory value is not in Isuzu's best interest, certain supplier relations are protected to ensure their survival:

Although the supplier rated as having the highest value would generally win the order, firms that had a reputation for being good suppliers were often awarded at least part of the order even if their products did not have the highest value. Examples of such companies included Yuasa for batteries, Toyo Valve for valves, and Nihon Seiko for bearings. These firms were awarded partial contracts to maintain their relations with Isuzu. (Cooper and Yoshikawa 1994a, 5)

Olympus has not developed such a sophisticated approach to its suppliers. Instead, it relies upon internal resources to support its parts requirements. Even so, it follows three steps to ensure the lowest prices: "(T)he cost of purchased parts was lowered by (a) implementing strict controls to ensure that target costs were met; (b) widening the sources of procurement to obtain lower costs; and (c) identifying multiple suppliers for each component to create competitive pressures" (Cooper 1994j, 8).

Target Costing and Maintaining the Balance of Power

The cost management relationship between Tokyo and Yokohama is driven by Tokyo's target-costing system, which is used to identify the price at which Tokyo is willing to buy parts from its suppliers. From Yokohama's perspective, the target-costing system of Tokyo Motors sets the price at which it can sell its products to Tokyo Motors. To remain profitable and independent of Tokyo Motors and its other major customers, however, Yokohama has to create an environment in which it is self-sufficient. To do this, Yokohama first must ensure that no single customer is sufficiently large to dictate selling prices and other conditions; second, it must create a culture that allows the firm to say no to unprofitable business; and third, it must create circumstances in which trade-offs within the survival triplet are possible.

To ensure profitability, Yokohama has recently adopted a new strategy that includes a resolution to not sell unprofitable products:

Under this new strategy, Yokohama resolved that any new product that was not going to generate an adequate profit margin across its life would not be introduced. . . . One of Yokohama management's objectives was to create a corporate culture that enabled them to say "no" when they could not identify a way to

make a product profitably. . . . Yokohama's management believed that developing such a culture was critical to its survival
because it ensured that the firm did not become dependent on
its customers. (Cooper and Yoshikawa 1994d, 3, 5)

Because the level of communication between customers and
suppliers is high, selling prices have to be considered "public
information," which strengthens the importance of maintaining
selling prices:

> Yokohama occasionally refused to sell products at the target
> price identified by the customer. Several forces drove this deci-
> sion. First, Yokohama as a separate company had to remain
> profitable in order to survive. If it accepted too many un-
> profitable contracts it would become insolvent. Second, Yoko-
> hama dealt with a sufficient number of customers that losing a
> single order from any one of them did not place the firm at sig-
> nificant risk. Third, if the same product was supplied to other
> firms then an effective market price for that product existed. If
> Yokohama sold that product to another customer below its effec-
> tive market price, there was a substantial risk that once the new
> price leaked out that it would rapidly become the market price
> for that product. (Cooper and Yoshikawa 1994d, 5)

On the other hand, Yokohama's automotive customers—including
Nissan, Isuzu, Mazda, and Toyota as well as several European and
Korean automotive firms such as Volvo, Volkswagen, and Hyun-
dai and other major customers including Komatsu, Fuji Heavy
Industries, Control Systems Company, Ltd., and Daewoo Heavy
Industries—use multisourcing to ensure that their suppliers do not
become too powerful and charge monopsony rents. Yokohama
reacts to this strategy by trying to find ways to become the best
supplier through quality-function-price trade-offs. It achieved this
objective by creative management of the survival triplet across
organizational boundaries.

The Quality-Function-Price Trade-Off

The QFP trade-off is designed to weaken the power of the customers' target-costing systems by challenging the size of the survival zone that Tokyo Motors and other customers try to enforce (see Figure 9-2). If Yokohama can prove that the survival zone can be relaxed, then it can produce the part at a lower cost (see Figure 9-3). If Yokohama can keep at least some of the difference in cost in doing so, the firm can be more profitable. Yokohama is best served if it can reduce the quality and functionality of the part and leave the target price unchanged (i.e., not reduced to reflect the relaxation of the other two characteristics):

Figure 9-2
How Tokyo Motors Tries to Shift the Survival Zone of Purchased Components

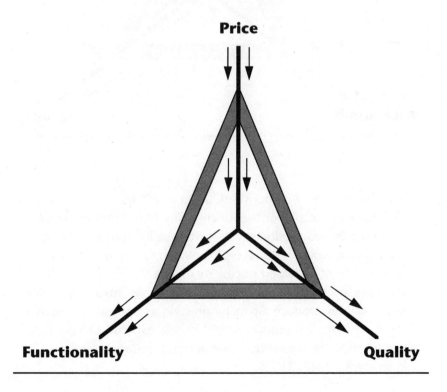

Figure 9-3
**How Yokohama Tries to Shift the Survival Zone of Components
Purchased by Tokyo Motors**

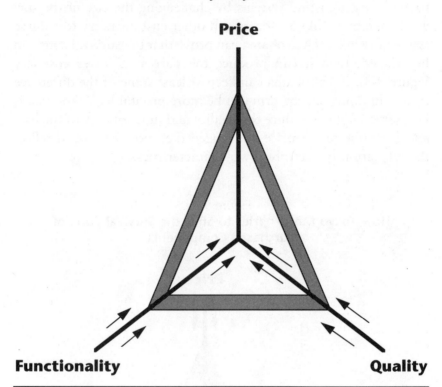

Price

Functionality

Quality

If Yokohama could demonstrate using a QFP tradeoff that relaxing either the quality or the functionality of the product would not result in end products with lower quality or functionality, then Nissan would often accept the change in product specifications in lieu of increased prices. Yokohama viewed these QFP tradeoffs as critical to its survival. For example, Yokohama might find a way to produce a part by pressing as opposed to machining it. The pressed product would be less expensive to produce but it would be inherently lower in quality. (Cooper and Yoshikawa 1994d, 5)

If it is not possible to reduce quality and functionality to an extent that will permit Yokohama to manufacture the part profitably, Yokohama's customers are sometimes willing to relax target prices. The relaxing of the target price is temporary: "Most major customers usually would not agree to long-term changes to target prices. However, they would sometimes allow the price to rise above the target for the first few years after introduction to allow Yokohama time to find ways to reduce their costs sufficiently to make an acceptable return at the target cost" (Cooper and Yoshikawa 1994d, 3).

There are other conditions under which the target price may be relaxed, though again, such a reprieve is only temporary:

> Another opportunity to negotiate occurred when Yokohama was heavily involved in the design process and in the scheduling of the product. Under those conditions, it was difficult for competitors to intervene as Yokohama was acting in many ways like a captive supplier. If Yokohama was unable to meet the target price under these conditions, the customer was often forced to accept a higher price that provided Yokohama with an adequate return. However, even under these conditions, only a temporary reprieve was given; in the long run, Yokohama was expected to sell the product to the customer at the target price. (Cooper and Yoshikawa 1994d, 5–6)

Another opportunity presents itself when Yokohama is the sole source of a product:

> If a product was sold only to one customer such as Nissan, Yokohama would give them a preliminary breakdown of the cost structure of the product. This cost breakdown allowed Nissan to determine the profit margin that Yokohama *expected* to earn on this product. If this margin was too low this would provide Yokohama with a rationale for using QFP to try and negotiate some change in either the target price or the specifications of the product. (Cooper and Yoshikawa 1994d, 5)

While these opportunities help Yokohama to maintain its profitability, sometimes other departments in Tokyo Motors make decisions that are not favorable to Yokohama:

> Major customers had substantial bargaining power over Yokohama during the pricing negotiations. Yokohama managed to remain profitable by taking advantage of QFP trade-offs wherever possible. Yokohama was also protected to a certain extent by its strong reputation and good relations with well established customers. However these were not always sufficient. For example, the Nissan Parts Design Department was highly supportive of Yokohama. The engineers in that department wanted to maintain good relations with Yokohama and were more accommodating about price and functionality than other Nissan departments such as Purchasing. Occasionally, Purchasing would intervene in the negotiations between Yokohama and the Parts Design Department and cause the contract to go to a competitor with a lower bid. (Cooper and Yoshikawa 1994d, 6)

It is difficult to explain this behavior. It can be interpreted either as the purchasing department ensuring that no single supplier becomes too important, thus protecting the integrity of the target-costing system, or as a harmful intervention that damages the effectiveness of the interorganizational blurring that exists between at least one of Tokyo Motor's departments and Yokohama.

The QFP trade-off can only be used for products that can be differentiated to some degree. While commodity products do not fit this requirement, Yokohama occasionally does produce some of these products:

> Yokohama . . . avoided such products because the ability to negotiate QFP trade-offs was limited. Sometimes however, it was not possible to avoid manufacturing commodity products. . . . There were over 30 identifiable competitors in the air conditioner industry. The leader in both terms of volume and price

was Nippon Denso. All of the other competitors were effectively forced to follow their price leadership. However, even under these conditions, Yokohama often found ways to negotiate. In particular, if it could develop a quality, cost, or delivery time advantage, it could use this advantage to negotiate the conditions of the order. (Cooper and Yoshikawa 1994d, 4)

Minimum Cost Investigations

Tokyo Motors implements minimum cost investigations (MCI) in order to reduce the inefficiencies introduced by having multiple firms involved in the production of a purchased part. MCI allows all of the players to get together and design a part as if they were employees of a single company. The technique was developed originally by the Jamco Consulting Company to help reduce costs. It consists of five major steps:

1. Gather cost information about each function of a product.
2. Search for ways to minimize costs.
3. Propose alternative ways to reduce costs and develop guidelines for ways to develop inexpensive products.
4. Perform feasibility studies for the proposals in step 3.
5. Develop an implementation plan for the cost reduction proposals approved in step 4.

It is not unusual for engineers from Tokyo, Yokohama, and Kamakura, one of Yokohama's suppliers, to come together for MCI meetings. These meetings allow parts to be designed so that all of the steps from raw material to finished product are more efficient:

For example, engineers at Kamakura Iron Works Co., LTD., a supplier to Yokohama of metal forgings, would design a forged part so that the amount of machining required at Yokohama to complete it was reduced. Yokohama was willing to pay more for

such a component because it cost them less to complete it.
(Cooper and Yoshikawa 1994d, 4)

The MCI process begins with Tokyo's target-costing system by setting a target cost for the part. Yokohama will request an MCI meeting if it believes that it cannot manufacture the part profitably at its target price. The MCI meeting enables everyone involved to make suggestions about how to minimize production costs. Once design and production processes that enable the two firms to meet Tokyo's target cost are established, Tokyo engineers set the transfer prices from Kamakura to Yokohama and from Yokohama to Tokyo. Thus, under MCI, Tokyo determines, through negotiations, the profit margins for both Yokohama and Kamakura.

Life at the End of the Chain

Kamakura, the firm at the end of the chain, produces castings and forgings that are subsequently machined by firms like Yokohama and then sold to firms like Tokyo Motors. Kamakura has found a niche in which it can produce castings and forgings and sell them at a small profit. Kamakura is forced to survive by being as efficient as possible:

> Kamakura specialized in producing low-volume products. This strategy was adopted because most of the firm's customers could produce forgings in high volumes in-house. It was not unusual for a part that was initially outsourced to Kamakura because of its low volume requirements to be taken in-house when its volume increased, or for a part initially produced in-house to be outsourced to Kamakura when its volume requirements declined.
>
> As a result of its strategy, Kamakura relied upon manually intensive production processes that could be cost-justified for low-volume production. (Cooper and Yoshikawa 1994b, 2)

Even with its small size, Kamakura is expected to share its innovations with other firms:

> Because Kamakura had been identified as a superior supplier by Yokohama, Kamakura employees were invited to give a presentation on their value engineering techniques. Value engineering techniques were used at Kamakura only on new products. . . . Although most product designs were provided by the customer, Kamakura personnel would review the submitted designs and, if appropriate, suggest how they could be improved to make them easier to forge or less expensive to finish. These reviews were conducted by multifunctional teams drawn from marketing, production, engineering, production control, and quality assurance. Kamakura held technical exchange meetings with its customers four or five times a month. Most of its customers, including Yokohama, were not knowledgeable about forging technology. Kamakura would often get involved in the design process by requesting functional specifications from customers and then working with their engineers to design the appropriate part. (Cooper and Yoshikawa 1994b, 3)

Although Kamakura can create a fairly broad customer base, it is too dependent upon its customers to act as a truly independent concern. While Yokohama has some mechanisms available to it to reduce the power of its customers' target-costing systems, these mechanisms are not available to Kamakura:

> Selling prices for most of Kamakura's products were established either by the market or by customers' target costing systems. . . . For new products, the customer would either identify the target price using its target costing systems or would ask Kamakura to bid for the work. The approach used depended upon the nature of the new product. When the new product was similar to existing products, then the target price would be set based upon the price of the existing part. If a part was different from existing products, then a bid would be requested.

When asked to bid on a new product, Kamakura would determine the expected cost of the new product using its price estimation system. The firm's bid would be based upon the expected cost of the part, the customer in question, and general market conditions. Even for these products, the customer would usually compare Kamakura's bid price with the price generated by its target costing system. (Cooper and Yoshikawa 1994b, 4)

Kamakura's customers are sensitive to the firm's predicament and are willing to relax the target costs of some products, at least temporarily.

Often, Kamakura's bid would be considered too high by the customer and the two firms would enter into price negotiations. The primary purpose of these negotiations was not to allow Kamakura to set prices but to allow it to explain why it could not produce the product at the desired target price. Kamakura's objective for these negotiations was to get the customer to make some price concessions. Major customers like Yokohama (and even minor customers) dominated these negotiations and, after listening to Kamakura's arguments, would set the selling price. However, Kamakura had considerable leverage in these negotiations because of its three areas of strength relative to other suppliers: its high technological capacity, high quality standards, and reputation for delivering products on time. . . .

If Kamakura could demonstrate that by increasing the product's quality it could reduce the customer's overall costs (by reducing defects and rework), then the customer would be willing to increase the selling price accordingly.

Only rarely would Kamakura agree to sell a new product at a loss. It was more likely to refuse to manufacture a part than accept an unprofitable contract. Most of Kamakura's customers accepted this constraint; because they understood Kamakura's cost structure, they would rarely press for an unprofitable price. . . . When Kamakura's management considered a product's production volume to be too low to be economical (under 60% of full production volume), Kamakura would press for a higher price to cover the higher costs associated with low production volumes. (Cooper and Yoshikawa 1994b, 4)

Kamakura's weakness also causes the information it shares about its costs with its customers to be greater than the information Yokohama shares with its customers:

Kamakura was expected to share most of its cost information with its customers. For example, Yokohama used a formal cost estimation document that had to be returned with each bid. This document required Kamakura's bid to be divided into eight categories: material cost, mold cost, facility fees, labor costs, heat treatment costs, shot blast costs, management fees, and profit. . . .

In theory, if every customer agreed to pay the selling price determined by this estimation procedure, then Kamakura would earn a pretax profit of 7%. However, actual profitability during the early 1990s was running at about 2%. The 5% difference was mainly attributed to overly optimistic estimates for products that experienced a decrease in production volume or that were subjected to price cutting, to decreased efficiency, to a shortening of product life cycles, or to products taking longer than expected to machine. (Cooper and Yoshikawa 1994b, 5)

Kamakura is unable to earn the return that it feels is appropriate because of the power wielded by its customers. However, sometimes Yokohama will intercede on Kamakura's behalf in MCI meetings to ensure that Kamakura remains solvent:

To protect Kamakura from excessive downward price pressures, Yokohama would often intercede on Kamakura's behalf in the MCI negotiations. One of Yokohama management's objectives was to create a corporate culture that enabled them to say "no" when they could not identify a way to make a product profitably. They were trying to install the same culture at

Kamakura to help protect that firm from excess supplier pressure. Yokohama's management believed that developing such a culture was critical to their survival as it ensured that they did not become a slave to their customers. (Cooper and Yoshikawa 1994b, 5)

Summary

This chapter documents how firms in a Japanese supplier chain in the automobile industry have developed interorganizational cost management systems. These systems are just one example of the many ways the firms have chosen to blur their organizational boundaries. Besides cost information, the firms share information on production and quality control, use of new materials and technologies, and research and development findings. The three firms in the TYK supplier chain have adopted interorganizational cost management systems in an attempt to ensure their long-term survival. The primary objective of these systems is to enable the entire supplier chain to become more cost efficient through the sharing of product design and cost information. Improved efficiency has become a prerequisite to survival because of the intensely competitive environment of the Japanese automobile industry.

The systems are designed to achieve three objectives. First, they create conduits that transmit the competitive pressures faced by Tokyo to the other two firms. Tokyo's target-costing system, for example, is designed to transmit its customers' demands for increased functionality at the same or lower cost to the other firms in the supplier chain. If functioning properly, target-costing systems will spread the cost reduction pressures among the three firms equitably. Second, the systems allow the product engineers at all three firms to jointly design products that can be manufactured more cost efficiently than if the firms acted independently. More formally, they can design to a single global minimum cost as opposed to three separate local minimum costs. MCI negotiations, for example, are designed to achieve this objective by enabling the costs of production in all three firms to be considered during the design process. Finally, through QFP trade-offs, the cost management systems create a way for the specifications that Tokyo sets for the parts that it purchases to be modified. These modifications allow the product to be sold at its target price, while still generating an adequate return for all three firms. Such interactions are necessary as Tokyo frequently demands excessive QFP values because its engineers do not have detailed knowledge of the design considerations that Yokohama and Kamakura must make.

The success of these systems depends heavily upon a cooperative relationship between the firms. It is critical for each firm in the chain to trust the one above it not to use the shared information to its sole advantage. It is critical because despite the cooperative nature of the relationship among the three firms, Tokyo dominates Yokohama, which in turn dominates Kamakura. While the dominating firms control the profitability of the dominated firms to varying degrees, each is aware of the importance of the other firms to its long-term survival. Even so, the dominated firms have acted to protect themselves against expropriation of their profits in two ways. First, they have implemented and enforced rules against selling unprofitable products. These rules allow them to say no when a customer asks them to accept an unprofitable order. Second, they have diversified their customer base sufficiently that they can afford to say no when appropriate.

Given these checks and balances, the firms in this supplier chain are willing to share detailed cost and product design information that would normally be considered highly confidential. This shared information helps reduce product cost and allows Tokyo and Yokohama to relax their target costs, albeit temporarily, when presented with evidence that their costs are unreasonable.

These interorganizational systems have drawbacks, however. In particular, they create a pathway for technology diffusion that inhibits each firm's possibilities for developing a sustainable competitive advantage through technology over its competitors. This pathway consists of Tokyo's sharing Yokohama's innovations with its other suppliers (who are Yokohama's direct competitors) and vice versa. Since Yokohama and its competitors also supply

Tokyo's competitors, any innovation rapidly spreads to all firms in the industry.

The increased rate of technological diffusion that results from establishing horizontal linkages across firm boundaries reinforces the intensely competitive environment in which confrontational strategies emerge. Firms are thus confronted with a paradox: they cannot stop sharing design and cost information because to do so would leave them strategically disadvantaged and, unless they stop, the possibility of achieving a sustainable competitive advantage remains elusive.

PART FOUR

MANAGING THE COSTS OF
EXISTING PRODUCTS

2,952 people were required in 1972 in watch movement production; by 1980 it was down to 2,520, and by 1990 it had fallen to 1,542.

Citizen Watch Company, Ltd.

INTRODUCTION

Just because a product is profitable when it is launched does not mean that it will remain profitable across its production life. As survival zones change shape over time (as competitors launch new products or consumers' preferences change), products may fall outside their survival zones and become unprofitable. In markets in which prices are falling, a firm must monitor product profitability and take appropriate actions to ensure that products that are unprofitable or at risk of becoming unprofitable are subject to corrective actions. Such actions include cost reduction, redesign, discontinuance, and outsourcing.

Unless the product is redesigned, functionality and quality levels are essentially established. Therefore, three cost management techniques are used to help manage the costs of existing products: product costing, operational control, and *kaizen* costing (see Figure IV-1).

Product costing systems are used to report the cost of existing products so that their profitability can be monitored. Reported product costs are used to manage the range of products offered, set selling prices, identify products that require additional cost reduction efforts, and select products for outsourcing, replacement, and discontinuance.

Operational control techniques are used to create cost reduction pressures at the product and production process level. These techniques hold individuals responsible for the costs they can control and then report variances from expected results. Results can either be standard costs or anticipated costs that reflect the savings from the firm's *kaizen* costing system. *Kaizen* costing

Figure IV-1
The Systems Used to Manage the Cost of Existing Products

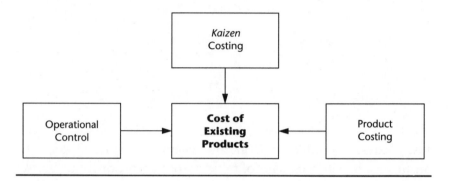

systems focus on making improvements to the production process of existing products. The improvements are designed to increase the effectiveness of the production process, improve the quality of production, or increase safety. If they increase the efficiency of the production process, they reduce product costs.

Both operational control systems and *kaizen* costing systems play a critical role in reducing the cost of existing products. Usually *kaizen* costing systems are the more important of the two because they harness the creative abilities of the entire workforce. For this reason, the operational control system is usually used to monitor the *kaizen* costing system, not to create cost reduction pressures. Some firms use the synergy between the two systems to generate additional pressure for cost reduction by setting highly achievable targets for their *kaizen* costing systems and then creating open-ended pressure for cost reduction through their operational control systems.

CHAPTER 10

PRODUCT COSTING

Reported product costs are used to help support a number of product-related decisions, including setting selling prices, identifying unprofitable products, and identifying products as candidates for redesign, outsourcing, and discontinuance (see chapter 5). While some Japanese product costing systems designed to help manage the cost of existing products are highly innovative, the majority are quite conventional, and equivalent systems can be found in Western firms. There are several explanations for this. First, target-costing systems and associated VE programs are designed to remove costs from products while they are in the design stage. If this objective is achieved, the need to monitor product profitability during the manufacturing stage is reduced.

Second, production systems are so highly controlled that there is no need to use the firm's cost system to monitor product costs. Instead, the cost system is needed only once a year to determine the cost of existing products. At Kamakura Iron Works, for example,

> [t]he cost system . . . was run once a year at budget time to determine the profitability of all products and to create the overhead rates used during the year to estimate the profitability of new products.
>
> When a new product was introduced, these rates were used to calculate its production costs. It generally took six months before the production process completely settled down and the machine and labor hours stopped decreasing. However, most of the learning occurred in the first two months. The long-term

> profitability of the product could be established after two
> months, when reported costs were relatively stable. (Cooper and
> Yoshikawa 1994b, 5)

Although activity-based cost (ABC) systems have begun to attract more attention in Japan recently and some firms, including Yamatake-Honeywell, have begun to implement such systems, most firms do not use them for at least five reasons. First, other programs, such as the VE programs, already foster the reporting of accurate product costs and create incentives to design cost effective products (the two primary reasons for implementing ABC systems). Since many firms already have programs that stress higher usage of common parts, the need to develop product costing systems that create incentives to use common components, for example, is reduced. Second, the majority of firms do not produce low-volume products. Their careful segmentation of the market keeps production volumes high enough that the degree of distortion introduced by traditional systems is not that great. Therefore, the increase in accuracy of reported costs due to the adoption of activity-based concepts is lower than might first have been expected.

Third, the view that product lines should be complete reduces the need for accurate individual product costs. As long as the product line is relatively accurately costed, then major decisions (such as where to source a product line, whether to try to increase sales volumes, or whether to drop the line) are adequately supported. Indeed, some firms have recognized that so many decisions are taken at the product line level and so few at the product level that their product costing systems report only the costs of product lines, not products. These systems are less expensive to maintain because they do not have to report product costs. When product costs are required, they are determined on an *ad hoc* basis outside the cost system.

Fourth, the spread of a new technology takes time. ABC was introduced into the Western literature in 1988, and it has taken several years to gain a significant foothold in Western practice. Since a major set of articles on ABC did not appear in Japanese until 1992, the language barrier probably has slowed the emergence of these systems in Japan.

Finally, Japanese firms use their product costing systems to support their cost reduction programs rather than to obtain accurate product costs. Supporting cost reduction strategies requires fairly simple assignment schemes, not the sophisticated ones used in most ABC systems. For example, using direct labor hours or costs to assign costs to products, which frequently leads to distorted product costs, may reinforce a firm's decision to increase the degree of automation because such assignments make direct labor appear expensive. In Western firms, this practice would be criticized for leading to poor decisions that resulted in projects that reduced direct labor but simultaneously increased overhead. Since the primary cost reduction goal in many Japanese firms is to remove direct labor (not indirect, support, or back office expenses) from the production process, a labor-based cost system creates the appropriate incentives. In several firms, management is aware that such systems create the risk of initiating inappropriate labor cost reduction projects, so each project is reviewed to eliminate this risk and ensure that the project is cost justified.

A TRADITIONAL COST SYSTEM

The cost system at Nippon Kayaku, a pharmaceuticals and fine chemicals manufacturer, follows Western textbooks perfectly. It is a traditional unit-based system that relies heavily upon direct labor to determine product costs. Even so, it is not a simple system; instead it is a very sophisticated one. The system's complexity reflects the complexity of the production process, and the design of the system cannot be faulted from a traditional perspective. As long as the products are relatively high volume ones and do not differ from each other too much at the nonunit levels, the reported product costs are sufficiently accurate for management's purposes:

> Determining product costs required that numerous allocations be performed by the firm's cost accounting system. . . .
> The existing system was a combination of both standard

and actual cost systems. The standards were set every six months when the semi-annual budgets were produced. Actual costs were determined monthly and compared to the standards. . . . The cost system determined product costs by adding together the reported costs of the production processes required to produce a given dyestuff. Thus, the cost system was designed to report the cost of each production process separately. Approximately 1,000 processes were performed, and their costs determined, at the Fukuyama plant. (Cooper and Yoshikawa 1994c, 5)

The structure of the cost system highlights the importance the firm places on accurate product costs (see Figure 10-1). The focus of the cost system on the production process, rather than the product, is illustrated by the identification of direct and indirect costs. Production processes are treated as a mixture of cost centers and components. Product cost is determined by summing the costs of the processes required to produce each product.

The assignment of direct costs to production processes is straightforward. The assignment of indirect costs is, by definition, problematic. The use of intermediate responsibility centers highlights the importance of cost control. Indirect costs are assigned directly to these centers, which allows costs to be controlled before being allocated to the production processes. A step-down procedure is used to allow for the reciprocal service problem:

The indirect costs were first assigned to the service and factory management departments in which they were consumed. There were three service departments—power and wastewater, quality control, and inventory control—and one factory management department at Fukuyama. Each service department was treated as a separate responsibility center. The factory management department consisted of six responsibility centers: production management, research and development, facility maintenance, general affairs, environmental maintenance, and accounting. Service and factory management department costs were allocated to the production departments using a step-down process. (Cooper and Yoshikawa 1994c, 6)

Figure 10-1
The Structure of Nippon Kayaku's Cost System

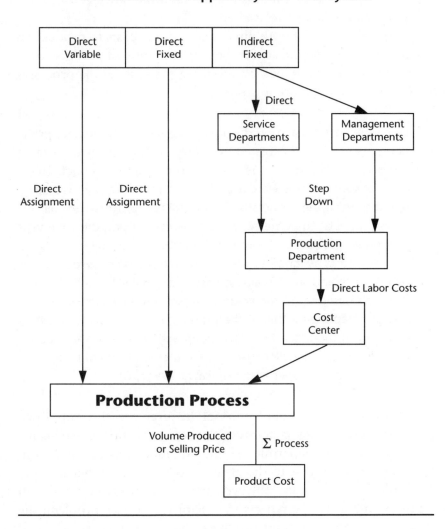

The heavy reliance upon direct labor costs to allocate costs to the production processes becomes clear in the next step when costs assigned to the production departments are allocated to the cost centers and then to the production processes contained in those centers. Indirect costs are allocated from the cost centers to the production processes through the use of direct labor costs for indirect labor expenses, maintenance costs for some machine-related costs, and special indexes (running hours × usage rates) for the remaining machine-related costs.

The assignment of both direct and indirect costs to production processes is the prerequisite for the determination of product costs. These costs are determined by summing the costs of the processes required to manufacture a product:

> Once the cost of each production process was determined, product costs could be calculated by simply adding up the costs of the production processes required to produce the product. The costs of each process were allocated to the products in two different ways. If the outputs of the production process were all main products, then the costs were allocated using the volume of product produced. If some of the outputs were byproducts, then the costs assigned to the byproducts were equal to their selling price and the remaining costs were assigned to the main products based upon the volume of each product produced. This last step meant that at the product level all costs were allocated. Even the costs that could be directly traced to the production processes were allocated in the last step of determining product costs. (Cooper and Yoshikawa 1994c, 6)

Nippon Kayaku's only unusual features are the step-down procedure used to get costs from the service factory departments to the production departments and the allocation of costs from the production process to the product, based upon either production volume or revenue. However, these two steps are handled in textbook manner: one reflects the reciprocal service problem; the other the existence of joint products.

SOME INNOVATIVE PRODUCT COSTING SYSTEMS

There are at least three types of innovative systems that reflect the economic realities of the competitive environments faced by firms, the nature of their production processes, and the types of decisions that management considered most important. The first type, used by Komatsu and Mitsubishi Kasei, report product line costs but not product costs. The second type of system, used by Shionogi, is traditional but highly accurate. The third type of system, found at Yamatake-Honeywell, is an ABC system.

The designs of these systems reflect trade-offs between the costs of measurement and the costs of errors from inaccurate product costs. For example, systems that report only product-line costs are used in environments in which individual product-related decisions are rare because the majority of decisions are taken at the product level. Similarly, the very sophisticated but traditional system at Shinogi reflected the demand for more accurate product costs created by the increasingly complex competitive and regulatory environment. Finally, the activity-based cost system at Yamatake-Honeywell was introduced to reduce distortions in the product costs reported by the firm's traditional cost system. The intense competitive environment required more accurate product costs than the traditional system could report.

Systems That Report Product Line Costs

Both Komatsu and Mitsubishi Kasei implemented new systems to avoid the distortions inherent in reporting the cost of product models through traditional unit-based allocation schemes. At Komatsu, a product category system (the primary level at which costs were reported) replaced a traditional system that reported costs at the product model level. At Mitsubishi Kasei, the new system reported costs at the level of the product line but not at the product model. The Komatsu system is interesting because it represents a planned devolution of cost system complexity. Admitting the inability of its traditional cost system to handle nonunit level costs, Komatsu managers designed a new cost system to be accurate at the product line level, but not at the product level.

The Komatsu Cost System. The old Komatsu system, which was a traditional unit-based cost system, used a relatively sophisticated first stage allocation procedure that drove overhead costs to the production centers (see Figure 10-2). Overhead was split into

Figure 10-2
Komatsu's Old Cost System

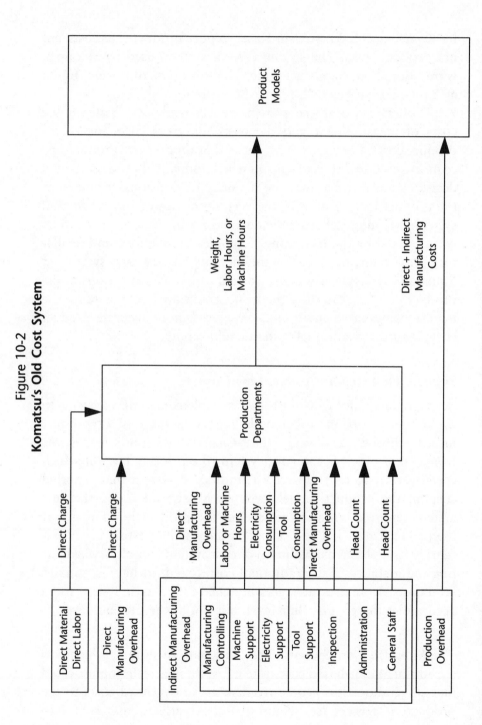

Source: R. Cooper, "Komatsu, Ltd. (B): Profit Planning and Product Costing," case study 9-195-061 (Boston: Harvard Business School, 1994), 11.

three major blocks, based upon the ease of assignment to the production centers. The first block was directly assignable; the second block was indirectly assignable using usage measures; and the third block was allocated through the use of a modified value-added approach. The second stage was again heavily conventional and used three different unit-level allocation bases: weight, machine hours, and labor hours. This system could be compared to the pre-ABC system at John Deere Component Works, for which it is isomorphic. Unfortunately, Komatsu's old system was unable to report accurate product costs:

> Analysis of how the old cost system allocated indirect manufacturing overhead costs to the product models indicated that reported costs were inaccurate. When the old system was designed, the number of production engineers supporting the shop floor labor force was relatively small; therefore, inaccuracies in how these costs were assigned to products was considered acceptable. Over time, as both overhead as a percent of total cost and the degree of automation increased, the use of direct labor hours as the only allocation basis for overhead produced greater inaccuracies. Eventually, the distortions in reported costs became unacceptable. (Cooper 1994f, 5)

Indeed, most traditional systems cannot assign overhead to products adequately when overhead costs are large and not unit based (i.e., not directly proportional to the number of units produced), and overhead at Komatsu has grown rapidly. The firm has identified four major reasons for the increase in overhead:

1. Increases in indirect labor wage rates that were not offset by increases in productivity.
2. Automation, especially the introduction of flexible machinery systems and computer-integrated manufacturing, that decreased the direct labor content of products while increasing their indirect content, including machine depreciation and technical support costs.

3. Increases in product diversity, which led to increases in the relative importance of indirect costs.
4. The shift to offshore production for some components and products, which increased their administration costs. (Cooper 1994f, 4)

Komatsu's new system is *not* designed to correct the distortions inherent in the old system. Instead, it is designed to report costs at the product category level:

Management decided to simplify the old cost system by combining indirect manufacturing overhead costs and production overhead costs into a single category called plant control overhead, and by allocating these costs to the product categories. Product categories consisted of end products, attachments, spare parts, prototypes, and an "other" category that contained miscellaneous items such as castings. The product category "end products" contained product lines, such as bulldozers and excavators. (Cooper 1994f, 5)

The advantage of this approach is the low cost of measurement that is required to support the system; its primary drawback is the lack of accuracy at the product model level.

The new system was designed to be accurate at the product category and line levels but not at the product model level. Its primary objective was to provide better cost control. Consequently, production floor managers were only held accountable for the direct manufacturing costs of the products. Support department managers were held responsible for indirect costs. Management was aware that the new system did not relate overhead to individual product models in ways that captured the consumption of overhead. However, the system was much simpler to understand, which highlighted the importance of managing overhead departments, and was less expensive to maintain. (Cooper 1994f, 5–6)

While the new system (see Figure 10-3) is simpler than the one it replaced, the assignment of costs to the product categories still has to be accurate. To ensure that it is, Komatsu has developed several specific allocation bases. The most commonly used allocation base is *production yen*. It is used to allocate the costs of the general, administration, and inspection departments and the technical center. The allocation base *adjusted production yen* is used to allocate the costs of planning, coordination, and purchasing. Production yen is adjusted to allow for the more complex management required for attachments, spare parts, and prototypes since it usually takes longer to manage these items than excavators, for example, because they are produced intermittently and because the customer frequently requires fast service.

A special two-stage procedure is used to allocate the costs of the planning, coordination, and purchasing departments. In the first stage, the costs of the planning, coordination, and purchasing departments are driven to the end products category using adjusted production yen. In the second stage, costs of the end products category are driven to the different end product lines (bulldozers and excavators), using head count, which is defined as the number of people in the overhead department dedicated to the product line.

Planning, coordination, and purchasing costs are allocated to the other four product categories using adjusted production yen. With the exception of spare parts, which are purchased from a separate department, no equivalents to product lines are identified. The cost of the spare parts department is charged directly to the spare parts category. The cost of in-house processing is used to allocate the costs of manufacturing engineering and manufacturing control to the product categories.

Japanese firms often solve problems like obsolete cost systems in two stages. The first stage is to declare the existing system invalid, and the second stage is to replace it with a new one. Komatsu, however, has taken a three-stage approach. The old system was not capable of providing either operational control or accurate costs at the product model level. The new system is an intermediate solution. It provides improved operational control

Figure 10-3
Komatsu's New Cost System

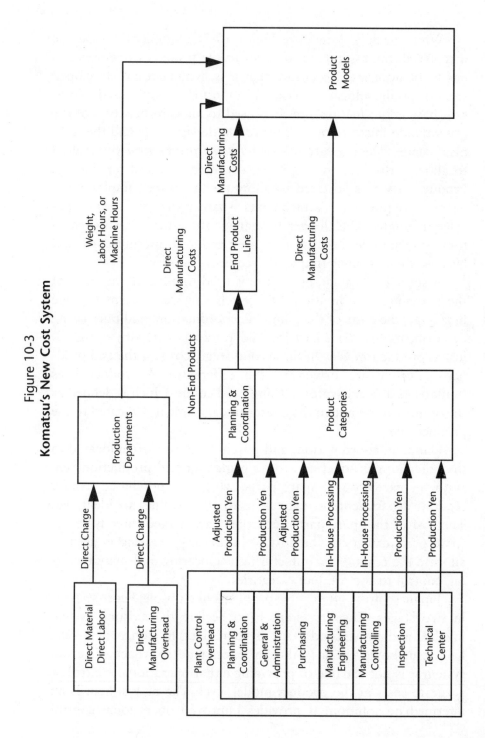

Source: R. Cooper, "Komatsu, Ltd. (B): Profit Planning and Product Costing," case study 9-195-061 (Boston: Harvard Business School, 1994), 12.

but less accurate costs at the product model level. Eventually, it will be replaced by a system that provides both enhanced operational control and accurate costs at the product model level. Although Komatsu's management considers the new system to be superior to the old one with respect to costing and believes that the system reports accurate costs at the product category level, no one in the firm believes that the reported costs of the product models are accurate. Therefore, managers are less likely to be misled by those reported costs than they were under the old system. However, this does not prevent reported costs from being used in making producted-related decisions:

> Despite concerns about the accuracy of the product model costs reported by the new cost system, Komatsu management relied upon these costs when making several product-related decisions, including transfer pricing, product mix management, and turning down orders. The cost information used in making these decisions included the allocation of indirect manufacturing and production department overhead. It was this use of reported product costs that caused management to be concerned with the new cost system. There was consensus that products and models differed in how they consumed overhead, and that these differences were not captured by either the old or new systems. Over time, the company planned to implement a new cost system that could better assign all manufacturing costs to products, thereby increasing management's ability to control overhead. (Cooper 1994f, 6)

The Mitsubishi Kasei Cost System. Firms must have individual product costs if they are to make individual product-related decisions. At Komatsu, enough such decisions are required that the firm developed a system that could report product costs even if they were inaccurate. However, as the number of such decisions declines, the need to report product costs through the firm's cost system comes into question. Mitsubishi Kasei's new system avoids the problem of inaccurate product (model) costs by simply not reporting them. The system is designed to report the cost of product lines, not products.

Except that it relied more heavily upon direct labor in the second stage, in many ways, Mitsubishi Kasei's old system was similar to Komatsu's old system. By traditional standards, the system was reasonably complex. It identified three major categories of costs: factory costs, direct selling costs, and administration costs (see Figure 10-4). Factory costs included the raw materials, utilities, labor, and overhead consumed in the production process; direct selling costs included transporting, loading, and insuring finished products; and administrative costs included marketing, distribution, and corporate administration expenses.

Factory costs were identified as either variable or fixed in nature. Variable costs included the costs of raw materials, the costs of receiving those materials, and the costs of the utilities consumed in the production process. Variable costs were charged directly to products unless the production process, such as the cracking of naph-

Figure 10-4
Reporting Product Line Costs in Mitsubishi Kasei's Old System

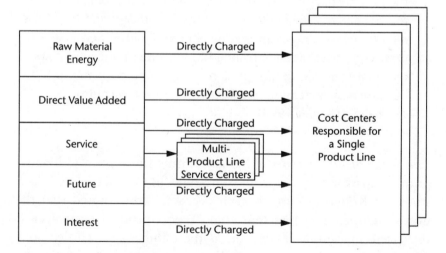

Source: R. Cooper, "Mitsubishi Kasei Corporation: Product Line Cost System," case study 9-195-066 (Boston: Harvard Business School, 1994), 17.

tha, resulted in joint products. In these cases, some form of allocation was unavoidable. Fixed costs included the costs of the direct labor workforce, depreciation, repair costs, and production overhead. These costs were split into direct and indirect fixed costs.

Direct fixed costs, such as direct labor, depreciation, or repairs, were charged to the production processes and, hence, to the products that consumed them. Indirect fixed costs were split into two categories—departmental overhead and factory burden—and allocated to the production processes. Departmental overhead, which included the salaries of the departmental general managers and the costs of the coordination and technical sections within the departments, was charged directly to production cost centers and then allocated to the products. Factory burden included the costs of wastewater treatment and central planning. These costs were allocated to the production cost centers and, subsequently, to the products.

Because they could be identified by product, direct selling expenses were charged to products. Administrative expenses were allocated to the production centers. The administrative functions, such as general affairs, personnel, and accounting, were split into a number of separate service cost centers. The personnel function, for example, was broken into five different centers: organization support, labor union window, training, welfare, and accounting for wages. The expenses of these centers were allocated to production areas, using bases that were thought to capture the workload created by the production areas in the service centers. For example, the expenses of the welfare department were allocated to the production cost centers using head count because the number of individuals in the production center captured approximately the amount of welfare support each center required.

The departmental overhead, factory burden, and administrative expenses were allocated from the production centers to the products in two steps. Indirect costs were allocated to the facilities within each production center and then to products. Thus, the system required three distinct allocation steps: to the production cost center, to the facility, and to the products. The costs of administration expenses were allocated from the production center to the facility level by using the same base that was used to allocate the costs to the production centers. For example, welfare costs were allocated to the facilities using head count. Because the allocation base used in the earlier steps was frequently unavailable at the product level, these allocations relied on a different base, usually direct labor hours or a managerial estimate of usage.

In 1987, this system was replaced by a computerized system that was designed to overcome many of the old system's limitations. In particular, the new system had four major objectives:

1. To allow explicit attribution of responsibility for all costs.
2. To increase the firm's ability to control service costs.
3. To allow departmental and section managers to control costs according to planned objectives.
4. To allow individual product costs to be determined as required. (Cooper 1994h, 4)

The unique characteristic of this new system is its inability to report product costs. Instead, it reports product line costs (see Figure 10-5). Although most decisions are made at the product line level, occasionally product-related decisions are needed:

There were three major reasons why individual product costs were required. First, they helped determine individual product prices when the same product line was used in various ways. For example, polyethylene was injection-molded to form products such as beer crates, buckets, and plastic toys. It was also blow-molded to produce products such as detergent bottles, and extrusion-molded to create films. Each application required different types of resin, and these resins had different production costs. For the sales force to be able to sell these resins, they had to know their costs. Second, individual product costs were important to decisions about what grades of a product line to manufacture. Product mix decisions of this class were usually made when a plant reached capacity and orders had to be turned down. Under these conditions it made sense to accept the most

Figure 10-5
Reporting Product Line Costs in Mitsubishi Kasei's New System

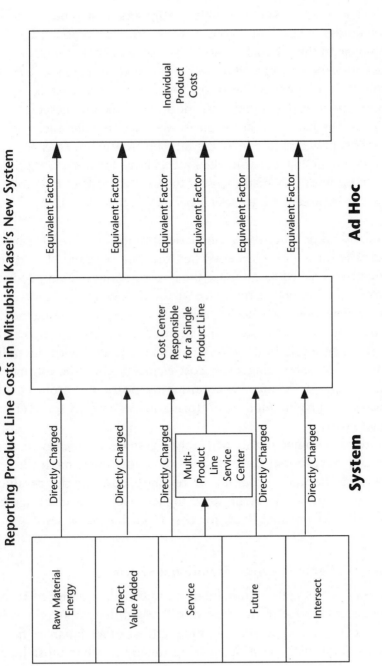

Source: R. Cooper, "Mitsubishi Kasei Corporation: Product Line Cost System," case study 9-195-066 (Boston: Harvard Business School, 1994), 19.

profitable orders where possible. Finally, individual product costs were used to check the profitability of individual products by comparing the product's costs to its selling price. Individual product costs were compared to selling prices when there was a risk that they were being sold below variable cost. Export sales were often made at prices that were much lower than domestic prices. The higher domestic prices were due to tariffs and special services provided to domestic customers. Mitsubishi Kasei accepted these low prices to keep plants busy. However, accepting such business only made sense if the variable costs of the products sold exceeded their selling prices. (Cooper 1994h, 6)

Individual product costs can be determined on an *ad hoc* basis outside the formal cost system when they are required. To do so, an engineer is asked to estimate the cost of an individual product based upon his or her experience of the production process. The engineer develops cost factors for each of the five cost elements identified by the cost system. These cost factors are used to estimate the magnitude of the cost elements associated with the individual product. Summing these cost elements gives the estimated product cost. For financial accounting purposes, inventory is valued using the product line cost information as a proxy for average product costs.

Both the Komatsu and Mitsubishi systems are designed primarily for operational control, but both show the same trade-off being made between accuracy of reported costs at the product model level and accuracy at some higher level of product aggregation, such as product lines, for cost reporting purposes.

Shionogi's Highly Accurate Traditional System

Shionogi's cost system, while highly traditional, is designed to be highly accurate. One of the most interesting differences in the way cost systems are managed at Shionogi and at other Japanese firms is the location of the cost accounting function. While most Japanese firms locate the cost accounting function at their headquarters, Shionogi locates its cost accounting function in its plants

(Cooper 1995a, 4). Only by locating the function in the plants can the system be kept sufficiently up-to-date to maintain the accuracy Shionogi requires. As will be discussed in chapter 12, locating the system in the plants allows the *kaizen* costing and product costing systems to be more closely integrated.

Shionogi first began working on its system in 1974:

> The Shionogi cost system had been under development for over 15 years. Its continuous evolution reflected the demand for more accurate product costs as the competitive and regulatory environment that the firm faced became more complex. The conceptual work on the system began in 1974 when the four categories of cost elements recognized by the then existing system were increased to nine. The original four categories were raw material, packaging material, labor, and "other expenses." The additional five categories were developed by splitting the category "other expenses" into six new ones; utilities, equipment repair, testing, subcontracting, direct overhead, and indirect overhead. (Cooper 1995a, 4–5)

The additional categories of cost elements are identified so that costs can be more accurately assigned to departments or cost centers and then to products. To achieve this degree of accuracy both the first stage (in which costs are assigned to the departments) and the second stage (in which costs are assigned to products) must be accurate:

> The advantage of the increase in the number of overhead categories recognized by the system lay in its ability to get those costs more accurately assigned to the departments where they were consumed. In the old system, "other expenses" were allocated to the departments and products using the basis of direct labor hours. This increase in system sophistication was required because, as the level of automation in the plant increased, the accuracy of assigning the "other expenses" based upon direct labor hours became more and more questionable. This accuracy problem was further compounded by a shift in the nature of the

work performed by the labor force from direct "touch" operations to more indirect activities such as technical development
and process monitoring. (Cooper 1995a, 6)

To reflect the complexity of the production process, three types
of departments are identified. This permits the nature of their
activities to be individually recognized:

Three types of departments—production, service, and indirect—
were recognized. Three different types of production departments were recognized one for each of the three major
production steps. Service departments covered the support activities supplied directly to the production departments and included the equipment repair, utilities, and testing. Indirect
departments supplied services only indirectly to the production
departments and included the general administration, general affairs, finance and accounting, production planning, and technical development departments. (Cooper 1995a, 6)

The identification of three types of departments forces the
assignment of costs in the first stage to be undertaken in two steps.
The first step consists of assigning direct costs to all of the departments. In addition to the directly assigned overhead, direct costs
include raw material, packaging material, and labor. While the first
cost assignment step is simple, the second is not. Costs assigned
to the service and indirect departments must be allocated to the
production departments before they are allocated to products. In
the second step, the direct costs of the service and indirect department costs are allocated to the production departments using a
three-stage step-down procedure. The first stage takes the direct
costs of the service departments and allocates them to the indirect
and production departments. To remove the problem of reciprocal
services, this stage starts with the costs of the repair department
and allocates them to the other service departments as well as to
the indirect and production departments. The costs of the utilities
department are allocated next and followed by the costs of the
testing departments.

After allocating the service department costs, the costs of the indirect departments (including their share of the service department costs) are allocated to the production departments. Two different types of indirect departments are recognized. The first type captures the costs of the technical development associated with each production department. The cost of the technical development dedicated to each of the three production processes is driven directly to the production departments. This procedure is relatively straightforward since production-oriented technical development expenses are monitored at the process level and thus are directly assignable to the production departments.

The second type of indirect departments are departments that supply common services, such as general administration. The costs of the indirect departments that cannot be directly assigned to the production departments are allocated to these departments, using the sum of the direct costs of the production and service departments.

This highly complex and accurate system is required to support the product mix decisions that the firm faces. In the highly competitive pharmaceutical environment, Shionogi's management believes that accurate product formulation costs are critical if the company is to achieve its profitability targets.

The Yamatake-Honeywell ABC System

In June 1992, Nobuyuki Takai, Yamatake-Honeywell's chief financial officer, instructed the cost section of the management department located within the Shonan Factory to replace the existing cost system with an ABC system. The decision to change systems was brought about by concern over the effect of distortions created by the existing system on business decisions. Two months later, part of the new system was running and reporting costs for the firm's control valve products. Control valves were chosen for three reasons. First, they were simple products with only three production lines. Second, the lines contained few variants. Third, the firm strongly suspected that the product costs reported by the old system were highly distorted.

[B]ased on the information from the old system, the firm's small control valves appeared to be highly competitive while the large control valves were apparently noncompetitive. This perception made the firm reluctant to accept orders for large control valves. Because manufacturing was convinced that both sizes of valves were equally competitive, the only viable explanation for the differing levels of profitability was that the cost system was introducing serious distortions into reported product costs. (Cooper 1994p, 2–3)

The old system had been highly conventional and consisted of a single cost pool for each product line. This overhead pool contained the costs of the indirect production departments, including production control, production engineering, quality control, and purchasing. Direct production overhead costs were accounted separately and classified as *burden, material burden,* and *labor burden.* The total overhead for each product line was divided by the total direct cost of that line to give the burden rate for the line. Total direct costs included direct materials, direct labor, and the costs of the tooling and equipment depreciation. The reported cost of each product was obtained by multiplying the direct costs of the product by one plus the burden rate for the appropriate product line (see Figure 10-6).

The overhead associated with each product line was determined by taking the indirect costs for labor and expenses semiannually for each department and multiplying them by the appropriate factor from the department's load table. The load table identified the amount of time spent on each product line by everyone in the department. Load tables were required because most personnel within each indirect department worked on all three control valve product lines. Therefore, some allocation scheme to assign their costs to the different product lines was required. The load tables contained information on the 100 separate operations required to complete manufacture of the products. The load factors, which were determined by interviewing the group leaders, were reevaluated every six months. Clearly the old system was not activity based and would report distorted product

Figure 10-6
Existing Cost System at Yamatake-Honeywell

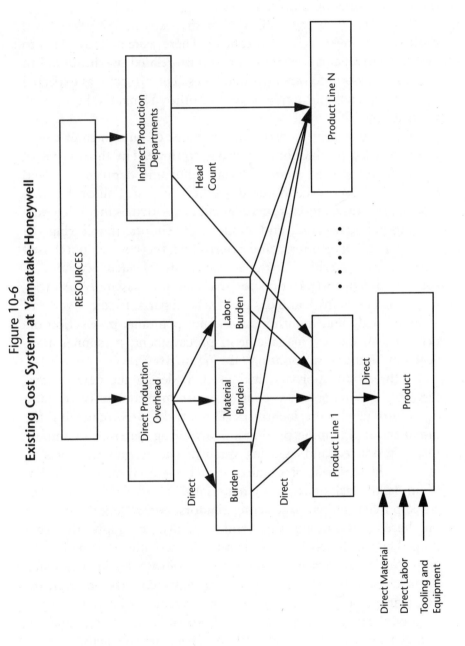

costs if overhead activities were performed in different ratios for the various sizes of control valves.

The portion of the ABC system that was initially developed dealt with material-related overhead. There were already plans to develop subsystems for labor and facility-related overhead and to extend the system to other product lines. The project was expected to be completed and implemented in other Yamatake-Honeywell factories by 1995.

The new system increased the number of burden rates calculated for each product line from one to three. The three types of overhead recognized were material, labor and depreciation, and facility-level overhead. Material overhead included all of the costs associated with material procurement, i.e., activities involving purchasing parts, selecting and supporting vendors, monitoring the quality level of vendors, and controlling the cost of purchased parts. Labor overhead included the costs of such activities as product design, preparation for manufacture, assembly of products, delivery control, and design of special parts. Facility overhead included daily and monthly production planning, production order control, factory management, procurement, personnel management, and cost accounting (see Figure 10-7).

A three-step approach was used to design the new system. First, the five major tasks required to produce control valves (and other products) were identified. These tasks were managing the organization, planning production, acquiring materials, manufacturing products, and assuring quality. The second step was to identify the major steps required to achieve each major task. For example, the task of acquiring material was broken into five major steps: purchasing parts, selecting vendors, controlling the costs of purchased parts, monitoring vendor quality, and supporting vendors. The third step was to identify the activities that had to be performed to achieve each major step. For example, the major step of purchasing parts was broken into eight activities—receipt, order, management of delivery dates, management of actual delivery of goods, payment, materials supply to subcontractors, cancellation/changes to the schedule, and database management.

Each department was responsible for developing its own

activity-based model and identifying the major tasks and steps performed in the department as well as the time spent on them. Some of the support departments performed activities that supported more than one major task. For example, the Production Control Department had two primary functions, production control and purchasing. The production control function was part of the task of manufacturing products and therefore was considered part of the labor-related overhead. In contrast, the purchasing activity was part of material procurement and therefore was material-related overhead.

The sections within each department were responsible for identifying the activities they performed and their full-time equivalents (FTEs). The section estimates were determined using job content questionnaires that were made up from all activities described in the ISO 9000 protocol. The questionnaires were prepared by Saburo Shimada, manager of the cost accounting section in the fiscal control department and completed by members of the cost section in the Shonan Factory. Since each department contained several sections and the accounting department did not

Figure 10-7
ABC System at Yamatake-Honeywell

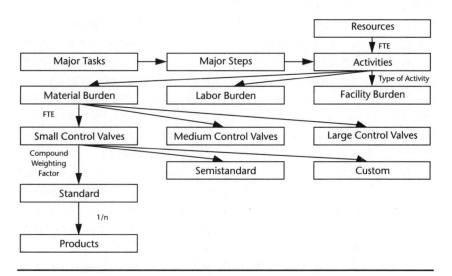

want the model to become too complex, each section was only expected to summarize its activities. For example, the field instruments production group contained five sections: production planning, procurement, production control, process engineering, and quality control. Their respective activities were summarized as organizational management, production planning, procurement, product manufacture, and quality assurance.

Once a section had identified the activities and related FTEs it performed, Nobuyuki Takai identified the activities that were to be assigned to the three burden pools. Activities were assigned on the basis of the reason the activity was performed. In other words, activity costs were assigned to the material burden pool if they were performed in order to supply material to production. If they supported production, they were assigned to the labor and depreciation pool, and if they supported common functions, they were assigned to the facility level pool.

The costs within the cost pools associated with each product line were then assigned to the different product types in each production line. To do this, objective information from the firm's mainframe production control system, known as the final assembly daily explosion (FADE) system, was required. FADE included an MRP system that was used to schedule production and purchasing. Three classes of products were recognized by FADE. Standard products, products that were manufactured for inventory, made up the first class of products. The parts lists for these products was maintained on FADE and used to generate purchase orders. Custom products that were made to customer order made up the second class. Because the parts lists for these products were not maintained on the FADE system, their purchases were not scheduled by FADE. Finally, there were hybrid or semistandard products that contained both parts that were and were not maintained on FADE.

Determining whether or not a part was maintained on FADE was critical to the design of the new cost system since parts that were on FADE were less expensive to procure, because they were ordered and purchased automatically, than parts that were not and therefore had to be manually procured. If the new system was to be accurate, then, it had to assign more costs to special parts than to standard ones. To do this, a compound weighting factor was developed. This factor was created from the workload factor, i.e., how long it took for standard and special parts. For semistandard products, the weighted average workload factor was based upon the average mix of standard and special parts used across all control valve lines. This workload factor was then weighted according to the volume of products produced for each product type. The resulting compound factor was used to assign production control costs to each product type.

Dividing the total cost of the product type by the number of units produced gave the materials burden cost per unit of each product type. Thus, the two-stage procedure for the determination of the material burden rate for each product type was determined by using a head count in the first stage to create the cost pools, one for each product type, and then by using the compound weighted factors to drive the material burden to the different types of products in the product lines. For the control valve cost system, there were three cost pools (one each for small, medium, and large control valve product lines) and three types of products in each product line (standard, semistandard, and custom control valves), giving a total of nine material burden rates for control valves (one for each product line product type pair).

The cost of consumables and the depreciation of dies and molds were added to the material burden flat fee. These additional portions of material burden were assigned to specific products whenever possible. For example, the dies that are used to produce control valves are often specific to a particular valve. Therefore, the depreciation cost of the die is divided by the planned material cost of the valve to give the ¥/material ¥ burden charge for die depreciation. Usually each die is used in a number of different variants of a given product, not just a single product. In this case, the total material cost of the variants produced is used to give an average ¥/material ¥ burden charge for that variant family. Thus, the total material-related burden for a given product was made up of three distinct elements: the activity-related costs, the costs of the consumables, and depreciation of dies and molds.

The material burden portion of the activity-based system at Yamatake-Honeywell was highly sophisticated and corrected for many of the errors in the old system. The activity, and hence cost, differences between small and large valves were captured, and the new system did indeed report more accurate product costs. Interestingly, it did not differentiate among activities that are performed at the unit, batch, product, or facility levels. Clearly, some of the material-related activities are nonunit related so some distortion will remain. If the production volumes for the various valves in each product line/size category are similar, the distortion will be small.

SUMMARY

The product costing systems at the firms discussed in this chapter varied from highly conventional to highly innovative. Only one of the systems was an ABC system. Other innovations included systems that could only report the costs of product lines, not products. The conventional systems were similar, if not identical, to their Western counterparts. The lack of innovation reflects the heavy reliance placed upon target costing and value engineering, which, when coupled with careful management of the product mix, does much to remove the requirements for reported product costs using activity-based principles.

The decision by Komatsu and Mitsubishi Kasei to report at the product line, as opposed to the product level, reflects a cost-benefit trade-off. Since few decisions are made at the product level and target costing, coupled with the short lives of many of the products, makes it virtually impossible for products to become unprofitable before they are replaced, the value of accurate product costs is diminished. Furthermore, at most production facilities, product lines are manufactured in dedicated areas of the factory. Therefore, it is relatively easy to assign costs directly to the product lines but not to the products. By reporting accurate product line costs, the firms are able to monitor profitability at the level they make decisions, the product line.

Under most conditions, traditional systems cannot report

product costs as accurately as ABC systems. Consequently, in environments in which accurate product costs are required, ABC systems are apt to be present. While Shionogi requires highly accurate product costs, its system is not activity-based. Instead, it is a highly sophisticated system that relies upon identifying multiple categories of costs and assigning them to numerous production centers, using direct measures wherever possible. The costs of the service department and indirect departments are allocated to production departments using a step-down procedure that relies upon three allocation bases that are designed to capture the usage of the indirect and service departments by the production departments.

Yamatake-Honeywell is in the process of implementing an ABC system. The system identifies five layers of activities. The lowest layer are the activities that are used to cost products. While the system is highly sophisticated, it does not take advantage of the hierarchy of manufacturing activities.

CHAPTER 11

KAIZEN COSTING

By reporting product costs, product costing systems identify products that are either unprofitable or at risk of becoming unprofitable. Once these products are identified, *kaizen* costing is put into action. *Kaizen* is the Japanese term for continuous improvement. *Kaizen costing* is continuous improvement applied to cost reduction in the manufacturing stage of a product's life. While it is through *kaizen* costing that the costs of existing products are reduced, *kaizen* systems do more than just reduce costs, they also increase the quality of products and the safety of production processes.

Not all firms undertake *kaizen* costing. At Nissan's assembly plants, for example,

> [u]nless the production cost exceeded the target cost, no cost reduction efforts were undertaken during the production stage. Management had determined that the incremental savings from such efforts were more than offset by disturbances they created to the production process. When inflation or other factors caused costs to rise, pressure was exerted upon the suppliers to find ways to keep component costs at their final target levels. Similarly, pressure was exerted on the assembly plants to achieve the assembly target costs. (Cooper 1994i, 7)

Kaizen costing, then, is deemed inappropriate when the cost of the disruptions caused by changes to the production process is greater than the savings. To reduce the cost of disruptions, many firms introduce changes to production processes only when the cumulative savings or improvements are considered sufficient to justify them. Thus, changes in the production processes may occur only every six to twelve months. For a month or so after a change, a production process will generate negative variances until it is brought back under control.

Like target costing, *kaizen* costing systems are most effective when a cost reduction objective is set. Unlike target costing, *kaizen* costing does not concern itself with product design, focusing instead on the production process related either to a given product or to the processes in general. The aim of a *kaizen* costing program is to remove unnecessary inefficiencies from production processes. As a *kaizen* costing program achieves its objectives, the overall cost of production, and hence reported product costs, falls.

The primary difference between *kaizen* costing and target costing is the degree of freedom each has to reduce costs. In target costing, product design is not finalized; therefore, functionality can be changed. In *kaizen* costing, the product is in production; therefore, only minor design changes can be undertaken. This constraint reduces the degree of cost savings that can be achieved. According to one estimate, approximately 90 percent of a product's costs are frozen once its design is approved (Blanchard 1978). If this estimate is correct, then *kaizen* costing can only influence the remaining 10 percent. Even so, *kaizen* costing programs are seen as important parts of a firm's overall cost reduction efforts.

The focus of a *kaizen* costing system is determined by the strategy of the firm and the way in which the firm feels it can most effectively reduce production costs. At Citizen, for instance, the *kaizen* costing program focuses on labor reduction. The major way to reduce labor is to alter the time required to operate or support the production machines. Alterations can be achieved in two ways. First, the running speed of the machines can be increased so that more parts per hour can be produced. Second, a single employee can be used to operate more machines. For Citizen, then,

[t]he success of this program was illustrated by the turning machine department. The 150 turning machines in the department were operated by 15 people during the day shift and only 2 people on the night shift. The high ratio of machines to people had been achieved by paying considerable attention to what events caused downtime and eradicating them. The 15 people on the day shift were primarily involved with setting up the turning machines, troubleshooting, and keeping the machines loaded with wire. Only 2 people were required on the night shift because high volume components that did not require changeovers were produced at night. The only task of the night shift was to keep the machines running. If a machine broke down or drifted out of tolerance, it was left for the day shift to troubleshoot. (Cooper 1994a, 7)

In contrast, at Sumitomo Electric Industries, product material content is high and labor content low. Consequently, the firm's *kaizen* costing system, which can trace its origins back to the earliest days of *kaizen,* focuses on material rather than labor. The evolution of Sumitomo's system sheds light on the motivation of the company's workforce and management team:

A cost-reduction orientation emerged at SEI around 1955 because the union leaders believed that any salary increases they demanded should come out of their own efforts, not out of the pockets of the firm's other stakeholders. Responding to union requests, the firm began to invest heavily in human resource management (HRM). . . .

At the heart of SEI's HRM approach was a willingness to increase the pay of the work force as it became more efficient. This HRM policy allowed the work force to demand higher pay in exchange for higher productivity. The success of this policy created a work force willing to become more efficient and to change the nature of their jobs as required. This flexibility allowed SEI to very rapidly and effectively introduce mass production despite the dislocations it caused in the workforce. (Cooper 1994m, 3)

The reward system that Sumitomo developed in the 1950s is unusual in that it specifically includes a monetary reward, known as productivity enhancement:

> salaries consisted of three elements: base salary, bonus, and productivity enhancement bonus. Each year, the pool of funds provided to employees for their productivity efforts was determined for each facility based upon its productivity. Each individual's productivity enhancement bonus was determined by multiplying the individual's base pay (excluding bonus) by the appropriate factory's productivity ratio. This ratio was determined by dividing the total funds in the productivity pool by the total salary base of the participating employees. Thus, the pay scheme was designed to create positive pressure for increased productivity throughout the organization. (Cooper 1994m, 3)

For the scheme to work, the firm has to be able to accurately measure improvements in productivity. To help Sumitomo do this, several systems were developed or modified. Among these systems were the total budget system and the direct cost system as well as blue collar and staff cost reduction target programs. These cost reduction target programs were at the heart of the firm's *kaizen* costing program.

> Daily plans were developed at each facility to determine ways to reduce costs. These plans were based upon the monthly budgets, which reflected the savings anticipated from the kaizen programs. The objectives of the daily meetings were to discuss the savings achieved the previous day and how they compared to the budget, and the savings expected to be achieved that day. The rate of achieving these cost savings was measured against the monthly budgets [see Figure 11-1]. Cost reduction plans were prepared at the facility level and then consolidated at the

Figure 11-1
SEI's Rate of Achieving Cost Reduction Targets

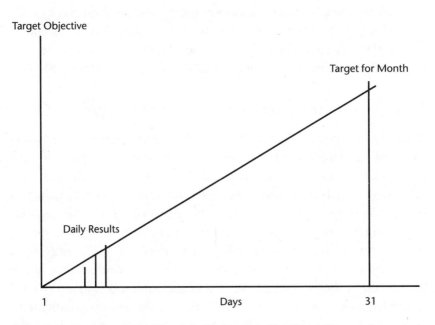

Source: R. Cooper, "Sumitoma Electric Industries, Ltd.: The Kaizen Program," case study 9-195-078 (Boston: Harvard Business School, 1994), 13.

divisional level to see if they provided an adequate cost reduction objective for the division. (Cooper 1994m, 5)

Attention to detail is critical to the success of a *kaizen* program. No improvement, however small, can be ignored. For this reason, many firms reward individuals who identify savings. Usually the rewards are not monetary but instead bring attention to the individual's achievements. At Citizen, for example,

[t]o create incentives for the work force to identify savings, picture boards were placed throughout the factory. These picture boards contained pictures of the before and after improvements and identified the group and individual who identified the savings and the degree of savings. For example, one set of before

and after pictures covered a reduction in the time required to read a set of meters. The person reading the meters determined that the time he required to read them could be reduced by shifting them. Prior to moving them, it required 2 minutes and 58 seconds to read each meter. After they were moved, it required only one minute and 30 seconds. (Cooper 1994a, 8)

SETTING *KAIZEN* COSTING OBJECTIVES

While *kaizen* costing programs are the responsibility of the workforce, most firms use a top-down pressure to ensure that sufficient savings are achieved. Because the work groups set their own cost reduction targets and then negotiate with senior management, this top-down pressure is sometimes difficult to observe. The negotiations, an interesting mix of top-down and bottom-up philosophies, usually result in cost reduction targets that are more aggressive than originally planned. The power of the negotiations lies in the commitment they create to the cost reduction targets at every level of the firm, even when those targets are set by senior management.

At Sumitomo Electric, the negotiation process to establish the final cost reduction targets is as follows:

Each facility was broken into a number of distinct manufacturing processes, each run by a self-directed work team. Usually, these groups were treated as cost centers and were responsible for collecting cost information. However, sometimes there were several groups within a cost center, in which case costs were collected at the group level, not at the cost-center level. . . . Each . . . center was responsible for developing a six-month budget. Like other budgets, this was prepared with the first three months in detail and the last three averaged. The budget was expected to cover all of the center's expenses, including wages and salaries, overtime charges, travel, and office supplies. Each responsibility center submitted its budget to the division general manager for approval. Any discrepancies between corporate objectives and the center's budget were subject to negotiations before approval was received. (Cooper 1994m, 11)

This process creates a top-down pressure for the groups to achieve the targeted cost reductions. Sometimes this pressure was subtle, other times it was quite obvious:

> Some of the targets for the reduction of indirect costs were set by the budget section of the accounting department at the head office. This section was responsible for setting the corporate policy on indirect cost reduction. For example, it might set a corporate policy of reducing indirect costs by 3% for the year or reducing travel expenditures by 10%. These policies were communicated to the divisions and were expected to be incorporated into the divisional profit plans. (Cooper 1994m, 11)

The intense pressure to achieve cost reduction targets can only be maintained if the targets set for each group are achievable. At Sumitomo, for example,

> [t]he majority of groups achieved their cost reduction targets to within ±2%. Typically, between 10% and 20% of the groups failed to achieve their targets, with a similar percentage achieving higher savings. No statistics were kept on group performance because management considered it more important to monitor how each group performed rather than how close it came to its target. (Cooper 1994m, 6)

To help monitor performance, Sumitomo maintains charts on each group's performance (see Figure 11-2). Because the cost reductions achieved by each group are contingent upon the nature of the product, the maturity of the production processes, and the experience of the group, care is taken not to compare intergroup performance: "The level of expected cost reduction depended upon the product. Some products had the potential for high *kaizen* savings, while the costs of other, more mature products were difficult to reduce. For this reason, no attempt was made to compare cost reduction performance across groups" (Cooper 1994m, 6). This does not mean that other types of comparisons are not made and, indeed, used to increase overall efficiency:

Figure 11-2
**SEI's Profitability Chart of a Group Reaching between +/-2%
of Its Target**

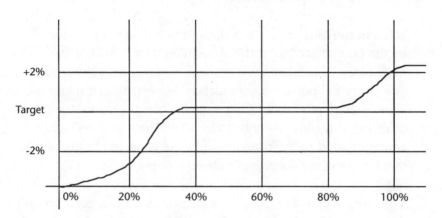

Source: R. Cooper, "Sumitoma Electric Industries, Ltd.: The Kaizen Program," case study
9-195-078 (Boston: Harvard Business School, 1994), 14.

When the market price of a product declined and the product
was at risk of becoming unprofitable, the staff cost reduction target was adjusted downwards. The extent of this downward shift
was determined by the rate of price decline expected in the fore-
seeable future. . . . This new cost reduction target, because it
was more aggressive than the previous target, required that
white-collar workers go beyond kaizen and find ways to fundamentally change either the design of the product or its production processes. (Cooper 1994m, 10)

KAIZEN COSTING EVALUATION

Because one of the objectives of *kaizen* systems is to reduce costs,
the systems affect the variances calculated by the firms' standard
cost systems.

Although *kaizen* costing programs and standard cost systems
are integrated in most firms, standard cost systems are not usually
viewed as the primary performance evaluation system for *kaizen*

costing achievements. Instead, more direct measures of productivity are used. At Citizen,

> [t]he success of cost reduction efforts was measured using an achievement ratio, which was obtained by dividing actual labor hours by standard labor hours. Achievement ratios were computed monthly for each group and semiannually for each product. The expected value of the achievement ratio was 100%, reflecting the incorporation of the cost reduction targets into the standards on a monthly basis. (Cooper 1994a, 7)

Citizen uses a mixture of self-directed teams and managerial oversight to ensure the efficacy of its *kaizen* costing program. As described in earlier chapters, under this approach group leaders are free to make their own decisions as long as targets are achieved. If group performance declines, managers are first asked to explain how they are going to correct the deficiencies. If performance does not improve, technical support is provided. If this does not help, the group leader is replaced:

> If the achievement ratio for a group was about 101%, then a review was triggered. At this review, the group leader would discuss ways to ensure that the following month's achievement ratio would fall to 100%. The standard was not changed for the first month that the achievement ratio was over 100%. This created additional pressure on the group to achieve its cost reduction targets. If the ratio remained above 100% for a second month in a row, then the standard was adjusted in the third month to reflect the failure to achieve the desired cost reductions. In effect, the cost reduction target for the group was revised downwards.
>
> Even though the target was revised, the review continued of why the targeted savings were not achieved and how they could subsequently be achieved. There was no direct reward or punishment associated with over- or underachieving. The reasons behind the failure to reach an achievement ratio of 100% were discussed thoroughly and fully analyzed. If the reason was

based on the manager's ability, the results would be reflected in
his or her personal evaluation and promotion potential. (Cooper
1994a, 7–8)

The allowable range of the achievement ratio before action is
taken is notable: only a 1 percent deviation is required before the
review process begins. Such tight tolerances indicate how carefully
the production environment is controlled in many Japanese firms.

In contrast to Citizen, Sumitomo relies heavily upon its workers' awareness of the firm's cost system to achieve targeted cost
reductions:

All blue-collar workers were very much aware of the cost system.
Charts were posted throughout the factory that indicated both
the cost of products and processes and the level of cost reduction achieved (the charts consisted of graphs or tables). This sharing of cost information was considered a critical part of the
firm's kaizen program. Only by sharing the relevant cost and
quality information could management expect the workers to be
able to most effectively achieve cost reduction by setting and
committing to sensible targets. (Cooper 1994m, 5)

This reliance upon cost information requires a workforce that
is capable of understanding the information. In the firm's view, the
easiest way to achieve this objective is to have the workers collect
the information:

For kaizen cost reductions, the trend was to delegate cost reduction to the factory level. In particular, management tried to use
accounting data at that level. . . . To transfer ownership of accounting information from the accounting department to the
shop floor, factory personnel began to prepare shop floor cost
management information, and subsequently some of it was used
by the accounting department to produce financial reports.
(Cooper 1994m, 6)

There were five major elements in Sumitomo's first effort to involve its workers in cost management:

1. Workers were provided with cost information and were expected to manage with it.
2. Accounting was performed in the plants as well as at headquarters.
3. Some investment decisions were made by the blue-collar workers.
4. There were separate financial and management accounting systems.
5. Monthly meetings were held with blue-collar workers to evaluate plant and divisional performance. (Cooper 1994m, 7)

To ensure that cost reduction targets are achieved, as the responsibility for the *kaizen* costing program and the generation of associated cost management information is spread lower in the organization, Sumitomo uses its accounting system:

The accounting system was used to determine when the division was not achieving its cost reduction targets. It was plant accounting's responsibility to draw attention to any cost reduction shortfalls and obtain an explanation from the division general managers as to why the planned cost reductions were not achieved. Every six months, a more thorough review was undertaken that included analyzing the cost reductions due to investments. Investment-related cost reduction analyses were only performed every six months because, unlike the blue-collar cost reductions, they required off-line calculations. (Cooper 1994m, 7)

While it is not absolutely necessary to provide workers with detailed cost information for *kaizen* costing programs to function, there is some evidence that programs that do provide this information are more effective. Under the old system at Kirin Brewery, for example, brewery workers were not aware of costs and this lack of information was felt to be one of the drawbacks of the system:

This lack of knowledge about cost and hence profitability made it impossible for the workers to see the magnitude of their contribution to the brewery, let alone to overall firm performance. For example, the percentage yield (not the cost of the lost beer) was used to measure the efficiency of the process of transferring beer from the fermentation vats to the storage tanks. Knowing that beer transfer efficiency had increased 5% during the year, however, did not indicate whether the resulting savings were significant or immaterial. Similarly, without some ability to benchmark the economic performance of the self-directed groups in each brewery, there was no easy way for management to evaluate how these groups were performing financially or for the groups to evaluate their own economic performance. (Cooper 1994d, 9)

The problem was not that the breweries were trying to trick or "game" the system but that nobody had enough financial information to make the appropriate trade-offs between, for example, the cost of overtime and temporary workers. This problem was corrected in the new system (see chapter 11), which made cost information widely available.

THE MATURING OF *KAIZEN* COSTING SYSTEMS

As *kaizen* costing systems age, they become less effective. The primary problem appears to be that the workforce runs out of ideas about how to improve productivity. After many years of making suggestions, it is not surprising that the number of suggestions and the magnitude of savings falls. At Citizen, for example,

[l]abor content was reduced primarily in two ways: either production engineering would change the way the product was produced or the work force would find ways to become more efficient. In the early 1990s, about 80% of all cost reductions were expected to be achieved by production engineering changes. Only 20% was expected from the work force, because

it had already spent years becoming more efficient and management believed that any remaining savings opportunities were limited. (Cooper 1994a, 6)

The loss of effectiveness of the programs reflected their maturity rather than a failure on the part of the workforce. Sometimes the program also reached some physical limit that made it virtually impossible to achieve any more savings. In this case, a firm's workforce may begin to make investment decisions to find ways around that limit. At Sumitomo Electric,

[i]n the early days of the kaizen program, all investment recommendations were made by the staff engineers. Over time, the blue-collar workers began to make investment recommendations. This shift was driven in part by the kaizen objectives having been achieved for many of the production processes. These mature processes were so efficiently run that the workers could no longer see ways to improve them without investment in new equipment. For example, the rate of production of polyethylene-coated cable could only be increased if new coating equipment was purchased. (Cooper 1994m, 9)

Reacting to the maturity of *kaizen* costing programs, some firms develop new systems that are designed to revitalize their *kaizen* costing programs (see chapters 13 and 14). At the Kyoto brewery of Kirin beer, cost reduction programs "typically identified four or five targets for improvements each year. This continuous change of focus helped keep the programs active" (Cooper 1994d, 8).

The increase in overhead that drove the development of new cost systems at several of the firms discussed in chapter 10 also affected the focus of *kaizen* costing programs. At Citizen, for instance, the focus shifted toward indirect costs:

The workload of each indirect person was reviewed to see if the position could be eliminated or the duties reduced. This analysis typically resulted in a new job description, which was prepared by the cost center group to which the indirect person belonged and reviewed by the general managers. At the heart of this cost reduction exercise was the belief that if the work did not go away there would be no long-term savings. The second approach was to identify the necessary indirect activities, and where possible automate them so that they could be performed less expensively. (Cooper 1994a, 8)

In addition to changing cost reduction targets, sometimes modernization of the production process creates new *kaizen* costing opportunities. At Kirin,

changes in market demand and brewing technology created new processes on which to focus the cost reduction programs. For example, while pasteurized beers had been very popular in the past, draft beer, which was unpasteurized, had gained popularity. The resulting changes in the brewing process were subjected to cost reduction programs soon after they were introduced. (Cooper 1994d, 8)

Finally, the proliferation of products often requires changes in physical facilities and production processes, which may create new opportunities for cost reductions. There are, however, limitations to the effectiveness of these techniques to improve the vitality of *kaizen* programs. For example, at Kirin, "despite a continuous change in focus of the cost reduction programs, management felt they were losing effectiveness" (Cooper 1994d, 8). Similar sentiments were expressed at Olympus, "The decision to introduce a new program was driven in part by the observation that the savings from the 1987 plan had reduced in recent months" (Cooper 1994j, 10).

SUMMARY

Kaizen, the philosophy of continuous improvement, played a critical role at many of the firms studied, especially those with products having relatively long lives. Length of the product life was important because longer-lived products provided more opportunity for *kaizen* than shorter-lived ones.

The potential savings from the *kaizen* costing systems were lower than those from a firm's target costing system because the degrees of freedom for cost reduction were fewer. In particular, the product's design was already established. The primary objective of these *kaizen* costing systems is to make production processes more efficient. Therefore, *kaizen* costing operates at the product level.

For a *kaizen* costing program to be effective, its objectives must be achievable. Objectives are set through a mixture of top-down and bottom-up approaches. The top-down portion of the negotiations sets the overall cost reduction objective. The bottom-up portion assigns cost reduction objectives to the individual groups. Attention to detail and continuous feedback are keys to the success of the program. Picture boards, graphs, and charts are frequently used to provide feedback on the progress of the programs.

For *kaizen* variance analysis to monitor the effectiveness of a *kaizen* costing program, the standards built into the cost system must reflect the savings expected from the *kaizen* costing program. Therefore, variances are zero only if the anticipated savings were achieved. If a positive variance is detected, it means that greater than expected savings have been achieved. If a negative variance is detected, it means that the anticipated savings have not been achieved and that remedial actions are required. Some firms created additional cost-down pressures by rewarding groups that achieved positive variances. This double approach to cost reduction—a specified cost reduction objective coupled with rewards for achieving greater than expected savings—creates the maximum pressure for cost reduction.

The process of evaluating the performance of a *kaizen* program typically usually relies upon such nonfinancial measures as Citizen's achievement ratio. If this ratio exceeds 101 percent, the group leader is expected to explain why the cost reduction objective has not been achieved and what actions are going to be taken to achieve it. If the situation is not corrected, more severe actions by the central support staff are taken, including the replacement of the group leader. Cost information appears to play an important role in the success of *kaizen* programs. Workers who have access to cost information appear to be better able to direct their efforts.

There is some evidence that *kaizen* programs at some firms are maturing and beginning to lose their effectiveness. In these situations firms may change the focus of their programs by changing objectives, paying particular attention to recently introduced production processes, or by introducing systems designed to "harness the entrepreneurial spirit."

CHAPTER 12

OPERATIONAL CONTROL

There are two cost management techniques that Japanese firms use to increase the efficiency with which they manufacture their existing products: *kaizen* costing systems and operational control procedures. Often, these two techniques are used to reinforce each other. In these situations, operational control systems signal the existence of a problem and *kaizen* costing systems are then used to develop solutions to the problem.

An effective operational control system requires identifying the nature of costs, the establishment of responsibility centers, and the development of a process of variance analysis through the application of standard costs. Responsibility centers are necessary to help individuals understand what costs they will be held responsible for. Therefore, the identification of the nature of costs and the creation of responsibility centers occurs in tandem. Individuals should be responsible only for costs that they control. Costs outside their control should be ignored when operational control systems are developed. Variance analysis is used to monitor how well individuals are controlling their controllable costs. Variance analysis can be used to monitor how well an individual is achieving his or her budget or how well the individual is achieving his or her *kaizen* costing objectives. Firms vary in the way they established standard costs. Some use last period actual, others use estimated actual, and others, expected at the end of the period.

IDENTIFYING THE NATURE OF COSTS

For an operational control system to be effective, it must differentiate among four types of costs that are created by two sets of dichotomous definitions, one set that defines direct and indirect costs and another set that defines variable and fixed costs. The differentiation between direct and indirect costs is necessary if individuals are to be held responsible for the costs they control. The differentiation between variable and fixed costs is necessary if the system is to generate meaningful variances.

A direct cost is one that is assigned directly to a cost or profit center. No allocation procedures are used and the association of the cost with the center is both causal and accurate. For example, a person spends 60 percent of his time in the center; thus, 60 percent of his salary can be attributed to that center as a direct cost. An indirect cost is one that is allocated to the center. While a causal relationship may have been identified between the indirect cost and the center, the accuracy of the assignment is not given. For instance, assume that the cost of electricity is assigned indirectly to three departments and one department increases its consumption. The indirect assignment may show the electricity consumption (and thus cost) of all three departments as increasing, even though only one department has changed its level of consumption.

Many cost systems differentiate between both direct and indirect costs and between variable and fixed costs (see Figure 12-1). At Nippon Kayaku, for example,

> [d]irect costs were those costs that could be directly assigned to a production process. Indirect costs were those costs that could not be directly assigned to a production process but had to be allocated. Variable costs were those costs that varied directly with the level of production at the plant. Fixed costs, in contrast, were those costs that tended not to vary with the level of production. Only direct costs could be variable, but not all direct costs were variable. Thus, the direct costs contained both variable and fixed elements, while indirect costs contained only fixed elements.
>
> The two variable cost elements were direct material and direct other. Direct material costs consisted of the costs of all mate-

Figure 12-1
Nature of Costs at Nippon Kayaku

	Direct	**Indirect**
Variance	Direct Material Direct Other	
Fixed	Direct Labor of Production	Indirect Material Indirect Labor Indirect Other

rials that could be directly assigned to a production process. These materials were predominantly the primary ingredients for the chemical reactions required to produce the dyestuffs. Direct other costs included power, water, and subcontractor-related expenses. These cost elements could be assigned directly to each production process because their consumption could be measured at the process level. Power and water expenses allocated to products using standard consumption ratios. Actual subcontracting-related costs were assigned to each process.

The direct fixed costs consisted of the direct labor costs of the production processes. The labor costs were considered fixed because of lifetime employment contracts, which made it impossible to adjust labor levels to match production levels. Although some labor reassignment between processes was possible, overall labor levels could not be adjusted in the short term.

The indirect fixed costs consisted of three major elements: indirect material costs, indirect labor costs, and indirect other costs. Indirect material costs included supplies, tools, office equipment, repair parts, and fuels. Indirect labor costs included indirect labor salaries, part-time employee wages, bonuses, reserves for retirement, pension, and welfare expenditures. Indirect other costs consisted of depreciation, insurance, local taxes, leases, maintenance, disposal of industrial wastes, and travel expenses. (Cooper and Yoshikawa 1994c, 5–6)

However, when a new cost system was designed for Mitsubishi Kasei, it did not refer to fixed or variable costs because the fixed and variable cost perspective was considered too simplistic. Instead, the system identified five distinct cost categories, which managers felt gave them a better handle on how costs behaved as decisions were made:

1. Raw material and energy costs (the expenses of the raw material and energy consumed in the production process)
2. Direct value-adding costs (the direct costs of the processing and manufacturing departments)
3. Service costs (the costs of various support services)
4. Interest costs (the costs of funds procurement, determined by subtracting interest receivable from interest payable)
5. Future costs (costs from which benefits are expected in the future).

RESPONSIBILITY CENTERS

In an effective operational control system, all controllable costs are assigned directly to responsibility centers. Indirect cost assignments make it impossible to know if changes in resource consumption are due to distortions in the indirect assignment process or to an actual change in the level of consumption. Therefore, cost systems designed to provide operational control rather than accurate product costing contain few indirect cost assignments. For example, at Mitsubishi Kasei,

allocations made it impossible to hold managers responsible for costs; instead, they allowed them to make excuses. To reduce the number of allocations to the absolute minimum, the new cost system was designed around cost centers that were associated with a single product line. For example, the costs of production, distribution, marketing, and administration for a specific product line were charged directly to production and service cost centers that were responsible only for that product line. (Cooper 1994h, 4)

To clarify the concept of responsibility and to reduce the number of allocations required to report product line costs, Mitsubishi Kasei increased the number of cost centers and changed their structure:

To ensure that explicit responsibility for all costs was achieved, the number of cost centers in the new system was much higher than in the old one. In the old system, cost centers were either production plants that contained multiple facilities or service centers that were responsible for providing services to the entire firm. These cost centers were so large that numerous cost allocations were unavoidable. In contrast, cost centers in the new system were predominantly production facilities and service centers that were responsible for only a single product line. Management called these cost centers "cost boxes" because they were concerned not with how costs were incurred within the centers but with the total amount of costs consumed within them. (Cooper 1994h, 6–7)

There are interesting similarities between cost boxes and amoeba in the Kyocera system (discussed in chapter 14). Both represent the lowest level in the firm at which reporting is performed, but amoeba are profit centers, while cost boxes are cost centers. It is possible that the Mitsubishi Kasei system is an intermediate form of the internal competition system described in chapter 14.

It was not always possible for Mitsubishi Kasei to split up cost centers so that they only served a single product line. Multi-product-line cost centers forced the firm's new system to rely on allocations to determine product line costs:

Some services were provided on a centralized basis and responsibility for several product lines was unavoidable. The costs of such services were charged directly to these multiproduct-line cost centers and then subsequently allocated to the individual product lines serviced. These allocations, where possible, used bases that captured the underlying reasons for consumption by the product lines. For example, the costs of wastewater treatment were allocated to product lines based upon the volume of wastewater and the level of pollution they produced. (Cooper 1994h, 5)

Even so, it was considered critical for the allocations that occurred in the new system to be meaningful to the managers responsible for the costs:

These unavoidable allocations were carefully chosen to be both understandable and believable by the product line managers. These characteristics were considered important because they ensured that even though some allocation was involved, pressure to reduce costs was created on product line managers. For example, with respect to wastewater treatment, incentives were created to reduce the volume of wastewater and level of pollutants produced. (Cooper 1994h, 5)

Thus, by carefully designing cost centers and cost assignment procedures and by shifting the level of reporting to the product line level, the number of allocations was kept to a minimum. Furthermore, the focus of the reported costs became the same as the focus of operational control.

VARIANCE ANALYSIS

Traditionally, variance analysis is used to monitor how well an individual is controlling costs. Its aim is to ensure that budget is achieved. At Komatsu, the variances are calculated as part of the general bookkeeping process, exactly as they are in any number of Western systems:

Labor costs and overhead expenses were debited to the production overhead account as they were incurred. As the production of a product was completed in each cost center, production overhead was transferred to the work-in-process account at actual volume and standard price. The monthly difference between the labor and overhead expenses was charged to the production overhead account and divided into two variances: the budget and operation volume variances. The budget variance was a spending variance that captured the difference between the budgeted and actual level of expenses. The operation volume variance was the production volume variance, which captured the unabsorbed overhead due to actual production volume being different from planned. (Cooper 1994f, 3)

The labor and overhead variance is split using a two-way analysis that differentiates spending from volume absorption variances. The only variation from the standard textbook in the Komatsu system is the combination of labor and overhead variances. In a more traditional approach labor efficiency variances would be developed. Labor rate variances would not be generated because the labor wage rates are set by contract and do not vary. This treatment of labor reflects the view that labor is a fixed cost and has the general properties of an overhead item.

In the Komatsu system, variance analysis is not considered a major cost control technique. Instead, it is viewed as an accounting mechanism that keeps the financial accounting and managerial accounting systems compatible, as the combination of the five variances into two aggregated variances indicates:

The five variances—inventory, operation volume, budget, and the two purchase price variances—were aggregated into a production overhead and material cost variance. The material cost variance contained both of the purchase price variances and the direct material portion of the inventory variance. The production overhead variance contained the other variances. (Cooper 1994f, 3)

Variance analysis only makes sense when the production process is well controlled. At Mitsubishi Kasei, however, the realities of the economic environment and chemical processes made variance analysis and a standard cost system infeasible:

> The new cost system, like the one it replaced, was an actual not a standard cost system. A standard cost system was not considered appropriate by management because of the large unavoidable variances that it would have generated. There were two primary reasons that a standard cost system would have reported major variances at Mitsubishi Kasei. First, the changes in the price of raw materials, such as oil, and fluctuations in exchange rates would have caused the raw material price variances to be large. Second, the yield would decrease after each production processes' annual overhaul for a couple of months until the process was brought back under control. This reduction in yield could not be estimated with any accuracy. Therefore, for the two months after the overhaul, the material usage variances would be large because the performance forecasts were too inaccurate to be useful. (Cooper 1994h, 7)

In environments in which *kaizen* costing systems are operating, the standards that are used to evaluate the systems either reflect the improvements expected from *kaizen* activities or the variance analysis must be modified. At several firms, the standard cost system and the *kaizen* costing system are so integrated that the program and the system support each other. To achieve this level of integration, the anticipated *kaizen* improvements are embedded in the standards. This approach is used at Citizen, Topcon, Yamanouchi, and Olympus. At Topcon, "The cost reduction, or cost down (CD) goals, as they were known, included the cost reduction plans of the engineering, purchasing, and manufacturing departments. These plans included changes in material specifications, product design, and procurement sources" (Cooper 1994o, 5).

Unlike the other firms, Topcon creates another cost reduction pressure in addition to its *kaizen* costing program through its operational control system. This pressure is created by rewarding cost reductions above and beyond those anticipated by the *kaizen* costing system:

> Although TOVs [the firm's name for its cost system] anticipated expected cost reduction efforts, the system created pressure for the workers to achieve even greater savings via the calculation of the income from production. This income number was calculated by subtracting the actual cost of production from the TOV cost for the same product mix. If the income from production was positive, then the efficiency of the firm was higher than expected; if negative, then it was lower. When the income was lower, the business unit was expected to find ways to improve performance and bring the income number back under control. (Cooper 1994o, 7)

Yamanouchi Pharmaceutical uses a similar technique:

> Standards were set once a year. The standard labor hours were extracted from negotiation between the production centers and production control and were recorded in the process master. These standards reflected all anticipated cost reductions and other savings that were likely to occur.
> The expected variances were not zero because the production department was expected to become more efficient during the period; these improvements were not reflected in the standards but they were in the budget. Therefore, the overall budget-to-standard variance was expected to be positive. In 1991, the expected improvement was ¥300 million, up from ¥200 million the previous year. This ¥300 million was expected to come primarily from improvements in the yield of production processes, the purchase price of materials, and the direct and indirect expenses of production. (Cooper 1994q, 10–11)

The firm determines the standard direct labor cost of each product by applying the standard labor rate to the product's standard direct labor content. The standard labor rate is the expected standard labor rate for the period including any anticipated wage revisions. The rate is identified in the annual labor contract and does not change during the year. The standard direct labor content is determined through industrial engineering data issued by the engineering department. Standard direct labor hours are established as attainable goals, assuming that the cost-down targets for labor content reduction are achieved by the manufacturing, materials, and engineering departments.

At Olympus, variance analysis is used to monitor the progress of the firm's cost reduction programs.

> The production cost control and reduction program focused primarily on removing material, labor, and some overhead costs from products; the division's profit plan identified cost reduction targets for these costs for each product. . . . The standards were set every six months and included the anticipated reductions that would be achieved in the next six months. . . .
>
> The material price variance was computed for each product by comparing the actual material cost to the standard material monthly target. This target was the average of the material costs for the previous six months adjusted for any anticipated changes in material costs in the upcoming month. The work improvement variances were the difference between the actual labor hours and the standard labor hour monthly target, and between actual machine hours and the standard machine hour monthly target. Their target was calculated by assuming that labor cost reductions would occur evenly over time. To these linear cost reductions were added any specific reductions due to planned changes in the production process. The actual "budgetary other" costs, which included general expenses of the factory, were compared to budgeted costs to determine the other budgetary variance. (Cooper 1994j, 8)

Not all firms modified their standards in this way. At Sumitomo Electric Industries,

> [e]very month, variances were calculated that determined the difference between the standard and actual amount of each major

element of conversion costs. These conversion cost variances were determined for each department. . . . Each month, the conversion cost variances were plotted on the department's variance chart. Because the standards were set each April and based upon the previous year's performance, positive variances were expected to result from the various cost reduction efforts; these variances were expected to increase as the year progressed. (Cooper 1994m, 9)

Shionogi's system identifies two sets of standards. The first set is the budgetary standards. These are not updated during the year for anticipated changes in operating conditions:

The budgetary standards, which were set once a year, were based upon the actual performance achieved in the last month of the prior year. These standards were modified to reflect any anticipated improvements in production equipment and process planned for the upcoming year. For example, if a new piece of equipment was expected during the year or a major change to the production process then the standards were set to reflect the expected actual operating efficiencies. (Cooper 1995a, 14)

The second set is called the updated standards; these are used to monitor the *kaizen* costing program and are updated during the year:

While the budgetary standards for the cost system were only set once a year, a second set of standards called updated standards was revised from time to time. These standards reflected the results of the kaizen program. They were used to evaluate the workforce's current performance. Updated standards were used as a basis for comparison for every lot. The usage variances calculated from these standards provided up-to-date feedback on the current progress of the kaizen programs.

The difference between the two standards measured any changes in manufacturing costs since the budgetary standards were set. (Cooper 1995a, 15)

The importance of these variances is illustrated by their availability to production supervisors. Variance information is not used solely at the management level to identify problems. Instead, it is used at the production supervisor level to help workers improve efficiency:

> Production supervisors had on-line access to the updated standards and the actual production results for each lot and hence the kaizen variances. Their access, however, was limited to variances specified in terms of units. They were not provided with access to variances specified in monetary terms. On-line availability was considered important by management as they felt it caused the workforce to be highly cost conscious. Workers were neither rewarded nor punished for creating variance. However, overall performance, including variances, was taken into account in reviews that lead to both promotion and pay raises.
>
> More detailed financial analysis, including some data expressed in monetary terms, was also available but not on-line. These reports were available to management and some production supervisors. (Cooper 1995a, 15)

The operational control role of the cost system and the *kaizen* costing programs clearly intersected. At many firms great care is taken to ensure that the two systems do not create conflicting pressures. At Shionogi, for example,

> it was not permitted to create cost reduction pressures by setting the budgetary standards at an unrealistic level compared to the current actual. This constraint was placed on the standard setting group because they might be tempted to influence the direction of the kaizen process by the way they set the budgetary standards. (Cooper 1995a, 15)

The dynamic nature of the control process is illustrated by the interaction between the workforce and the technical development group:

The work force reported to the technical development depart-ment after every lot was completed to discuss the effectiveness of their kaizen activities. The workers were expected to identify the portion of the variance that was due to kaizen. Once the standard setter and the workers responsible for that chemical process had agreed on the level of kaizen improvement, the up-dated, but not the budgetary standards, were adjusted accord-ingly.

Updating standards required three steps. First, the technical development department tested a new process in the laboratory or pilot plant to see if it achieved the anticipated improvement. Second, once the improvement was confirmed, the technical de-velopment staff asked the production staff to run the new proc-ess on the production line, and checked the result. Finally, when the anticipated result was attained, the production staff repeated the same process on their own and confirmed the improved re-sult by themselves. When all three steps were successfully com-pleted, the management authorized the new standards as official and the firm's databases were updated.

If the new updated standard created negative variance in the future, because it was too difficult to consistently achieve, it was reduced to more accurately reflect reality. Thus, the vari-ances determined from the updated standards were expected to be either zero or slightly positive due to kaizen activities that were yet to be reflected. However, natural variations in the yield of the chemical processes sometimes caused these variances to be negative. (Cooper 1995a, 16–17)

The primary function of the standards—to create downward pressure on costs—requires that the standards are carefully set. There is no point in setting standards that cannot be achieved. Rather, standards should create achievable targets that require stretching on the part of the workforce:

The primary role of the standard setter was to ensure that the standard setting process achieved its objective. That is, both budgetary and updated standards reflected the most up to date information and were accurate: the budgetary standards on an annual basis and the updated standards on a monthly or as needed basis. If a standard setter set updated standards that were too difficult to achieve, these standards were usually revised after a few months to make them more realistic. (Cooper 1995a, 17)

The standard setting process is taken extremely seriously at Shionogi. Standard setters are

selected from among the most highly knowledgeable, skilled, and reliable workers in the technical development staff. Many were holders of a masters degree in chemistry or pharmacy. They were usually assigned from the beginning to a technical development department. Sometimes, standard setters were temporarily assigned to the production floor to increase their in-depth understanding of the production process. This increased knowledge was considered valuable because it allowed them to set more accurate standards. (Cooper 1995a, 11)

KIRIN BREWERY COMPANY, LTD.

At Kirin, the competitive environment was changing to one in which satisfying the customer was becoming more critical. This trend was accelerated by the introduction of a new beer, Super Dry, by Asahi, a competitor of Kirin Brewery. Super Dry rapidly gained over 25 percent of the Japanese market, mostly from Kirin.

The introduction of Super Dry forced Kirin to change its orientation from one of "product-out" to one of "market-in." This new approach relied on increasing customer satisfaction through the continuous introduction of new products, the objective being to draw consumer attention away from the dry beer market dominated by Asahi. The firm achieved this objective by developing a more generic new beer market in which Asahi did not have a first player advantage. In 1988, Kirin began to introduce a steady stream of new products. In that year, the firm introduced three new beers, including Kirin Dry. The next year, it introduced three additional beers, followed by two more in 1990. In 1991, two more beers were introduced, but four beers were withdrawn. The pattern of introducing new beers, while withdrawing the less successful offerings continued. In 1992, the firm introduced three new beers and withdrew two. Finally in 1993, the firm introduced one new beer and withdrew one. The number of products offered thus increased from eight to fifteen over the six-year period.

In order to increase its flexibility in the face of the challenge presented by Asahi, Kirin shifted from a functional to a divisional form. As a result of the new organizational form, the management team in charge of the Beer Division for the first time had responsibility for planning and controlling its profits. To help sales and brewery management cope with these new responsibilities, divisional management introduced two new profit planning and control systems: the sales office management reporting system (SOMRS) and the plant management reporting system (PMRS). These systems took about two years to design and implement. SOMRS was implemented in 1990 and PMRS in 1991. These two systems illustrate the relationship between strategy and cost management in Japanese firms.

Sales Office Management Reporting System

The SOMRS was designed to report the overall profitability of each sales office and the level of the expenditures under the control of the sales manager. It was implemented to help control the rapidly growing sales force that was needed to support the firm's new customer-oriented strategy and the more complex beer market created by the introduction of numerous new products. Kirin's sales and marketing function contained seventeen sales head offices (SHOs), each of which was located in a major city, such as Tokyo, Osaka, and Nagoya.

The SHO profitability report (see Figure 12-2) started with the sales of the office. The variable cost of sales and the variable sales expense were subtracted from the sales figure to determine the office's marginal profit. The variable cost of sales, which repre-

Figure 12-2
Sales Head Office Profitability Report

	Budget	Actual	Variance
Sales			
Variable Cost of Sales			
Variable Sales Expense			
Promotion (variable)			
Distribution			
Marginal Profit			
Fixed Cost of Sales			
Fixed Sales Expense			
Promotions (fixed)			
Advertisements			
Direct Profiit			
Branch General and			
Administration Expenses			
Allocated Corporate			
Overhead			
Operating Profit			
Extraordinary Items			
Profit Before Tax			
Sales Volume			

Source: R. Cooper, "Kirin Brewery Company, Ltd.," case study 9-195-058 (Boston: Harvard Business School, 1994), 14.

---

sented only the variable portion of the direct costs of the beer, was determined by adding the costs of the raw material, utilities, and inside transportation and then subtracting any revenues from by-products. Variable sales expenses were primarily made up of variable promotion and distribution expenses.

The fixed cost of sales and fixed sales expenses were subtracted from the marginal profit to give the SHO's direct profit. The fixed cost of sales consisted of the plant's labor and overhead expenses. The fixed sales expenses consisted of the fixed portion of promotions and the advertising expenses of the SHO. Promotion expenses covered items such as pamphlets, price-cutting programs, giveaways, and up-front payments to new liquor stores to entice them to adopt the firm's products. Advertising expenses covered local advertising designed to promote sales within the SHO's region and national advertising which was charged to the SHOs using an appropriate allocation method.

Operating profit was determined by subtracting the SHO's general and administrative expenses and any corporate overhead allocated to it from the direct profit. The general and administration expenses included secretarial support, order processing, invoicing, accounting, and branch level personnel expenses. Finally, the branch's profit before tax was determined by adjusting the branch's operating profit for any extraordinary items, such as disposing of defective products or merchandising goods.

The SHO manager was held responsible for advertising, salaries, and administration expenses, even though any changes in the level of salary and administration expenses had to be negotiated with the head office. The primary measure used to evaluate SHO performance was the difference between actual profit and planned profit before taxes. The difference, rather than the actual amount, was used so that any advantages due to location and product mix were factored out of the evaluation. This approach was necessary because SHOs responsible for districts with historically high market shares were inherently more profitable than SHOs responsible for historically low market share districts as fewer sales, promotional, and advertising efforts were required per yen of sales due to lower levels of competition. Product mix had to be factored out because canned products were more profitable than bottled ones. Consequently, any SHO that sold a higher percentage of canned beer than another was automatically more profitable.

Each SHO was subdivided into sections and branches. Sales sections were located inside the SHO, while sales branches were located outside it. A typical sales section or branch contained between five and six salespeople and was responsible for marketing Kirin's products in a relatively small geographical region. Each section or branch was held responsible for some of the rebates provided in its region, nearly all of the promotion expenses for the region, and some of the advertising expenses. They were held responsible for only some of the rebates because rebate levels in a given geographical area reflected decisions made at the head office and the branch as well as the section.

The SHO reporting system reported branch or section profitability and contribution margin. These reports were used to monitor how well each branch or section was managed. Every year, a budget was prepared for each branch and section. Actual results were compared monthly to budget figures to monitor the level of branch and section revenues and expenses. The monthly marginal profit, or more precisely, the contribution to profits generated, was considered the key to monitoring branch and section performance. This monthly contribution was accumulated for the year and was used to determine the level of the year-end incentives paid to each branch and section. Individual line items within the budget were not monitored closely because managers were expected to make their own decisions regarding the amount of promotion and advertising undertaken. Before increasing the overall levels of these costs, however, a section or branch manager was required to demonstrate to his direct supervisor that the additional expenditures would increase the unit's marginal profit. Poorly performing branches or sections were not punished, but the branch or section's result was known to the SHO management and above, and the circulation of poor results had been known to influence the promotion of branch or section managers: "No benefits were awarded to individuals under the incentive system. Management believed that employees were rewarded by seeing their section or branch become more successful. Superior performance was not ignored, however; individuals tended to be promoted from successful sections" (Cooper 1994d, 6).

The beer division had developed an incentive plan to provide successful SHOs with additional promotion and advertising funds for the last six months of the year. The majority of these funds was used to promote products during the December year-end holiday season when beer consumption was much higher than in the other winter months. For example, while only 30 percent of annual sales occurred in the four winter months, December accounted for one-third of those sales, or about 10 percent of annual sales. The additional promotion and advertising funds allowed the branches and sections to increase their year-end sales despite intense competition.

The SOMRS is a classic profit center control system that is designed to make a manager responsible for the revenues and costs under his control. From the Western perspective, the only surprising things about the system are the number of sections that are monitored and the reward system. While the number of centers is quite large by Western standards, with only five to six people in each center, the profit pressure is driven to the bottom of the sales organization. Everyone in the sales division is aware of the system and interacts with it on an ongoing basis. The reward system is typically Japanese. Workers are not directly rewarded or punished for their performance. Association with a more successful branch or section is the individual's reward. The leader of the unit benefits from an improved chance of promotion.

Plant Management Reporting System

The PMRS has two primary objectives: to improve cost management and to introduce the concept of profit control. Kirin's management felt that it was important to improve the brewery's ability to manage costs because overall costs had continued to rise despite more than ten years of aggressive cost reduction programs.

Under the old system, cost reduction programs focused on reducing material, personnel, and facility investment costs, not on brewery profitability. Thus, brewery managers knew their cost reduction objectives and how well these objectives were achieved, but they did not know how profitable their breweries were. Furthermore, managers could not be certain that the cost reductions were improving the brewery's profitability:

> For example, the corporate head office might initiate a program to reduce overtime costs. At the end of the year, the head office would report back to the facility that it had saved a certain amount of money by reducing overtime by such a percentage. Unfortunately, there was no way to be certain that the reported savings represented real profits. The overtime might have been reduced not by becoming more efficient but by increasing un-

monitored costs, such as those associated with temporary workers. (Cooper 1994d, 6)

Management felt that a profit-oriented approach would create pressure to increase revenues, which was considered especially important given existing market conditions. The introduction of new beer products made it more difficult to maintain production efficiencies. For example, a bottling line's capacity was decreased when additional products were introduced because the number of required changeovers increased. Furthermore, even with beer sales increasing at only 2 percent per annum, existing breweries were reaching their capacity. Consequently, it was important to create pressures that would lead to increased output volumes, thus avoiding the need to build new breweries:

> The PMRS generated pressure to increase production volume because it converted the breweries to profit centers. Since breweries could boost their profits both by increasing production volume as well as by decreasing costs, including revenue in the evaluation metric changed the incentives for brewery personnel. For example, when a brewery was treated as a cost center, management would view overtime negatively because it increased costs. If a brewery was considered a profit center, overtime would be viewed positively if the additional revenue it generated exceeded its costs. Thus, shifting to a profit center orientation enabled each plant manager to act like an entrepreneur and maximize brewery profitability. (Cooper 1994d, 7)

The costs used to set prices were based upon the actual results of the first ten months of the prior year. These costs included both variable and fixed expenses. The budgeted costs included any cost reductions that had been achieved in those ten months but were not adjusted for any anticipated savings during the coming year.

Reported profits were used to determine the size of the incentives awarded to the plant at the end of the year. Again, individual employees did not benefit directly from the incentive plan. Instead, the general manager of the plant was free to use the incentive funds to improve the morale of the workforce. He could, if he wished, throw a party, purchase a karaoke set for the employees, plant a garden, or even purchase a new piece of equipment that, while not cost justified, would improve working conditions. Unlike the sales office incentive system in which the incentive was awarded in the same year as it was earned, the plant incentive scheme awarded the incentive at the beginning of the next year.

The profit of each brewery was monitored monthly using a brewery profitability report that was similar in structure to the SHO profitability report. The variable costs of production were subtracted from the monthly sales of the brewery to the SHOs to give the marginal profit. Variable production costs included the major raw material expenses, major material expenses, variable processing costs, and any carryover from semifinished goods. Fixed costs of production were subtracted from the resulting marginal profit to give the operating profit. Fixed costs included the fixed portion of processing costs, labor expenses, depreciation, and general and administrative expenses. Any extraordinary items, such as the disposal of excess raw materials and the sale of scrap, were subtracted from or added to the operating profit to give the plant profit. Finally, payments to headquarters were subtracted to give the final plant profit. A simplified Plant Profitability Report is shown in Figure 12-3.

The cost-oriented variance between actual and planned profit was the primary measure used to evaluate plant performance. This number was used because it factored out the effects of the plant's scale and product mix on productivity. The volume-oriented variances were not considered the responsibility of the plants because changes in sales levels and, hence, production volumes were outside the control of plant management.

The PMRS is a classic control system that could be found just as easily in a Western firm as in a Japanese firm. What is most interesting about it is the way in which it was expected to increase the output level of the breweries, a direct outcome of the application of the profit pressure.

A second and somewhat unexpected benefit of it was the pressure the breweries felt to become more effective and efficient.

Figure 12-3
Plant Profitability Report

	Budget	*Actual*	*Variance*
Sales			
Variable Costs			
Major Raw Material Cost			
Major Material Cost			
Variable Processing Cost			
Carry Over of Semi-Finished Goods			
Marginal Profit			
Fixed Costs			
Fixed Processing Costs			
Labor			
Depreciation			
General and Administration			
Operating Profiit			
Extraordinary Items			
Plant Profit			
Payments to Headquarters			
Final Plant Profit			
Production Volume			

Because under the old system breweries were treated as partial cost centers, the data to support cost management systems were not available, and the breweries had not developed sophisticated cost management systems The conversion of Kirin's Kyoto brewery into a profit center increased the financial information available to brewery personnel and led directly to the emergence of the Kyoto brewery system.

SUMMARY

Operational control is achieved in two ways: first, by ensuring that individuals are held responsible only for the costs they control; second, by using variance analysis to evaluate how well those individuals control their costs. To ensure that individuals are held responsible only for the costs they control, it is necessary to establish responsibility centers. For responsibility centers to be effective, however, costs must be assigned directly to them, not allocated. The desire to hold individuals responsible for costs means that firms must differentiate costs, on the basis of how they are assigned and on their behavior. Consequently, many systems categorize costs based upon their direct or indirect assignment and variable or fixed nature.

In firms in which operational control systems are considered important, great care is taken to ensure that as many costs as possible are traced directly to the centers. This objective is often achieved through the careful definition of the cost center structure. When allocation is necessary because costs cannot be assigned directly, care is taken to ensure that the allocation process is meaningful. This objective is achieved by capturing causal relationships between the costs being allocated and the allocation base being used.

By increasing the number of cost centers many firms increase responsibility for costs. As the size of the cost centers is reduced, it becomes easier to hold individuals responsible for the direct costs of that center. At Mitsubishi Kasei, for example, the cost centers were the lowest level of cost analysis in the firm. The only matter of interest was the total cost of each cost center, not how those costs were incurred.

The evaluation of how well costs are controlled is achieved through variance analysis. At some firms, the variance analysis system is highly traditional and used simply to monitor cost control. At other firms, the variance analysis systems are integrated into the *kaizen* costing systems and used to monitor the effectiveness of these systems.

Kirin converted its sales offices and breweries from cost centers into profit centers and created two new systems designed to increase the degree of responsibility of center managers and to make them place more energy into increasing revenues as well as reducing costs.

PART FIVE

HARNESSING THE ENTREPRENEURIAL SPIRIT THROUGH MICROPROFIT CENTERS

There is good water, wherever fine sake is produced.

Ancient Japanese Saying

INTRODUCTION

The cost management techniques discussed in parts 3 and 4 which are used by firms that have adopted a confrontation strategy focus on the product and the production process. The aggressive use of these techniques allows firms to reduce the cost of products over time, but for some firms, these reductions have not been sufficient. Therefore, these firms have developed additional cost management techniques. The techniques are fundamentally different from the techniques discussed previously in that they do not focus on the product or the production process. Instead, they focus on the group leaders. The effectiveness of these techniques is the result of the increased pressure placed on the leaders of the self-directed teams to perform. These techniques do not take new approaches to cost management; rather, they use a known technique, the creation of profit centers, in innovative ways.

The first of these techniques is the conversion of cost centers into pseudomicroprofit centers. This technique increases the pressure on group leaders to perform. The second technique reduces firm size by breaking the firm into numerous, highly autonomous, real microprofit centers.

The advantages associated with making cost centers into profit centers derive from the creation of increased responsibility and the awareness this brings to group members of the effect of their actions on the profitability of the firm. This awareness causes group leaders to try to improve group performance in ways that increase profits. Because profits are simply revenues minus costs, changing cost centers into profit centers intensifies the pressure to reduce costs and creates new pressure to increase revenues.

The creation of small profit centers reduces the growth of organizational bureaucracy yet allows the firm to respond quickly to changes in its competitive environment. Firms that have adopted confrontation strategy cannot afford either the extra costs of unnecessary bureaucracy or the slowing of the firm's reflexes that such a bureaucracy causes. By keeping the effective firm size small, "empire building" becomes almost impossible, and a firm can maintain its ability to adapt quickly to changes in competitive conditions.

These two techniques are highly interrelated. It is not possible to reduce firm size without first creating profit centers. Three factors play a critical role in determining whether a firm creates pseudo- or real profit centers and whether it sets out to create business managers or to manage firm size. The three factors are

1. the ability to identify someone with the skill to manage the profit center;
2. the existence of external customers who are willing to buy the intermediate outputs of the profit centers; and
3. The willingness to sell the intermediate outputs of the profit centers to external customers.

The three firms that developed systems creating business managers without changing effective firm size were either unable to find customers who were willing to buy the intermediate outputs or were unwilling to sell the intermediate outputs. Two of the firms, Higashimaru Shoyu and Kirin breweries, could not find customers because they produced products from a continuous production process and the intermediate outputs (such as koji and moromi for soy sauce and the wort for beer) were not in a condition to be sold. In contrast, the outputs of the groups at Olympus Optical could be sold, but the firm was unwilling to do so because the interim outputs could only be used in cameras and, therefore, could only be sold to the firm's direct competitors. Since many of these outputs provided the firm with a competitive advantage, Olympus was unwilling to sell them externally. The inability to sell interim outputs made it impossible for arms-length market prices to be established. Consequently, Higashimaru Shoyu and Kirin breweries used cost-plus transfer prices. These prices were not meant to be realistic economic prices. At Olympus Optical, however, the existence of arms-length market transactions allowed the firm's technical department to set what were believed to be realistic market prices.

In contrast, Kyocera and The Taiyo Group were willing to sell the outputs of their groups, and were able to find internal and external customers, which allowed them to convert their production processes into real profit centers. This ability allowed them to reduce effective firm size in order to hinder the development of bureaucracy. Kyocera achieved this by creating pseudofirms, called amoeba, that were highly independent profit centers. In contrast, at The Taiyo Group, the profit centers were legally distinct corporations that were totally independent. At both firms, mechanisms were in place to ensure that individual profit centers operated in a way that was beneficial for the group as a whole. At Kyocera, the managerial reporting systems achieved this objective and at The Taiyo Group, group presidents, acting as consultants to each other, ensured that the centers were beneficial to the group.

Underlying the development of business managers and the creation of small, independent profit centers is the desire to harness the entrepreneurial spirit of group leaders. When a group is treated as a cost center, the leader's task is to manage costs. When the group becomes a separate business entity, the group leader must manage profits. This leads the group to treat revenues as part of their responsibility and increases the pressure the group places on itself to reduce costs. Each technique relies on individuals taking an entrepreneurial stance. In this discussion, entrepreneurial spirit is used to mean self-motivated and directed workers.

There could be hidden costs to these systems, however, because they reduce the ability of the firm to take advantage of economies of scale through the loss of the ability to share resources across the profit centers. In addition, there may be a risk of increased negotiations and conflict among the profit centers. At

Kyocera, organizational philosophy and strong communications among both profit centers and upper management were used to reduce these problems. At the Taiyo Group, president-consultants and strong relations between firms were used to help avoid the destructive outcome of excessive internal competition.

CHAPTER 13

PSEUDOMICROPROFIT CENTERS

Many of the cost management techniques documented thus far rely heavily upon the creativity of the self-directed groups that run the factories (see chapter 6). Although these groups usually have leaders, they have no formal organizational hierarchy. Believing that the way in which individuals view their responsibilities can sometimes be as important as the responsibilities themselves, several firms developed systems to convert groups from cost centers into profit centers. At Higashimaru Shoyu, for example, "The objective of the PCS [price control system] was to instill a profit-making attitude in the groups. Group leaders were expected to act like presidents of small firms" (Cooper 1994b, 9).

The firms that decided to convert from cost centers to profit centers identified two primary benefits arising from such a change in perspective. First, the systems would force the group leaders and group members to take responsibility for revenues as well as costs, which would cause the groups to try to improve the yields and quality of the outputs they managed. Second, the impact of any improvements would be seen directly on the firm's bottom line. Increased visibility would increase the pressure the groups placed on themselves to perform, particularly the energy they expended on cost management. Thus, the creation of profit centers was seen as a powerful technique for cost management. Kirin's Kyoto brewery identified four major objectives for its profit center system:

1. Employees would have a stronger sense of belonging to the company because they could see their own contributions to company performance.

2. By publicly acknowledging the profit centers and their managers who consistently achieved superior performance, such behavior would be reinforced.
3. Individuals could evaluate their own performance and thereby motivate themselves by comparing their performance to that of other centers.
4. The cost reduction programs would be given a new lease on life. (Cooper 1994d, 9)

As Olympus believed its cost reduction programs were beginning to lose their effectiveness, the objective of its functional group management system, which split the production process into a number of autonomous groups, was to increase pressure to reduce costs. The new system was expected to revitalize the cost management programs by changing the mind-set of the workforce: "Top management felt that holding the groups responsible for their profitability would promote greater pressure to reduce costs, and hence increase profitability, than would any conventional cost reduction program" (Cooper 1994j, 10–11).

Because there were no available market prices for their outputs, the profit center systems at Higashimaru Shoyu, Kirin breweries, and Olympus Optical broke the production processes into pseudo profit centers. The way in which the three firms established selling prices varied greatly. Of the three firms, Olympus expended the most effort in trying to get its transfer prices close to estimated arms-length prices. The other two simply used variants of cost plus pricing.

The Higashimaru Shoyu and Kyoto brewery approaches are very similar, which is not surprising because they share a common history. The Higashimaru price control system, which was developed by Toshio Okuno (see chapter 6), was shown to visiting executives from Kirin's Kyoto brewery who then implemented their own version of the system. The Olympus functional group management system was somewhat different from these systems but similar to an approach used by Texas Eastman.

THE HIGASHIMARU SHOYU PRICE CONTROL SYSTEM

The price control system (PCS), which was introduced in 1980, broke the soy sauce production process into six distinct steps and converted each step into a pseudoprofit center. Six groups—koji preparation, fermentation, moromi management, pasteurization and filtration, bottling, and shipping—were responsible for the major production steps. Each profit center bought its inputs from either the central section (raw materials) or the preceding production process profit center (work-in-process). Outputs were sold either to the next profit center in the process (work-in-process) or to the central section (finished goods). The transfer prices between groups were set by Okuno. The budgeted cost per unit of each group's output was increased by 0.5 percent to give the transfer price. Thus, a 3 percent profit was generated (6 × 0.5%) across the production process. This 3 percent profit did not equal either the actual or the expected profits generated by the production process, because Okuno had decided that it would be too complex to try to tie the profitability figures generated by the PCS into actual or expected profits. Instead, Okuno decided that each profit center should have the ability to generate a small profit each month if it operated at expected efficiency.

A similar approach was adopted for raw material prices, which were kept constant over a three-year period. Okuno believed that varying raw material and selling prices would make it too difficult for the groups to observe the effects of their improvements. Furthermore, Okuno wanted the PCS to remain a simple system, not an accounting system with variances and other forms of reconciliations. Therefore,

[t]he monthly profit earned by each group was calculated by subtracting the sum of its monthly expenses and purchases from its monthly revenues. Monthly expenses were determined from the group's annual budget. The input purchases were determined by multiplying the volume of inputs consumed by their PCS transfer prices. Monthly revenues were calculated by multi-

plying the quantity of output sold to the next group in the production process by the appropriate transfer price. (Cooper
1994b, 4)

Because, for example, the input provided to moromi management by koji preparation determined the amount of raw soy sauce
that could be produced, it was virtually impossible for any one
group to significantly increase its output. However, the groups
could improve the quality of their output. Under the PCS, groups
were paid a higher price for any output that was above a preset
quality level. For example, moromi management was paid ¥500
extra for every ichi shiire (a standard weight) of mold the group
produced that ranked above the 0.3 standard measure of enzyme
activity set by the research and development department. The
group received ¥500 less if the enzyme activity level measured
below the 0.3 standard. The incremental prices for quality were
set by the plant manager, and their primary objective was to
generate both cost and quality awareness.

Because soy sauce production is seasonal, more workers are
needed at some times than at others. To motivate the efficient use
of personnel, the groups were allowed to buy time from other
groups. The transfer price for a worker's time was set at its
approximate costs, about ¥14,000 per day. There were also three
production support groups covered by the PCS: inspection, machinery maintenance, and water treatment. Inspection was responsible for inspecting the bottling and packing processes. Machinery
maintenance was responsible for providing all equipment maintenance. Finally, water treatment was responsible for processing all
wastewater so that it could be released into a local river. To make
the production groups use support services more efficiently, the
groups were allowed to charge for their services. Machinery maintenance, for example, was allowed to charge 50 percent of the
labor cost of any unexpected repair but only 20 percent of the
labor cost of any planned repair. The percentages were chosen to
enable machinery maintenance to be profitable. Because it also
sold repair services and steam, it was not necessary to charge 100
percent of labor charges. Partial charging for labor costs allowed

the group to report a 0.5 percent profit. Two different rates were permitted to make the production groups think carefully about how they treated their equipment.

To make the PCS more concrete to his group leaders, Okuno created within the production control section the Higashimaru Bank, which printed its own money, modeled after old Japanese bank notes. Six denominations—¥1,000, ¥10,000, ¥100,000, ¥500,000, ¥1,000,000, and ¥2,000,000—were printed and stamped with the firm's seal in red to validate them. Every month, the PCS books of account were closed by the group leaders and summarized by the section manager. Each leader went to the next leader in the process and presented a bill for goods rendered. In addition, each group had to pay headquarters for the labor it employed, raw materials it consumed, and the depreciation on the equipment it utilized. All bills were paid in Higashimaru money.

After each group had paid its bills and collected its revenues, its monthly profits or losses were determined by the value of the remaining bank notes. When a group ran out of money, it could borrow from the Higashimaru Bank. While Okuno had considered making each group pay interest on money it borrowed, he decided that such a process was too complex and abandoned the idea. For the first few months that the PCS operated, all of the groups were profitable. Suddenly, however, all of the groups reported losses because Okuno had forgotten to include semiannual employee bonuses in the profit calculations. Since a bonus was equivalent to approximately 2.7 months of pay, it easily dominated the 0.5 percent profit generated on revenues. The system was subsequently modified to allow for semiannual bonuses.

After running on an experimental basis for a year, the PCS was declared a success by the group leaders and formally introduced. Over the next ten years, the system played a critical role in helping the firm to become more profitable. Some of the actions taken to improve a group's profitability reduced head count:

> [T]he bottling group reduced the number of its employees by installing new servo-mechanisms to test each bottle to ensure that it was a 2-liter soy, not a 1.8-liter sake, bottle. Testing was re-

quired because the glass soy bottles were returnable and some-times a sake bottle would get mixed in with the soy ones by ac-cident. The application of servo-mechanisms to make the size tests was suggested by group members when the employee who usually performed that test left the company. Normally, the group would simply have requested a replacement. However, the group wanted to see if it could reduce its head count by in-troducing the new equipment. The automated equipment was successful, and after a year of operating without the replace-ment person the group's head count reduction was made perma-nent and its budget adjusted for both the increased equipment and the reduced labor expense. (Cooper 1994b, 6)

Other actions reduced the cost of the services provided by the support groups:

[T]he koji preparation group, among others, reduced the size of the monthly bill it received from the machinery maintenance group by paying more attention to the way it monitored the temperature of the electric motors used to stir the fermenting koji, operate conveyor belts, and run machinery. By placing tem-perature sensors on the motors, it was possible to detect when they were overheating. By reducing the speed of rotation or, if necessary, stopping the motor completely, burnout could be avoided. If the motor was undamaged, no service call was re-quired. If the motor was at the end of its useful life, these pre-ventative actions allowed the machinery maintenance group to make a scheduled, as opposed to unscheduled, visit to replace the motor. (Cooper 1994b, 6)

Introducing thermal sensors allowed koji preparation to re-duce its demands on machinery maintenance, avoid the extra 30 percent surcharge for emergency repairs, and thereby increase its profitability. Workers who were no longer required were released to other groups, thus reducing the number of new hires.

Koji preparation also discovered that reducing the speed of the stirring motors could cut its electricity costs. The mold had to be stirred continuously, which used a lot of energy. By experimenting with slower rotation speeds during the early phases of koji preparation, the group was able to reduce its electricity costs to below their standard level of 3.2 percent. Additional savings were achieved by making moromi at night instead of during the day. Night-time preparation took advantage of the cheaper evening rates for electricity. Some of the actions taken were fairly simple but effective:

> The koji preparation group was the first to reduce its wastewater charge simply by picking up rubbish and brushing the floor clean before it was washed. The reduction in wastewater was significant because this part of the production process required very clean conditions and the floors were washed thoroughly several times a day. While wastewater only represented 1% of the group's budget, the savings were still considered important. (Cooper 1994b, 6)

Other actions were designed to improve the safety of the plant and thus avoid the accidents that led to absenteeism. The bottling group, for example,

> focused on the high cost of employee absenteeism because it had to pay more for an employee it borrowed than one it loaned. The bottling process used many conveyors and workers were forced to either climb over or under the conveyor belts. Occasionally, a worker would be injured by the conveyor equipment. The group decided to monitor these small accidents to see if it could reduce their frequency. To reduce injuries, it placed soft, sponge-like material where people were likely to bump their heads, removed sharp edges that were likely to cause cuts, and placed warning signs where appropriate. (Cooper 1994b, 6–7)

Some of the benefits brought about by the PCS affected the profitability of more than one group:

289

[T]he bottling group noticed that the task of checking and adjusting the acidity of the wastewater created when the returned bottles were washed in a weak solution of caustic soda and detergent did not keep the worker responsible for that task completely occupied. . . .

Close to the bottling group was a boiler that a member of the machinery maintenance group was to monitor. This individual had to monitor the boiler on an ongoing basis but was also not particularly busy. To increase the profitability of both groups, the bottling group and the machinery maintenance group negotiated to share the two tasks. As a result, the machinery maintenance group agreed to perform the acidity testing and adjustment process for a fee of ¥40,000 per month. This agreement allowed the bottling group to reduce its head count by one, thereby saving ¥150,000 per month. Thus, both groups increased their profitability. (Cooper 1994b, 7)

The success of the PCS, which reduced costs by 7 percent in its first year, drew the attention of numerous companies, including Matsushita (the giant electronics company), Yukijirushi (a manufacturer of dairy products), and Kirin (the country's largest beer manufacturer), which then implemented its own version of the PCS at its Kyoto brewery.

THE KYOTO BREWERY SYSTEM

The Kyoto brewery system (KBS) converted the Kyoto brewery into a number of profit centers and then rewarded center managers who improved the profitability of their centers and thus the profitability of the brewery. Kyoto managers adopted a profit control approach because they felt that over the years their cost reduction programs had fostered a negative attitude toward continuous improvement and that the new approach would foster a positive view.

Under the KBS, financial information was shared freely because each group had to be able to calculate its profitability, which meant that group members had to know the group's revenues and costs. This sharing of information was in direct contrast to the previous system under which little financial information was available to the group. Under the new system, responsibility for setting the brewery's cost reduction objectives resided at the brewery rather than at headquarters:

> Under the old cost reduction programs, the brewmaster would set specific non-financial cost reduction targets for each major step in the production process. . . . These targets were communicated to the work groups, which were expected to find ways to achieve those targets.
>
> Under the new approach, the brewmaster would set an overall profit target for the brewery and the working groups would set their own financial targets. When taken together, the targets set by the work groups were expected to be more aggressive than those set by the brewmaster so that if all of the groups achieved their targets, the overall profitability of the brewery would exceed the brewmaster's profit objective for a six-month period. (Cooper 1994d, 9–10)

The KBS gave the groups a high degree of autonomy in setting their own cost objectives as long as the overall cost reduction targets satisfied the brewmaster:

> If the targets set by the work groups were not sufficient to at least achieve the brewmaster's objectives, then the work groups were asked to develop more aggressive targets. No targets were ever set for the groups. Management believed it was better to allow the line workers to identify the level of cost reduction they could achieve rather than set targets in the budgeting process, because line workers were more familiar with the production process than were engineers or management. Management likened this feature of the new plant system to total quality management programs. (Cooper 1994d, 9)

To increase the pressure to control profits, and hence costs, the number of centers in the brewery was increased from five to nine. In the old system, three of the centers (brewing, kegging, and packaging) were related to the production process and two (maintenance and administration) were related to support activities. In the new system, six of the centers related to production and three to support. The nine centers were:

1. Brew House and Fermentation
2. Storage and Filtration
3. Mini Brewery
      Brew House and Fermentation
      Storage and Filtration
4. Kegging
5. Pasteurizing and Packaging
6. Logistics
7. Engineering and Maintenance
8. Utilities
      Wastewater
      Other Utilities
9. Service
      Administration
      Factory Tours
      Other Service Activities
   (Cooper 1994d, 10)

Since revenues from beer sales could only be identified with the first six centers, these centers were treated as profit centers. The other three centers did not handle the product and no sensible revenue figures could be associated with them. Therefore, they were treated as cost centers and were not covered by the KBS.

Under the KBS, both revenues and costs had to be measured for the six profit centers. Revenues were based upon internal sales either between the profit centers in the brewery or, in the final instance, between the brewery and the sales offices. The prices used to determine each center's revenues were based upon budgeted costs and determined from the annual budget of the brewery. A small profit was built into the system by including ¥50 million of profit in the price determination. This built-in profit avoided the situation in which a profit center that performed exactly to budget would not make a profit. Management believed that the small profit buffer created an incentive to achieve at least budgeted performance. The top two performing profit centers were awarded a small incentive bonus every six months. The award, which was smaller than the award given in the PMRS (see chapter 11), was used to fund a group outing or other such event.

To measure costs so that profits could be determined it was necessary to increase the number of cost measurement points in the brewery. For example, to monitor electricity usage at the profit center level, additional meters were installed throughout the factory. Separate metering was considered important because it allowed each center to determine and monitor its actual electricity costs. If these costs were deemed too high, the center could introduce cost reduction programs. Prior to the introduction of the KBS, no real attention was paid to the consumption of electricity at the center level because only brewery management had access to the cost of electricity.

The success of the KBS was evidenced by changes in the behavior of the groups:

- The brew house produced a large amount of hot water when the wort was boiled. Though some of it was used productively elsewhere in the plant (e.g., to sanitize pipelines and storage tanks), much of it was wasted. To find ways to use more of it productively, the fermentation center created a multicenter working team to find new uses for hot water in the other centers.
- The storage and filtration center created a working team to explore ways to reduce the cost of filtration materials.
- An intercenter working team was created between the utilities cost center and the other centers to find ways to reduce energy consumption.
- A working team in the brew house and fermentation profit center was studying ways to increase the extract yield when the wort was pressed. (Cooper 1994d, 11)

Unfortunately, because the old system generated little financial information, management was unable to prove that overall cost reduction under the new system was higher.

Clearly the systems at Kirin and Higashimaru Shoyu have much in common. The objective for both systems is the same: to create pressure to increase revenues and decrease costs. The major differences between the two systems appear to be the lack of a central bank at Kyoto and the way in which the profit for the centers was developed. While profit is based upon a percentage of "sales" at Higashimaru, at Kyoto it is based upon a flat fee above expected costs.

THE OLYMPUS FUNCTIONAL GROUP MANAGEMENT SYSTEM

Like the PCS and the KBS, the functional group management system (FGMS) at Olympus used pseudoprofit centers to motivate cost reductions in the production process:

> To motivate each group leader to act appropriately, the production groups were evaluated based upon the profits they generated. Each group was treated as a profit center by estimating the revenue it would have generated if it was a separate company that sold its output to Olympus. Top management felt that holding the groups responsible for profitability, as opposed to cost, would increase the motivation to reduce costs while simultaneously generating an increase in outputs. (Cooper 1994k, 7)

Each group leader was given full management responsibility for his area of responsibility and was expected to manage his group as if it were an independent company. There were, however, some significant restrictions on the leaders' freedom to act. For example, a group leader was not able to choose the components the group would buy externally or to negotiate purchase prices. Instead, he had to go through the material purchasing group for externally acquired components and purchase internally produced components from the other production groups. Furthermore the degree of change that the groups could make to their production processes without top management permission was fairly limited and included such minor improvements as increasing the processing speed of the machines, introducing unmanned operations, and reviewing current processing methods to find ways to improve them. The range of actions that any group could take was limited to the level of expenditures they were allowed to make and personnel considerations.

Once each group had set its own target profit and gained its acceptance from plant management, monthly targets were established. If a group did not reach its monthly target, the group's leader was expected to explain at the monthly group leader meeting why his group had not met target. Other group leaders at the meeting were usually supportive and would offer suggestions about how to achieve target. Theoretically, if a group consistently failed to achieve its objective, its leader would be replaced, but no group leader consistently failed to meet targets. Indeed the groups usually outperformed their plans.

The revenue for the four production groups created by the FGMS (Machining, Assembly 1, Assembly 2, and Assembly 3) was estimated by the technical manufacturing group. This group used its knowledge of production processes and the costs charged by the firm's external suppliers and subcontractors to estimate the price the firm would have to pay external suppliers for each component and assembly produced by each group. The estimated prices were then multiplied by the output of each group in the current period to produce each group's estimated total revenues. Because trial production and other activities that are designed to improve future products do not generate revenues, great care had to be taken when estimating group revenues. There was no point in identifying a group as unprofitable simply because it performed experimental production that was not immediately cost justifiable.

The selling price of a group's output was updated every six months. Since the firm's suppliers were becoming more efficient, the selling price (group management standard) was continuously decreasing. Thus, only groups that could remain at least as efficient as the firm's suppliers could remain profitable. If no way could be found to make a group profitable, the product would become a candidate for outsourcing. Thus, the FGMS placed production groups in competition with the firm's suppliers, thereby creating an intense pressure on the groups to improve performance. The only exceptions to outsourcing were experimental production lines that were testing ways to increase the level of automation for new products. These lines were protected because management felt that they were too strategically important to outsource.

Each group's profits were determined by subtracting its total costs from its total revenues. Thus, each group's performance was captured in three numbers: its revenues, costs, and profits. Of the three performance measures, profit was considered the most important, followed by costs and, finally, revenues.

Because support departments are difficult to convert into profit centers as their revenues are not easily calculated, only the purchasing department became a profit center. The department's revenue was determined from historical data about the rate of reduction of the selling prices of purchased components. These price reduction rates were used to predict the future prices of purchased components and these prices were used to determine the department's revenues for the period. Revenues were defined as the estimated selling prices of the parts purchased multiplied by the volumes purchased. Costs of the department were defined as the actual selling prices of the parts purchased multiplied by the volumes purchased. As a result, the purchasing department generated profits only when it could find ways to increase the rate at which the price of the parts it purchased fell. To achieve profitability, then, the department had to change the way in which it related to suppliers and the two technical groups. Traditionally, the department went to the market to find the cheapest source for each of the parts that it had to purchase, subject to quality constraints and long-term vendor relationships. The FGMS was designed to make the department work with design, engineering, and production to find innovative ways to reduce the costs of purchased parts. Management believed there were two major benefits from this change:

First, the purchasing agents were able to generate more compelling arguments about why the purchase prices should be falling more rapidly. For example, instead of simply using a desired percentage for purchase price reduction, they could now discuss technological changes that affected pricing. This additional knowledge enabled the agents to be more aggressive in the way they interacted with suppliers, thereby increasing the rate at which prices fell. Second, the purchasing agents were able to identify technological solutions that were fundamentally cheaper (e.g., by reducing the specifications of a part or finding new ways to manufacture the part). (Cooper 1994k, 9)

Suppliers also benefited from the change. For instance, the manufacturing process for light emitting diodes (LED) usually produced products with variable light intensity, but only the brightest of the intensities satisfied Olympus' requirements. The technical staff found a way to adjust the intensity of the LEDs that allowed the firm to use all the intensity levels. This advance not only reduced Olympus' purchase price but also the supplier's costs because the weaker LEDs were no longer considered defective.

The introduction of the FGMS benefited the firm in four ways. First, the system created a change in the mind-set of factory workers from a passive "wait for instructions" to a more active one in which they pursued their group's profit target.

Unlike the firm's cost reduction program in which group leaders recommended cost reduction targets that were then reviewed and either accepted or renegotiated until the savings were acceptable to divisional management, each group determined its own targets. The targets were set through a budgeting process in which each group set its own revenue and cost objectives. Since the FGMS would not be effective if each group went its own way, group objectives had to be coordinated with divisional objectives. Consequently, group budgets were established within a set of unifying themes that were incorporated into the corporate/divisional objectives:

> The corporate/divisional objectives identified the sales goal for the factory. These sales goals were divided into output goals for each group. By finding ways to increase their output levels, the groups increased their ability to generate "revenues" and hence profits. As the groups increased their revenues, the capacity of the factory also increased. (Cooper 1994k, 6)

Rather unexpectedly, the introduction of the FGMS ended the tendency to understate cost reduction estimates. There were two reasons for this. First, under the objective of increasing profits, "padding" cost estimates led to reduced profits and meant that the group was performing below its expected level. Second, the FGMS proved so effective that management did not find it necessary to try to increase improvement estimates.

Third, to increase output levels and revenues, groups interacted more with the technical production group to increase capacities. After the FGMS was introduced, several groups discovered that they needed additional support to achieve increased profits. "Because the engineering groups were not treated as profit centers, no charge was made for their services," and the groups needing help turned to them (Cooper 1994k, 8). In the first three years of the program, approximately 80 percent of the profit improvements were from changes that increased output:

> Under the functional group management system, the changes to the production processes that were envisioned were not expected to be substantial. Only minor changes to the equipment and fixtures were anticipated. The normal objective of these engineering changes was to increase output (i.e., capacity) though some of them did reduce costs. (Cooper 1994k, 8)

The remaining 20 percent of improvements were from cost reduction initiatives, such as the increased use of unmanned processing and shortened processing time. The dominance of the output-related improvements initially surprised Olympus management, which had expected a more even balance between the two sources of increased profits. Imbalances between the production rates of the various groups were controlled through the products order system so no significant inventory developed between the two groups.

Fourth, the Technical Production Group provided improved support to the groups to help them increase their levels of automation. This was achieved, for example, by increasing the processing speed of machines, introducing unmanned operations, and reviewing processing methods to generate ideas for new methods. The increase in the rate of automation led to reduced labor costs and improved product quality and, hence, higher group profits. As Olympus was dedicated to increasing the level of automation throughout its production process, the increase in automation that came about as a result of the FGMS was welcomed.

Finally, the firm's cost management system had to be modified to support the FGMS because the existing system did not provide group members with information about how the group's output contributed to the revenues or profits of the plant. Instead, the system simply informed the groups of their costs and how those costs compared to budget. The way in which standards were set also had to be changed. In the corporate cost system, standards were established every six months at the level of current performance. Therefore, as the groups improved their performance, positive variances were generated. However, the group cost system used standards that were based upon the mid-point of expected efficiency during a three-month period. Therefore, variances were unfavorable at first and became favorable as the improvements took effect.

Olympus management believed the FGMS helped the workforce become more flexible. This increased flexibility was considered critical for the future because major changes coming (the firm intended to move a majority of its production off-shore) and any increase in the workforce's ability to adapt to new conditions would help the firm.

SUMMARY

The desire to push the profit pressure deep into production systems has led several firms to split their production processes into pseudoprofit centers. Pseudoprofit centers, not real ones, were used because the firms could not establish market prices for the groups' outputs. By converting cost centers to profit centers, however, production groups at these firms were forced to consider ways to increase their outputs as well as reduce their costs. Only by making cost centers into profit centers could the firms achieve both objectives, since groups that are treated as cost centers have no incentive to worry about how cost reduction decisions affect revenues.

At Higashimaru Shoyu, group revenues were set by simply adding 0.5 percent to the standard cost of output. At Kirin's Kyoto brewery, revenues were determined by adding ¥50 million to the standard cost of the output. At Olympus, the technical manufacturing group set prices by estimating what the output of each group would cost if that output were acquired from outside suppliers. The built-in profits were designed to ensure that the groups would be profitable even if they simply achieved their standards. In all three companies, however, the groups increased their reported profits by becoming more efficient than the standards established by the firms' cost systems.

Because production processes at Higashimaru Shoyu and Kirin are highly coupled, it was not possible for groups to increase their outputs significantly. Instead, the groups focused on increasing the yield of the processes they controlled and the quality of their output. Each pseudoprofit center rewarded increased yield through reporting greater revenues and improved quality through higher unit prices, both of which led to increased group profitability.

For some support groups at these firms, it was not possible to determine a revenue figure because it was difficult to measure output quantitatively. These groups were usually treated as cost centers. At Higashimaru Shoyu and Kirin, the support groups charged for their services but sometimes at discounted prices. At

Olympus, the support groups did not charge for services. Olympus may not have charged for support services because it wanted the groups to become more automated, and by not charging for services, the production groups were encouraged to seek help in automating. At Higashimaru Shoyu, support departments that provided services (such as steam and hot water) directly to the production groups were treated as profit centers. By charging for support services, revenue is generated and profit can be calculated.

To make the price control system more concrete, the groups at Higashimaru Shoyu used "Higashimaru Money" to keep track of their profits. Each group was given operating capital and expected to buy and sell to the other groups. The other two firms did not utilize fake money but relied upon more conventional reporting techniques. In all the firms the conversion to profit centers appeared to create a highly motivated workforce that was willing to initiate and accept change.

One of the greatest benefits of conversion, according to management at all three firms, was the increase in intergroup activities. Once the groups understood the concept of profit, they rapidly realized that coordinating activities with other groups could increase profit opportunities. Coordinated actions included job sharing, multigroup cost reduction projects, and energy consumption management. While direct actions that improved group profitability could be identified, none of the firms had adequate records to prove that overall savings were greater than under their old systems.

Although the production groups at these three companies were treated as pseudoprofit centers, the groups had relatively little autonomy. At two other companies, however, the production process and the firms themselves were split into numerous real microprofit centers that were expected to compete among themselves. These systems were introduced because management felt that managing firm size could be a powerful cost reduction technique.

CHAPTER 14

REAL MICROPROFIT CENTERS

Firms that have adopted a confrontation strategy must compete aggressively using the survival triplet and be able to adapt rapidly to changes in competitive conditions. Heavy layers of bureaucracy cannot be allowed to slow the reflexes of the firm. While the size of an organization may not appear to be a cost management technique, it is, in fact, an important one. According to Kuniyasu Sakai, the founder of the Taiyo Group,

> It is the size of a company that matters. When a company gets too large it cannot respond in time. You need small flexible firms to survive. Breaking large companies into smaller independent units is a powerful form of cost management. . . .
>
> When you look at the sections you can see waste inherent to the old-style approach of large companies. Creating divisions is not sufficient; the sections have to become separate companies: that is the key to the *bunsha* philosophy. Being separate allows them to become more efficient. (Cooper 1994n, 1, 3)

At least two firms have developed systems that break each firm into a collection of small enterprises which have to be profitable to survive. While these systems have similar objectives and both require an increase in the number of business managers, they employ different approaches. The system used at Kyocera creates a large number of real profit centers called *amoeba*. These centers are not legally independent firms but highly independent pseudofirms that are responsible for selling products both internally and externally. The system used by the Taiyo Group creates separate legal entities that are responsible for a number of products.

At the heart of both systems is the assumption that small entities are more efficient and effective than large ones. This assumption is the basis for the amoeba system at Kyocera:

> As the firm got larger, Inamori wanted to develop an organization structure that allowed the sense of partnership to be maintained, that disseminated the concept of profits being generated during the production process, and that rendered highly visible the source of profits and losses. The divisional structure supported these objectives but as the firm expanded it was considered too aggregate, and thus the amoeba system developed. (Cooper 1994g, 3)

The *bunsha* philosophy at the Taiyo Group arose from the same assumption. The primary difference between the two systems is the degree of autonomy given to the profit centers. At the Taiyo Group, autonomy is absolute; at Kyocera, it is only partial:

> One way in which the freedom of amoebas was constrained in order to ensure that a coherent overall strategy emerged was in the range of activities they could undertake. Amoebas were assigned responsibility for a limited range of products. If an amoeba wanted to begin production of products outside its range, it had to get the permission of the division manager, who would make a judgement about the appropriateness of the proposed products in the firm's overall product line. If the division manager deemed the new product appropriate, he or she would also help the amoeba coordinate its introduction. (Cooper 1994g, 9)

THE AMOEBA PROFIT CENTER SYSTEM AT KYOCERA

The profit center system at Kyocera was named after the amoeba, a single-celled organism that can freely change its shape. The name was chosen to indicate that an organization can also freely change its shape. There are about 800 amoebas in the Japanese portion of Kyocera. Each amoeba is expected to form, expand, divide, and disband as appropriate. Since between twenty and forty changes to the number of amoebas occurs every month, the number of amoebas in the firm tends to vary daily.

Amoebas are relatively unstructured, and some amoeba contain teams that work on different shifts.

> Profit centers called "amoebas" were Kyocera's fundamental unit of operations. An amoeba had responsibility for all of the planning, decision making, and administrative activities attributed to it. Amoebas were the smallest organizational unit of operations inside Kyocera; they varied in size from a minimum of three members to a maximum of 50, with the average being around 15. Employees in different shifts belonged to the same amoeba. The size of an amoeba was determined by taking into consideration its visibility, communication requirements, and accountability. (Cooper 1994g, 2)

Sometimes task forces or project teams were created to work on tasks involving members from several amoebas, such as special cost reductions, special process studies for better quality, or new process technology implementations. Sometimes, team objectives were specified before formation; sometimes, teams were expected to identify their own objectives.

The head of the amoeba was responsible for reporting amoeba performance. Amoeba heads received few perquisites and had the same work space allotment as other members of the amoeba. Selection of the head was made by the person to whom he reported and based on the individual's ability to understand the technical aspects of the business, his leadership qualities, and his desire to make his amoeba the best. Seniority was not a major factor. While it was possible to replace the head of an amoeba that was performing poorly, the mechanisms in place to do so were designed to give the head another chance:

Occasionally, the cause of poor amoeba performance was identified as lack of leadership, in which case the amoeba head was
replaced. This decision was made by the individual to whom the
amoeba head reported, typically a section leader (though if the
amoeba was at the section level, it was a division manager). Before an amoeba head could be replaced, the approval of the division manager to whom the section leader reported, or the
corporate division manager to whom the division manager reported, was required. In addition, the replacement usually required the consensus of the members of an amoeba before the
division manager would approve a change of amoeba leadership. It was normal practice to transfer the poorly performing
amoeba head to another amoeba, not to simply demote him or
her. Great care was taken to ensure that this individual would fit
successfully into the new amoeba of which he or she was a
member. (Cooper 1994g, 7)

The amoeba system was designed to create an environment in
which individuals both enjoyed their work and were able to
influence the way in which it was performed. Effectively, amoeba
were separate little companies. Thus, members were expected to
act as if they were managers in an independent enterprise and
devote their attention and creativity to the operation of the
amoeba so that both the amoeba and their personal technical and
managerial skills would grow. The system prevented organizational bureaucracy by creating an environment in which all levels
of management could interact freely for the common purpose of
improving the firm's operations and pursuing its strategic objectives.

The system works because of the corporate philosophy instilled by Kyocera's founder, Dr. Inamori. Inamori believes individuals are most satisfied when their abilities, talents, and efforts
are dedicated to the betterment of the human organization to
which they belong rather than to their own individual interest.
Further guidance is provided by Kyocera's corporate culture,
which fosters originality and creativity while encouraging speciali-
zation. This culture is also strongly influenced by Inamori's per-

sonal philosophy, which emphasizes individual initiative and stresses the need to maintain creativity even in mundane and trivial tasks.

Creating and Disbanding Amoebas

Amoebas are concerned with process and product innovation. They are expected to find ways to improve production and to identify opportunities that will lead to higher revenues or lower costs.

> [A]ll employees, including those from production, sales, and administration, were expected not only to perform rotating tasks but also to devise creative innovations in every aspect of their jobs, no matter how small, to improve the contribution of their efforts to the company and to society as a whole. (Cooper 1994g, 10)

For this reason, new amoebas are created whenever amoeba members believe that such a group will be beneficial. For example, the printed circuit board design group had been part of an amoeba responsible for manufacturing ceramic printed circuit boards. However, as the group's activities expanded to include selling their services outside the firm, the group became an independent amoeba, selling its services based upon competitive prices. It is not necessary for a group to sell its products or services only outside the firm to become an amoeba. The ceramic firing department is an amoeba, even though it sells its output to other amoebas.

Amoebas are expected to grow and contract with their workloads. They are created either from "scratch" or by dividing existing amoebas. When the firm launches a strategically important new product and puts it into commercial production, a new amoeba responsible for manufacturing is formed to ensure that any improvements in the new product's profitability can be observed. Although existing amoebas are expected to develop new products in order to grow, when they become too large or when a new product becomes sufficiently successful to warrant the existence of its own amoeba, they are divided. Usually amoebas are disbanded or absorbed into other amoebas when a business opportunity vanishes. Members of the disbanded amoeba are assigned to other amoebas.

When an amoeba is expanding, it is expected to ask other amoebas if they have any excess manpower before looking outside for employees. This practice, which is critical to the effective distribution of manpower throughout the firm, is supervised by managers who are responsible for overseeing related amoebas in other groups. Personnel transfers occur either on a permanent or temporary basis, and managers and amoeba leaders are expected to react positively to transfer requests from other amoebas.

Amoeba creation and disbanding decisions occur at relatively low levels of the firm, which allows these decisions to be made quickly with a minimum amount of bureaucracy:

> Headquarter's administrative departments, including personnel, were not involved in the organizational planning of amoebas. An amoeba's manager was responsible for its operations, organization, and staffing levels. However, he or she could consult plant or headquarters' administrative departments for advice. Headquarters functioned as the "bank" for amoebas. Before funds could be borrowed, approval was required from the manager responsible for overseeing the amoeba. The level of this manager depended upon the amoeba in question; however, it was always at least one level above the amoeba leader. (Cooper 1994g, 5)

Kyocera has developed procedures to deal with occasional disagreements over changes in amoeba structure:

> Occasionally, a section leader or division manager would decide that a change in amoeba structure was required, but the existing amoeba head would disagree. When this occurred, an indepth and open discussion about the change in structure would take place between the amoeba head and his or her superior. In these discussions neither the amoeba head nor the superior was expected to make compromises simply to reach agreement. It

was important that such decisions be based upon logic, not egos. When agreement could not be reached, an upper-level manager would arbitrate and help the two come to a decision. (Cooper 1994g, 6)

Setting Selling Prices

If an amoeba cannot sell all of its output internally, it is allowed to market its products outside Kyocera. Therefore, the ability to identify market prices for the outputs of each amoeba is critical to the success of the amoeba system. Market prices are also the basis for setting the selling price between amoebas. For internal sales, however, the prices are slightly modified to reflect small differences in the product produced by the amoeba and that produced by external suppliers. To be able to negotiate effectively, amoeba members must be aware of the product offerings, quality levels, delivery performance, and prices of both internal and external suppliers and of the demands of both internal and external customers. Should two amoebas not be able to agree on a price,

the division manager who oversaw them would mediate the dispute. If the dispute was between amoebas in different divisions, the product group manager would mediate; and if the negotiations were between product groups, then the president would mediate. The role of the mediator was to help the two amoebas reach consensus, not to legislate a solution. (Cooper 1994g, 5)

If there are no market prices for its products, an amoeba uses cost plus pricing. When cost plus pricing is adopted, the overall profitability of the product is monitored until it is sold to an external customer. The rule that all amoeba involved in a product must make a profit on that product ensures that any internal sales eventually lead to external profits:

Considerable care was taken to ensure that even for internal sales where no external market existed, negotiations were independent and amoeba heads were not subject to coercion. This independence ensured that profits were not arbitrarily allocated. If, despite mediation, no agreement could be reached between the amoebas, then the purchasing amoeba would be allowed to purchase the goods externally. In most cases, the inability to reach internal agreement was seen as a sign that the selling amoeba was not competitive with outside suppliers. (Cooper 1994g, 5)

The decision to purchase internally or externally is driven primarily by strategic considerations. If there are good reasons to have an internal supplier of a product, then an amoeba is formed to make that product: "Amoebas were formed even when buying or selling their products or services externally appeared contrary to the overall profitability of the firm" (Cooper 1994g, 4). When an internal supplier is created, its performance is compared to that of outside suppliers. Amoebas are subjected to constant pressure to improve performance until they are superior to all external sources. This pressure comes from both the amoebas that use the product and higher management. Although internal suppliers are usually given priority, if an amoeba fails to outperform its external competitors, the amoebas that use the product it produces are allowed to go outside the firm for that product, especially if it can be shown that buying the product from outside will be to the long-term benefit of the corporation. The decision to use an outside vendor instead of an internal one is relatively rare and requires the approval of management above the amoeba level.

Amoeba Cost Systems

Because each amoeba is a small firm, complex cost systems are not required and the process of determining product costs is simple. Usually the raw cost data are sufficient:

[E]ngineers in each amoeba had access to most cost data relating to raw material, equipment, and other costs. Such access to cost data, combined with their up-to-date knowledge of changes in the production processes, allowed the engineers to calculate up-to-date costs for all of the products their amoeba produced. These cost estimates were used for pricing purposes. Thus, one of the advantages of the simplicity of the amoebas was that it allowed engineers to participate in the price-setting process. (Cooper 1994g, 8)

Some departments, such as quality control and production control, are treated as cost centers rather than amoebas because there is no way to identify meaningful selling prices for their services, which are intangible. The costs of these departments are allocated to the amoebas based upon an estimate of the benefit they receive. The simplicity of the amoebas allowed such allocations to be understood by all.

Maintaining Communication Levels

A flexible reporting environment allows senior executives, through their contacts with managers at all levels of the firm (including amoeba heads), to communicate a consistent sense of strategic direction and provide strategic guidance. By allowing amoeba heads to attend and participate at divisional meetings, communication among all levels of the firm are strengthened. To ensure that the amoeba acts in ways that benefit the firm as a whole, the head of the amoeba and the people to whom he reported are in frequent communication:

The interactions between amoeba heads and the section leaders and division managers to whom they reported were expected to be supportive. The various levels of management were meant to provide each other with advice on the most appropriate way to solve problems and increase profits. Occasionally, amoeba heads were dissatisfied with the advice they received from their direct superiors. Under these conditions, they were encouraged to go to that person's superior to discuss the problem. Such discussions were considered critical to the success of the amoeba system because they ensured that at Kyocera, senior management

was in regular contact with the heads of operating units.
(Cooper 1994g, 6)

Promotions usually are made internally to ensure that the
section leader and division managers understand the firm and the
amoebas for which they are responsible: "Amoeba heads were
usually promoted into the position above them. This meant that
most amoeba heads reported to individuals that had previously
been amoeba heads in the same division. This prior experience
allowed them to better understand the detailed operations of the
amoebas that reported to them" (Cooper 1994g, 6). Strong levels
of communication within and among amoebas are critical to offset
any risk that the firm will degenerate into individual profit centers
chasing local profit optima without worrying about the firm's
overall performance. Consequently, division amoeba managers
must ensure that the amoebas act in ways that are mutually
supporting:

> The long-term objectives of the amoebas were set by the divi-
> sion general managers; the identification of short-term objectives
> was the responsibility of the amoeba heads. . . . Division manag-
> ers were held responsible for all amoebas within their division.
> An important part of their job was to ensure that the amoebas
> were well-managed. In addition, they were responsible for ensur-
> ing that the amoebas received the personnel and material that
> they required to achieve their master plans. It was important for
> the division manager to maintain good communication with
> amoebas so that he or she could understand the problems each
> amoeba was facing, help the amoeba members resolve those
> problems, and provide a better sense of direction. Division man-
> agers were expected to maintain both formal and informal com-
> munication links with the amoebas in their division. They did
> this by frequently visiting the factories; some even organized in-
> formal parties for amoeba members. Section managers played a
> similar role on a smaller scale. However, they were more deeply
> involved in managing the operations of the amoebas in their sec-
> tion. (Cooper 1994g, 9)

A variety of formal meetings at the global (i.e., Kyocera-wide), corporate, product group, division, and amoeba level are used to keep communication open among different levels of management. Usually, the person responsible for the meeting begins with an overview of the operations and guidelines for future direction. After the initial address, the managers and leaders of the groups take turns reviewing the prior period's results and explaining plans for the coming period:

> The interaction between flexible reporting, monthly meetings, and corporate philosophy provided the integrating theme that ensured that the amoeba system was successful. In particular, the division manager was expected to create the strategic logic that held the division together. Without this integrating theme, there was a significant risk that amoebas would fail to create a coherent overall long-term strategy for the firm. (Cooper 1994g, 9)

Evaluating Amoeba Performance

There are two planning horizons at Kyocera: the first is for a year and the second is for a month. Amoeba sales targets and performance goals are set according to the amoeba's past performance and future opportunities, and each amoeba's performance is monitored against the annual (or master) plan on a monthly basis. The amoeba's performance against the monthly plan is monitored and publicized daily. The master plan is based upon the amoeba's strategy, and the monthly plan is viewed as a tool to help the amoeba achieve its strategy. Reflecting these roles, the master plan contains an ambitious target for each amoeba to achieve, but the monthly plan, which is more detailed, contains a more realistic estimate of an amoeba's likely performance. If conditions change, the master plan is revised in the middle of the year, and targets and goals are adjusted. Revisions are designed to keep targets ambitious but feasible. In contrast, monthly plans cannot be changed once they are implemented. Both the master and monthly plans are initiated by the members of the amoeba and discussed with upper management before implementation.

Amoeba performance is measured in quantitative terms, and certain key numbers, such as net production, added value, added value ratio to net production, and added value per hour, are monitored closely to help assess the overall performance of manufacturing amoebas. The business system's administration division is responsible for implementing the internal rules that govern the way in which amoebas report revenues and expenses. The rules are designed to ensure that reporting is both fair and equitable, thus ensuring comparability of results. The rules, which are simpler than conventional financial reporting rules, are designed to be easily understood and consistently applied to all amoebas. Because the business systems administration division controls the physical distribution of products, materials, and supplies as well as the computer systems that control these distributions, it can ensure that the performance reported by each amoeba follows the internal rules.

The primary measures of an amoeba's performance are how well it is achieving its plan and how much it has improved since the last evaluation:

> The basic evaluation system relied primarily upon two central measures. The first captured how well the amoeba was performing according to plan, and the second captured how much it had improved over the previous six months. The evaluation of how well the amoeba was performing according to plan compared its overall performance to both the annual master plan and to the more detailed monthly plan. The monthly plan evaluation mainly looked at orders received, shipments made, and value-added per labor hour for a sales amoeba. For a manufacturing amoeba, the monthly plan evaluation mainly looked at total production, production per labor hour, and value-added per labor hour. . . .
>
> The evaluation of amoeba improvement was based upon the increase in added value per hour achieved by the amoeba. This

measure was used because management believed that increases in an amoeba's added value per hour could only be achieved by increasing the fundamental productivity of the amoeba. (Cooper 1994g, 7–8)

Added value is defined as total shipments (both internal and external) minus total purchases (both internal and external) minus the operating costs of the amoeba, including depreciation, plant common expenses, and certain corporate charges. Corporate charges include charges for corporate research and development and "interest" on items such as inventories, properties, and in the case of marketing amoeba, accounts receivable. Thus, added value per hour captures the contribution that the amoeba makes to overall corporate profit. Added value per total output is determined by dividing the total added value by the amoeba's total output, which is defined as the sales of the amoeba minus purchases from other amoebas. This measure captures the portion of external sales associated with each amoeba. The total output per labor hour is determined by dividing the total output by the total number of hours that amoeba members work during the evaluation period.

To increase the pressure to perform, information about each amoeba's performance is announced or posted throughout the firm, but superior performance is not monetarily rewarded:

Although superior-performing amoebas were acknowledged, great care was taken to ensure that these amoebas did not consider themselves to be superior to other amoebas. Top management wanted to create an environment where amoebas competed for better performance for the sake of the entire company. An amoeba's superior performance was not to be considered for its benefit but for the benefit of the total firm, within which inferior-performing amoebas had to be sustained to develop their future potential. Therefore, the company recognized superior-performing amoebas by creating psychological, not monetary, satisfaction. In fact, it was against Kyocera's philosophy to motivate employees through material bonuses. Kyocera expected each employee to work for himself or herself, for his or her colleagues, and for society. (Cooper 1994g, 8)

THE TAIYO GROUP AND THE *BUNSHA* SYSTEM

The Taiyo Group calls its system *bunsha,* the Japanese word for company division. Unlike Kyocera, the *bunsha* system creates separate companies. Kuniyasu Sakai, the group chairman of the Taiyo Group, believes that the full energy of a large firm can be released through the creation of separate companies. Each company must have full autonomy. Indeed, as Sakai noted, the autonomy must be so complete that

> even the cost systems have to be allowed to differ. Under the divisional structure, all get the same cost system; it's a bit like every one buying suits with the same sleeve length. Under the *bunsha* philosophy, every company can develop its own cost systems so that they fit perfectly. (Cooper 1994n, 5)

Reflecting this philosophy, all of the companies in the Taiyo Group were relatively small and, like Kyocera's amoeba, would grow to a certain size and then split. These new companies were, in turn, expected to grow and split.

In 1992, the Taiyo Group consisted of approximately 40 small companies. If consolidated into a single entity consisting of a few divisions, the Taiyo Group would be considered a large firm by Japanese standards. Instead, it is viewed as a conglomerate of small to medium-sized companies. Unlike other Japanese firms of the same size, the Taiyo Group does not have a head office staff because Sakai views such staff as an obstacle to success. Furthermore, because all of the companies that make the group are small and autonomous, a head office staff is not required.

Sakai believes that the Taiyo Group has grown more rapidly under the *bunsha* philosophy than it would have if it had been more conventionally structured. In his eyes, one of the firm's greatest strengths is the opportunity it offers individuals to become leaders. According to Sakai, if the firm did not operate under the *bunsha* philosophy:

> Many of the people that are now presidents of bunshas would have left the group and become competitive enemies instead of the competitive allies that they are today. The presidents are all entrepreneurs and want to control their own companies and to demonstrate the ability to grow their companies. They would not be satisfied just being section chiefs or division heads. (Cooper 1994n, 4)

At the heart of the Taiyo Group's strategy is the need not only to meet the customer's requirements but also to be the "craftsman" of the industry. Each company is expected to have the highest skill level in its industry and to be able to supply its customers with what they wanted in ways that other firms cannot. A company knows it is successful when a customer asks it to extend into other domains. It is this process of extension that leads to the creation of new firms.

Companies within the *bunsha* group are expected to create long-term relationships with their customers. Sakai believes that companies can remain profitable only by satisfying customers and remaining small. It is far better, he believes, to create companies that, because of their customer relations, will be around in the long run, rather than to become large and famous:

> As soon as people think they need to become a big company, they are already on the road to disaster. It is much more important to think about existence and to plan to be around for 100 to 200 years. If the firm is not around for the long term then it is a great disappointment to the employees and managers. It is they who have worked hard and keeping the company around is their reward. (Cooper 1994n, 4)

Splitting Up a Company

Under the *bunsha* philosophy, the overall firm (The Taiyo Group) becomes a number of loosely connected companies, each of which serves a distinct group of customers. When one of the companies within the group became too large (by Sakai's standards), it was split up. The person who is the president of the firm does not run the firm but acts as a consultant to the individuals who are running the divisions. Thus division managers have all of the functions under their control, which allows cross-functional fights to be avoided.

This organizational form allows the split-off of the various divisions to occur over an extended period of time. Thus, even before being split off, the divisions can create a team-work environment, not a large company environment. The split-off process is not instantaneous. As divisions grow, they are readied for split-off. Customers that the two entities will eventually serve are identified and actions that will ease the separation are undertaken. When the division's sales are sufficiently large that it can stand alone, the division is *"bunshad"* and becomes a separate company. The division manager becomes president of the newly formed company and the president of the original company becomes chairman of the group of companies created by the original firm and the *bunshad* one. Even after the split-off, there is a protection period that permits the newly formed company to have time to learn how to stand on its own feet.

When a new company is split off great care is taken to ensure that customers do not suffer. During the protection period, the customer can go to the parent firm and get a bid for the entire job. When this occurs, the parent firm goes to the new company to get a quote on its part of the job. Only after the new company is established and can satisfy its own set of customers is competition between the parent firm and child allowed. The *bunsha* philosophy expects that the new company will eventually enter into direct competition with the parent firm and other members of the group. Indeed, competition is actively encouraged. Sakai believes that competition between at least three companies is required to encourage maximum creativity. According to Sakai:

> If a firm can stay lean and productive, it will never want for cus-
> tomers. But if any of our firms ever gives up constantly striving
> to be competitive, it will surely lose its position in the market be-
> fore long. In that case, I would rather see it sacrifice its market
> share to another Taiyo company and learn a lesson in the proc-
> ess. The group does not exist to subsidize poor performance
> among its member companies. (Cooper 1994n, 4)

In Sakai's mind, to apply the *bunsha* philosophy successfully new companies must be split vertically from their parents so that the parents retain the ability to make products that are competitive with those manufactured by the new company. Both the parent and the new company, however, will have its own distinctive competence, which allows the companies to attract different sets of customers and grow in separate ways. The insistence that each company have its own competence maximizes the rate of creation of new *bunshas*. For example, when the printed circuit board division of Taiyo Kogyo (the first company in the Taiyo Group) was *bunshad* to form Daisho Denshi, Taiyo Kogyo retained the ability to produce printed circuit boards. When Taiyo Kogyo later created another new *bunsha* (Daiwa), it also produced printed circuit boards but so did Taiyo Kogyo. In the next round, Taiyo Kogyo created Lexington, another circuit board manufacturer but still retained its ability to produce printed circuit boards.

Occasionally, an entire capability is split off, and the parent loses the ability to produce that class of products. For example, Taiyo Kogyo developed a computer division in 1968. The division was *bunshad* to create Daichu Denshi. At the time, however, Taiyo Kogyo retained a portion of the computer division, which was *bunshad* to form Daikin and Fanuc. The remaining Taiyo Kogyo computer division was *bunshad* to form Kodai High Technology. This time, however, the entire division was *bunshad* and Taiyo Kogyo lost its ability to compete in the computer market. In subsequent years, Daikin and Kodai High Technology, while still retaining their ability to compete in the market, *bunshad* their computer divisions to form Daikin Elecon and Kodai BIT, respec-tively. Now, Daichu Denshi, while retaining its ability to compete, is ready to split off Kiban. Thus, by the end of 1993, seven firms, all competing in the computer industry, had been *bunshad*.

When things go according to plan, the *bunshad* firms create their own offspring and the rate of new company creation increases geometrically. Some companies within the Taiyo Group try to ensure that still another company is forming at the time the new company is *bunshad*. To ensure the success of the *bunsha* process, companies are expected to create a number of "eggs," or fledgling businesses that may eventually become divisions and then be *bunshad* (see Figure 14-1). Usually these fledgling businesses deal with the application of new technologies. Daisho Denshi, for example, was undertaking research and development into the next generation of additive printed circuit board processing. Thus, while Daisho Denshi was getting ready to split off a new company to produce the first generation of additive printed circuit boards, it was also developing the next generation of additive printed circuit boards.

New *bunshas* are financed by the other members of the Taiyo Group. Each company president is given an opportunity for his company to invest in the new firm, and at least five presidents must agree to finance the new company. The compulsory minimum investment is ¥50,000, but companies can invest more if they choose. The maximum percentage ownership for any one company is 25 percent. Each *bunsha* is started with a capital of at least ¥25 million and may go to one of the Taiyo Group's banks for additional capital if it is required. Usually one of the stronger companies in the group will act as guarantor for the loan. If the group is unwilling to raise ¥25 million to finance the new entity, the division is not split off. This gives the presidents of the companies in the group some degree of control over the way in which firms are split off.

Because the *bunshas* are financed by other companies in the Taiyo Group, the companies are owned by each other. In effect, the group owns itself. No individual owns stock in any of the companies. Although there had been private ownership in the past, over the years, the Taiyo Group bought back all of the shares until

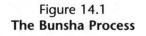

Figure 14.1
The Bunsha Process

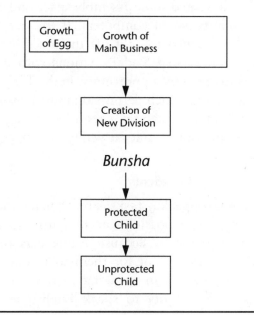

it became 100 percent self-owned. Sakai believes that self-owner-ship is critical to the success of the Taiyo Group as it allows the group to develop a long-term survival philosophy, not a short-term profit-oriented one.

Sakai does not always know what the companies in the Taiyo Group are doing. During one trip, for example, he discovered that Kodai High Technology had opened a new division that was assembling NEC personal computers. Such discoveries do not greatly concern him as he wants the individual companies to be truly independent and creative. In this case, Kodai High Technol-ogy had reacted rapidly to an opportunity created by the increased competition between NEC and several nondomestic computer manufacturers, including IBM and Compaq. In order to decrease its costs so that it could compete more effectively on price, NEC was outsourcing some of its internal operations, including the assembly of some of its personal computers. In response to this opportunity, Kodai rented some assembly space and developed the ability to assemble personal computers. If the new facility were successful, Kodai planned to split off the assembly facility as a separate firm. Sakai viewed Kodai's actions with pride: "Notice the fast response time to the opportunity. In the Taiyo Group there is no bureaucracy from which permission must be sought. As long as the firm can obtain the capital it requires through the bank, it is free to pursue any opportunity it wants" (Cooper 1994n, 7).

Developing Company Presidents

One of the Taiyo Group's key tasks is recognizing the potential of its employees as early as possible and preparing them to become presidents of new *bunshas*. Because young executives are promoted rapidly, it is important for them to recognize their own strengths and weaknesses. In speaking to new presidents Sakai often uses his own inability to speak English as an example, pointing out that he recognized his own shortcomings and hired people who could speak both languages to help him. For this reason, the entire resources of the Taiyo Group are available to the new presidents. New presidents are also encouraged to develop management teams that compliment their abilities.

As a result of the *bunsha* philosophy, the Taiyo Group has more presidents than would be found in an equivalently sized group, which would probably contain fewer, but larger, firms. Sakai believes the Taiyo Group benefits from its early promotions and greater number of presidents because

> [t]he responsibility of being president brings out people's abilities two to three times over being a division head. It is this expansion of abilities that creates our superior ability to satisfy customers. Just watching what others do and repeating it is not the best way to get costs down. Instead you have to desperately want to bring to the customer what he wants at the lowest cost. (Cooper 1994n, 7)

By promoting executives rapidly, the Taiyo Group builds their sense of loyalty and ownership, thus reinforcing their desire to succeed. Sakai described the reactions of one president to the *bunsha* approach:

> When one particular president joined the group his salary was lower than his contemporaries. However, he is now a president, while his contemporaries are still section chiefs and division heads. The president is very impressed with the *bunsha* process. He takes full responsibility for his company. He is very independent. The company's goals are his, the company is his, and so are its achievements.
>
> He wants to share his experiences with others in the group. He wants to *bunsha* as many times as possible in order to allow others to benefit from being president and having the ability to make their own decisions. Even a young company can *bunsha* because, if it is a good idea, the group will fund the expansion. (Cooper 1994n, 7–8)

Because all presidents of the various companies know each other and many have worked together in the past, relationships are positive, and problem sharing is common, even among presidents of rival companies: "Even though the presidents have lots of ability and are rivals, they fundamentally get on well together. Again, it is like brothers competing: they are still friends and get along well" (Cooper 1994n, 8). This sharing, an important mechanism for helping develop new presidents, allows the presidents to act as their own support group and helps to spread innovations around the firm.

There is no retirement age for presidents as Sakai believes that presidents who are thinking about retirement are no longer thinking about the long term. Presidents are also not rotated every few years as they are in other Japanese firms because Sakai feels that people who are rotated every few years tend to think in time frames defined by the rotation periods, which are fairly short.

Rewarding the Presidents

In the Taiyo Group, the salary of a president is made up of three elements. The first is the basic salary, which is the same for all presidents. The second is a bonus, based on company profits. The bonus allows the president's salary to reflect the size of the company that he manages. The president determines this portion of his salary. Finally, there are the *bunsha* receipts.

The primary objective of the Taiyo Group is not to grow or to be profitable, but to create additional *bunshas* so that a greater number of customers can be satisfied and more people can be developed. To ensure the creation of additional *bunshas* and prevent empire building, presidents who create new *bunshas* are rewarded financially. Once a new *bunsha* becomes profitable, it makes a payment, which is equal to the *bunsha* president's salary, to the president of the company from which it was *bunsha*d. The payment is to the president, not to the company. By creating numerous *bunshas* that are profitable, presidents can become quite wealthy. Some presidents in the Taiyo Group receive total remunerations in excess of ¥100 million per year.

The flow of funds from the *bunsha* to the president continues for as long as the *bunsha* is profitable, but in the first two to three years, while the *bunsha* is establishing itself, no payments are made. Since executive salaries at the Taiyo Group are typical of Japanese firms, *bunsha* payments are above industry norms. *Bunsha* payments are only made to a company that is the *parent* of the new company. No payments are made to *grandparents* or more distant forebears.

SUMMARY

Kyocera and the Taiyo Group both use company size to create additional pressures to become more efficient. While the objective of both firms is the same—the creation of numerous real micro-profit centers that work to control costs—the way in which the firms achieve this objective differs. Using its amoeba management system, Kyocera has created approximately 800 profit centers, each of which is given considerable autonomy but is subject to central control. At the Taiyo Group, 40 separate companies with complete autonomy have been created under the *bunsha* philosophy.

The amoeba system at Kyocera creates an environment in which individuals enjoy their work and are able to influence the way in which it is performed. Amoebas, which are the firm's fundamental unit of operation, are true profit centers. Adjusted market prices are used to set the transfer prices between amoebas. Amoebas must be profitable, or they are disbanded. The decision to create or disband an amoeba is made at fairly low levels of the firm hierarchy because, since amoebas are small, their individual reorganization is not considered strategically significant.

Amoebas were relatively unstructured. Each one is made up of three to fifty individuals. Each one contains a group leader, called the amoeba head. Everyone else is simply a member of the amoeba. Amoeba heads are chosen on the basis of their ability to understand the technical aspects of the business, their leadership abilities, and their motivation. Seniority is not a major factor in selecting an amoeba head. Usually, amoeba heads are promoted into positions above them. This promotion process continues up the organization, which means everyone reports to a manager who has had previous experience in the same division.

Amoebas are encouraged to sell their outputs both internally and externally. To be successful, each amoeba must know the markets in which it sells its products. As a result virtually everyone at Kyocera is highly sensitive to competitive conditions.

The decision to purchase internally or externally is driven primarily by strategic considerations. If it is considered beneficial to make a product in-house, an amoeba will be created. If a product is made in-house, other amoebas are expected to purchase the product unless they can demonstrate that an externally produced version is significantly superior.

Amoebas are evaluated on the basis of their past performance and their future opportunities. Two planning horizons are used: an annual one and a monthly one. Performance is measured in quantitative terms, based upon the value added to the amoeba's products. Performance data is public information and thus increases the pressure on the amoeba to perform.

At the Taiyo Group, internal competition is created by the firm's splitting off process in which the parent company retains the ability to compete with the new company. The process of splitting, or *bunsha,* is carefully managed. First a section of a company is identified as a potential candidate for splitting. If it grows, it is converted into a separate division and its customers prepared for the split. Eventually it is established as a new firm, and for a period of time, the two companies cooperate. Once the new company is strong enough to compete, cooperation ceases, and the two firms enter into direct competition.

New companies are financed by the other members of the Taiyo Group, and there is a minimum monetary commitment. Thus, the Taiyo Group is completely self-owned and only seeks external funding through bank loans. Once the new firm becomes profitable, it is expected to pay the president of its parent a sum equal to its own president's annual pay. This requirement discourages empire building and encourages the development of new companies.

Thus, by becoming a number of autonomous smaller entities, Kyocera and the Taiyo Group have been able to harness the entrepreneurial spirit of their employees and to use firm size as a mechanism to increase efficiency and cut bureaucracy. It may well be that the optimal size for a lean enterprise is smaller than it is for mass producers. The increased efficiency of the lean enterprise and its ability to produce products economically at lower volumes than its mass producer counterparts may have eliminated many of the economies of scale that have led to large firms. As Sakai has noted,

> [i]t looks good to be big but that only lasts 20 or 30 years, and then the company is gone. Large bloated firms cannot sustain their competitive advantage, despite their superior financial resources and market power. The Sakai family has been around for

over 400 years as a small business; we expect to still be around
in another 400. (Cooper 1994n, 5)

If the proposition that small firms are more efficient is true,
then firm size becomes a powerful technique for cost management.

CHAPTER 15

IMPLICATIONS FOR WESTERN MANAGERS

When an industry is dominated by mass producers, firms seek to develop sustainable competitive advantages. These advantages allow firms to avoid competition through the generic strategies of cost leadership and differentiation. The cost leader can avoid competition by threatening a price war, and the differentiator can avoid competition by satisfying customers to an extent that others cannot match economically. The only firms that do not avoid competition are those stuck in the middle, those that have not succeeded in securing sustainable competitive advantages. Without such advantages, they are forced to compete head-on with other firms that are in a similar position. Thus, typically the only mass producers that compete head-on are those that are not the leaders of their industries.

Competition among lean enterprises, however, is inherently different from competition among mass producers. Because lean enterprises are able to introduce products that match their competitors' offerings so rapidly, it is virtually impossible for any firm to create a sustainable competitive advantage. Thus, lean enterprises do not compete, they collide. When firms cannot create sustainable competitive advantages, they are forced to compete by repeatedly creating temporary ones that allow them to generate profits but do not enable them to differentiate themselves in the eyes of their customers. To survive, they adopt the generic strategy of confrontation. That is, they actively seek out their competitors and confront competition head-on. Because these firms can match their competitors' products, in time even the leaders of an industry are forced into confrontational competition.

When firms are engaged in confrontational competition, customers become extremely sophisticated and usually have little loyalty to a single firm. If a firm fails to deliver the products that the customer wants, the customer will turn to another firm without hesitation. To remain successful, then, firms must deliver products that satisfy their customers. They can only do this by paying careful attention to three product-related characteristics known as the survival triplet. When viewed externally, these characteristics are price, quality and functionality; when viewed internally, they are cost, quality, and functionality. Products that have values of the three external characteristics of the survival triplet that are acceptable to customers and generate adequate returns fall inside their survival zones. Because a firm can support lower prices over the long run only through lower internal costs, the firm that has adopted a confrontation strategy must become an expert at developing low-cost, high-quality products that have the functionality that its customers demand. To do this, the firm must monitor its customers' changing requirements, develop integrated systems to manage the cost, quality, and functionality of its products, and create an organizational context that will allow these systems to be successful.

It is the integration of these systems that manage cost, quality, and functionality that allows many Japanese firms to respond quickly to changes in economic conditions and to match their competitors' products. If the systems were treated as stand-alones, such a fast response rate would not be possible. Together, they create a firmwide discipline that ensures both future and existing products fall inside their survival zones. Unfortunately, Western literature has described the systems that have evolved to manage quality ("total quality management systems") and functionality ("time to market systems") in isolation and has almost completely ignored the systems that have emerged in Japanese firms to manage costs. These cost management systems should not be ignored because, in a world without competitive advantages, costs have to be managed both aggressively and intelligently. A firm that fails to manage the reduction of costs as rapidly as its competitors will find its profit margins squeezed and its existence threatened.

Therefore, cost management is a critical skill for firms that have adopted a confrontation strategy. These firms need overlapping systems that create intense downward pressures on all elements of costs and lead virtually every person in the firm to practice cost management. The systems must begin to operate when products or services are first conceived, continue throughout manufacturing, and end only when the product or service is discontinued. They cannot be limited to the four walls of the factory or to the boundaries of the firm. Instead, they must spread across the entire supplier and customer chains and create cost reduction pressures across the entire value chain of the products or services.

The cost management techniques that Japanese firms have adopted are designed to help a firm manage its product mix and the costs of both future and existing products. There are six distinct techniques used to manage the costs of products and production processes. Three of these—target costing, value engineering, and interorganizational systems—are designed to support the management of future products. The other three—product costing, operational control, and *kaizen* costing—are designed to help manage the costs of existing products. There are two other techniques that are used to manage costs through harnessing the entrepreneurial spirit of the firm's employees. The first of these techniques is to create pseudomicroprofit centers, and the second is to create real ones.

It is important to realize that most firms do not die either rapidly or easily. While it may be true that only the most efficient competitors survive, in practice it can take decades for a firm to go bankrupt, especially when the firm has been a successful mass producer. Such a firm can afford to generate poor returns for an extended period of time before coming to terms with its impending extinction. It is this survival ability that makes it difficult for many firms to come to grips with the need to adapt quickly to changing conditions. Thus, for these firms, the first challenge is to survive the transition from avoiding competition to confronting it.

SURVIVING THE TRANSITION

It is not clear that the number of competitors that can survive in a market dominated by mass producers is the same as the number that can survive in a market dominated by lean producers, nor is it clear that all firms can survive the transition. Each firm should evaluate its strengths and weaknesses and then decide if its probability of success is high enough to make attempting the transition worthwhile. For weaker firms, it may be better to withdraw from the market than to die a slow, extended death trying to compete with insufficient resources. The exact mechanism by which the firm withdraws depends upon the firm and its position vis-à-vis its competitors. Some may want to sell themselves to a competitor as quickly as possible; others may decide to treat the firm as a cash cow and then sell it or go out of business. Firms that believe they are strong enough to survive need to develop the systems, organizational context, and culture required for the aggressive management of the survival triplet. While each item is necessary for a firm, all three are required and must be in harmony for the successful adoption of confrontation strategy.

To succeed, these firms must create an organizational context that will support the integrated systems required to manage aggressively the survival triplet. Total quality management, product development, and cost management systems must be given a common theme. While integrating these three systems into a coherent program to manage the survival triplet will consume a considerable amount of resources, the right organizational context still must be created through the development of self-directed work groups that are committed to confrontation strategy. Without the commitment of the workforce, a firm will not develop the ability to manage the survival triplet as aggressively as necessary. The key point is that firms must learn to view the process of managing the survival triplet as a total systems solution, not a collection of independent techniques. For many firms undergoing the transition to confrontation, TQM and product development (time-to-market) systems function well, but the cost management systems fail to focus on the product design stage and are not adequately integrated into the firm's customer analysis program. Thus, of the three systems, it is the cost management system that requires the most attention.

Once a firm is ready to adopt confrontation strategy, it must carefully analyze competitive conditions to determine when its avoidance strategies are no longer appropriate. For many firms delaying the adoption of confrontation strategy is appropriate because they can use the transition period to prepare themselves for the harsh realities of a confrontational environment. This involves a thorough analysis of the competitive environment, product life cycle, and technological maturity to determine the cost management techniques that are most likely to be beneficial. Each technique is applicable during a different stage of the product life cycle, and depending upon several factors, some techniques may be more or less beneficial for a given firm.

The nature of competition does not change immediately as firms in an industry begin to adopt lean enterprise practices. Instead, it gradually changes from competition avoidance to confrontation. This rate of transition is logical because, just as the cost leader makes extra profits by allowing the differentiators to create a price umbrella, the lean leader makes extra profits in the early days by allowing the mass producers to determine the position of the survival zones. As more companies become lean, however, the nature of competition changes, and the lean players begin to define the position of the survival zones. In time, confrontation becomes the dominant strategy and the remaining mass producers see their profits disappear as the ability to create and maintain sustainable competitive advantages becomes extremely rare.

Firms that successfully developed sustainable competitive advantages in the old competitive environment may be tempted to make two mistakes at this point. First, they may expend too many resources trying to protect their existing (but no longer sustainable) competitive advantages. Second, they may expend too many resources trying to develop new advantages. Only if these investments extended the life of existing competitive advantages or led to the creation of new ones would the resources have been consumed wisely. Unfortunately, all too often these firms would discover that the resources they had committed to the extension or creation of sustainable competitive advantages had been wasted: management had risked draining the firm of the very reserves it required to adapt to confrontation.

Thus, the first step to surviving the transition is to accept that eventually the firm will have to adopt a confrontation strategy. This step is very difficult for many firms to take, given that adopting such strategies guarantees that profits will eventually fall below their historical levels. Firms that are used to being "profit-maximizers" and are now adopting a confrontation strategy need to determine the time frame over which they are trying to maximize profits. Short-term and long-term profit maximization behavior differs significantly when the market is shaped by lean producers. If too short a horizon is used a firm risks adopting strategies that will eventually lead to either bankruptcy or, at least, some very difficult years. It may, for example, chase profits that are associated with niches that are no longer growing and therefore are attracting lower levels of competition than the main market. While the lower level of competition allows profits to be higher, the niche is not attractive for the future.

More insidious, the profit-maximizing firm might become the high price supplier of low-quality and low-functionality products. Firms unwittingly develop this market position by trying to maintain profit margins at their historical levels either by increasing prices or by expending fewer resources on quality and functionality. This strategy can "succeed" for a while, but in the long run the underlying fallacies cannot be avoided. First, the firm is earning its high profit levels at the expense of customer loyalty. It is taking advantage of the loyal customers' willingness to accept products that lie on the edge (the negative one) of the survival zone or even slightly outside it. Once customer loyalty evaporates, the firm discovers that it must catch up to survive. Second, the extra resources that the firm's competitors are expending on quality and functionality might allow those firms to shift the minimum acceptable values of quality and functionality at a speed that the profit-maximizer cannot match. The profit maximizer's products rapidly fall out of their survival zones and the firm is forced to catch up or exit the market.

SURVIVING IN A CONFRONTATION MODE

Even when a firm transitions successfully to a confrontation strategy, it still faces the daunting task of surviving. Survival is achieved by creating an endless stream of temporary competitive advantages through the aggressive management of the survival triplet. Every product must be inside its survival zone. Three factors drive changes in the position of a survival zone: changing customer preferences; the way in which competitors manage the survival triplet; and the firm's distinctive competencies. Changing customer preferences is important because they help to determine which characteristics of the survival zone dominate. If the customer is demanding increased functionality, for example, and is not overly concerned with price, low cost, low functionality products are in trouble. While customer preferences may change survival zones, a firm can affect customer preference, and thus survival zones, by launching products with different trade-offs among the characteristics of the survival triplet. If a firm chooses to expend more resources on functionality than other firms in the industry, for example, it may gradually become the high functionality (and presumable high price) player. If the functionality of its products can be increased so much that customers change their preferences, then the firm can change the position of the survival zones for the products it sells, forcing other firms in the industry to catch up.

The challenge for firms in a confrontational market is determining when they can influence the customer preferences that drive their products. If a firm can identify one or more distinctive competencies, it should try to use them to differentiate its products, even though the differentiation will only be temporary. Olympus, for example, launched the Stylus line of compact cameras because it believed it had a temporary advantage in its ability to develop very small cameras. While its competitors can now match the Stylus, Olympus still dominates the super-small, compact camera market, demonstrating that, while first-mover advantages are reduced in confrontational environments, they are still real.

Firms become the lean leader by being better at managing the survival triplet than their competitors in one of two ways. The first is to find a way to quantum jump the competition. When a firm achieves a quantum jump, it dramatically reshapes the survival zones of products. Topcon's development of near-infra red technology is an example of such a jump. Competitors are forced either to catch up or to go out of business. Unfortunately, it is extremely difficult for a firm to quantum jump its competitors because doing so requires identifying a new way to deliver enhanced product functionality. Like sustainable competitive advantages, a firm should always take advantage of such opportunities but accept that it is risky to rely solely on them to maintain profitability.

The second way in which a firm can become a lean leader is by achieving superior management of the survival triplet through the continuous improvement of its products. Achieving a leadership position in this way is difficult because all of the firm's competitors are trying to improve at the same time. Usually each firm develops a "leadership" position in some of its products but not enough of them for customers to identify that firm as the leader.

A firm that is a lean leader and can maintain this position comes as close to developing a sustainable advantage as is possible in a confrontational market. The firm earns above average profits or gains market share by sustaining the ability to generate a continuous series of temporary, not sustainable, advantages. This difference in the nature of the competitive advantages is real. Sustainable competitive advantages suggest static equilibriums. Temporary advantages suggest dynamic ones. Firms that try to avoid competition are forced to protect the status quo. They rarely take actions that will lead to head-on competition. In contrast, when advantages are temporary, there is no status quo. Firms must actively seek to find ways to develop advantages over their competitors so that they can successfully confront them. A market dominated by confrontation contains firms that are actively seeking to destroy the advantages of their competitors while creating new ones for themselves. Because the advantages are temporary, these firms frequently destroy their own current advantages in order to create new ones. After all, there is no point in trying to defend an advantage if it will disappear in the near future.

There are two strategies open to a lean leader that will allow it to use its position to earn superior profits. First, it can use its leadership position to accelerate the rate at which survival zones shift. In doing this, the firm attempts to leave its competitors behind so that their products fall outside their survival zones. This strategy increases the leader's market share and hence profitability. It forces every other firm into a catch-up mode. Second, the leader can allow the other firms in the industry to dictate the rate at which the acceptable values of each characteristic of the survival triplet shift. This strategy allows the firm to make superior profits because it can deliver products at lower cost through better management of the survival triplet than its competitors. Under this strategy, profits increase but market share remains the same.

While many factors determine which of the two strategies the lean leader adopts, the primary ones are the ability of its competitors to learn from its products and strategic objectives. If a leader has the most advanced products (i.e., has first-mover advantages), then it should adopt the first strategy. However there is a risk in this strategy. Continuously launching products at the limit of the firm's ability allows competitors to learn from the products and thus may accelerate the rate at which competitors can catch up. Firms that follow this strategy adopt a role equivalent to the differentiator, without achieving that status in the eyes of their customers. It is the first-mover advantages that generate the superior profits. If the lean leader's first-mover advantages are small, it should think about adopting the second strategy. The extra profits that are generated by the firm's superior ability to manage the survival triplet reflect the firm's superior efficiency. Firms using this strategy adopt a role equivalent to the cost leader that allows differentiators to create a pricing umbrella from which to generate superior profits. However, as in the case of the first strategy, the firm does not achieve cost leadership status in the eyes of its customer.

If the leader's objective is to maximize profits (the traditional American objective), then the relative profits generated by the two strategies will determine which strategy is chosen. If the objective is to maximize market share (the traditional Japanese objective), then relative sales will determine which strategy is chosen. A profit-maximizing objective usually favors adoption of the second strategy. A growth objective usually favors taking advantage of the survival triplet by launching products with higher quality and functionality than its competitors but not charging more for them.

Firms that are not leaders are jockeying to find ways to become leaders and could easily become leaders in the future. This ability reflects the dynamic nature of confrontational competition. There are no firms that are "stuck in the middle" in Porter's sense (Porter 1990, 41). However, firms that do not aspire to leadership can enact confrontation strategy in a third way. They can "follow-the-leader." In doing this, the firm does little of the fundamental research and development required to introduce new products but instead uses value engineering and other techniques to match the new products of its competitors. This strategy works well if there are essentially two types of customers, trendsetters and copycats. Trendsetters buy new products as soon as they are available; copycats buy the products trendsetters have already bought. If the delay between the trendsetter buying and the copycat buying is less than the time it takes the follow-the-leader firm to introduce its products, then first-mover advantages are small and the follow-the-leader strategy can be successful. If first-mover advantages are strong, which happens when trendsetters are more numerous than copycats, the follow-the-leader strategy will not succeed. Follow-the-leader firms risk being left behind. If the firms undertaking research and development into new products can find ways to develop expertise in the application of technology that cannot be learned through value engineering techniques, follow-the-leader firms will fall behind. Alternatively, the firms undertaking research and development can license their new technologies to the other firms and thus earn above average returns.

Confrontation strategy, then, is not an excuse for senseless head-on competition. Instead, it is a deliberate strategy that acknowledges that lean enterprises do not compete in the same way as mass producers, which brings us back to the central message of this book: In industries in which lean enterprises are becoming dominant, only those firms that adopt a confrontation strategy *and* aggressively manage the survival triplet will survive.

Company Descriptions

Citizen Watch Company, Ltd.
This company is the manufacturing arm of the world's largest watch producer, Citizen, founded in 1930. It is responsible for manufacturing watches and other products that require expertise in watch technology, such as numerically controlled production equipment, flexible disk drives, liquid crystal displays for television and computers, dot matrix printers, and jewelry. Nonwatch products made up almost half of its revenues in 1990.

Higashimaru Shoyu Company, Ltd.
This company, which manufactures soy sauce, was formed in 1942 by the merger of Kikuichi Shoyu Goshi Gaisha and Asai Shoyu Gomeri Gaisha. Higashimaru produces eighty types of light and dark soy sauce, Japanese porridge, Japanese salad dressing, sweet sake, soup stocks, and noodle sauces. In 1992, the company employed 510 people, and its products generated approximately ¥21 billion in sales. Light soy sauce is its most important product.

Isuzu Motors, Ltd.
Isuzu originated in 1916 when Tokyo Ishikawajima Shipbuilding and Engineering Co., Ltd., began to manufacture automobiles. Based on units produced, Isuzu was the ninth largest automobile company in Japan in 1992 and faced ten large domestic competitors. Isuzu's 4 percent market share in that year is misleading because it does not reflect the firm's market strength in trucks and buses. In that year, Isuzu had a 10 percent market share in heavy- and light-duty trucks and an 11 percent share in buses.

Kamakura Iron Works Company, Ltd.

Kamakura was founded in 1910 as a blacksmith's shop. It is a family-run firm, located in a distant suburb of Tokyo. The firm has remained fairly small. In 1993, sales were nearly ¥6 billion, and profits were ¥35 million. The firm is a supplier of automotive parts and has twenty-one major customers that are either automobile manufacturers or suppliers to that industry. Among its customers are Yokohama Corporation (40 percent of sales), Isuzu Motors (20 percent), Hino Motors (15 percent), Jidosha Kiki Company (10 percent), and Yamaha Motors (5 percent). Other customers include Iseki, Kayaba Industries, and Shinryo Heavy Equipment. Although large portions of Kamakura's revenues are from vertically integrated companies, the firm is an independent company.

Kirin Brewery Company, Ltd.

Kirin began in 1870 as the Spring Valley Brewery, Japan's first brewery founded by W. Copeland, an American. Using its beer manufacturing technologies, the firm has diversified into a wide range of products, including biotechnology-based pharmaceutical products, new hybrid vegetable varieties, and optical sensing systems. It also produces products derived from by-products of the brewing process, such as carbonated drinks, yeast-related feed for fish and livestock, and yeast-derived natural seasonings. Kirin generates ¥1,800 billion and ¥90 billion in sales and operating profits.

Komatsu, Ltd.

Founded in 1917 as part of the Takeuchi Mining Co., Komatsu is one of the largest heavy industrial manufacturers in Japan. It is organized into three major lines of business—construction equipment, industrial machinery, and electronic-applied products—that account for 80 percent of its total revenues. The remaining 20 percent consists of construction, unit housing, chemicals and plastics, and software development. Together, these products generate revenues of ¥989 billion and net income of ¥31 billion. Since 1989, the company has been aggressively diversifying and expanding globally.

Kyocera Corporation

Kyocera was founded in 1959 by its chairman, Dr. Kazuo Inamori, and seven of his colleagues as the Kyoto Ceramics Company, Ltd. It considers itself to be a "producer of high-technology solutions" and specializes in developing innovative applications of ceramics technology. By taking on seemingly technically impossible jobs, Kyocera has established a strong reputation for innovation among major technical leaders in the semiconductor and electronic industries. The firm had sales of ¥453 billion and net income of ¥27 billion in 1992.

Mitsubishi Kasei Corporation

Formerly known as Mitsubishi Chemical Industries, Ltd., Mitsubishi Kasei is Japan's largest integrated chemical company with ¥710 billion in revenues and ¥5 billion in net income. Its three major groups are carbon and inorganic chemicals, petrochemicals, and functional products. The first two groups consist of high-volume and mass-produced products, but the third group—functional products—is made up of low-volume, high value-added products. This group is the result of the firm's successful diversification strategy.

Nippon Kayaku

Juntaro Yamamoto founded this first manufacturer of industrial explosives in Japan in 1916. In 1992, the firm had five major lines of business—pharmaceuticals, sophisticated products, agrochemicals, dyestuffs, and explosives and catalysts—that were divided into two groups, pharmaceuticals and fine chemicals. In that year, the firm's sales were ¥117 billion and its net profit was ¥2.8 billion. The firm's growth has been achieved through internal expansion and several acquisitions and mergers.

Nissan Motor Company, Ltd.

This firm was founded in 1933. It considers itself the most globalized of the Japanese automobile companies as it has 36 plants in 22 countries and markets in 150 countries through 390 distributorships and over 10,000 dealerships. In 1990, Nissan was the world's fourth largest automobile manufacturer, producing just over 3 million vehicles, approximately 10 percent of the world's demand for cars and trucks. Nissan has a stated policy of globalization through a five-step process that emphasizes localization of production, sourcing, research and development, management functions, and decisions.

Olympus Optical Company, Ltd.

As part of Olympus, Olympus Optical Company manufactures and sells optoelectronic equipment and other related products. Olympus, originally known as Takachiho Seisakusho, was founded in 1919 as a producer of microscopes. Major product lines are cameras, video camcorders, microscopes, endoscopes, and clinical analyzers. By 1990, Olympus was the world's fourth-largest camera manufacturer, with consolidated revenues of ¥219 billion and ¥8 billion in net income.

Shionogi & Co., Ltd.

This firm was founded as a wholesaler of traditional Japanese and Chinese medicines by Gisaburo Shiono in 1878. Shionogi is a research-and-development-oriented pharmaceutical manufacturer. It dedicates 12.4 percent of sales to R&D. Shionogi's strategy focuses on selling its products to hospitals and clinics. Although the majority of its revenues are generated through pharmaceutical products, it has other businesses, including animal health products, agrochemicals, industrial chemicals, diagnostics, and clinical testing services. It is recognized around the world for the quality of its antibiotics and other pharmaceutical products. In 1992, the firm generated ¥225 billion in sales.

Sony Corporation

Sony, one of the world's largest electronics companies, started as Tokyo Telecommunications Research Institute. In its earlier years, it generated revenues by repairing broken radios and manufacturing shortwave converters. The company's first really successful product was Japan's first magnetic tape recorder, which entered the market in 1950. The company grew rapidly and, by 1960, was a truly international firm with Sony Corporation of America and Sony Overseas, S.A., in Switzerland. In 1968 and 1970, the firm created Sony UK and Sony GmbH.

Sumitomo Electric Industries, Ltd.

This firm was founded in 1897 as Sumitomo Copper Rolling Works, a manufacturer of bare copper. Since its founding, Sumitomo Electric Industries (SEI), as it is now called, has continued to produce electric wires and cables. Indeed, it is the world's third largest manufacturer of these products. The firm adopted a diversification program in 1931 to take advantage of its distinctive competencies in the manufacturing of electric wires and cables. SEI's management considers the firm to be one of the most highly diversified in Japan.

Taiyo Kogyo Co., Ltd. (The Taiyo Group)

This firm was founded in 1947 by Kuniyasu Sakai and Hiroshi Sekiyama as the Taiyo Painting Company. As the firm grew and the Japanese economy expanded, it diversified into metal stamping and electronic equipment. The objective of the Taiyo Group's *bunsha* philosophy is to avoid bureaucracy through small companies with highly autonomous managers. This philosophy is based on Sakai's belief that "when a company gets too large it cannot respond in time." Sakai finds the flexibility of small firms to be a powerful form of cost management.

Topcon Corporation

Topcon began in 1932 as the Tokyo Optical Company, Ltd. It has diversified along its core competencies in advance optics and precision equipment processing. By 1992, Topcon sold four major product lines: surveying instruments, medical and ophthalmic instruments, information instruments, and industrial instruments. In that year, the surveying instruments business unit contributed approximately 36 percent of sales, medical and ophthalmic instruments 28 percent, information instruments 13 percent, and industrial instruments 23 percent. Topcon specializes in high-technology, high-margin, low-volume products. Because it relies on high technology for its profits, Topcon has invested heavily in research and development.

Yamanouchi Pharmaceutical Co., Ltd.

This firm was founded in 1923 to manufacture and sell pharmaceutical products. In 1992, Yamanouchi was Japan's second largest pharmaceutical drug company in terms of net profit. It is highly respected both in Japan and internationally. The company has a corporate philosophy of "Creating and Caring . . . for Life." In 1992, consolidated sales were ¥357 billion and net income was ¥33 billion. Pharmaceutical products accounted for 73 percent of sales, nutritional products 17 percent, and food and roses 10 percent. Yamanouchi acquired the Shaklee Group, which sells the bulk of its nutritional products, in 1989 as part of its diversification strategy.

Yamatake-Honeywell Company, Ltd.

Founded in 1906 as a small trading company, Yamatake & Co., Ltd., has grown into a group of six companies with consolidated sales of ¥196.8 billion and pretax income of ¥14.5 billion in 1993. In that year, the group consisted of Yamatake & Co., Ltd., Yamatake Keiso Co., Ltd., Yamatake Engineering Co., Ltd., Yamatake Control Products Co., Ltd., Yamatake Techno-systems Co., Ltd., and Yamatake-Honeywell Co., Ltd. Yamatake-Honeywell was formed in 1953, when Yamatake entered into a partnership with the American firm Honeywell. Yamatake-Honeywell has four divisions—industrial systems, building systems, control products, and factory automation systems—that carry out research and development for control and automation.

Yokohama Corporation, Ltd.

Yokohama was founded in 1939 as a joint venture between a Japanese automobile manufacturer and the Japanese government. It was first listed on the Tokyo Stock Market in 1955. Under license from a German firm, Yokohama was to manufacture hydraulic systems for automobiles and trucks and associated equipment. By 1992, the firm had 13 overseas affiliates, 7 liaison offices, a worldwide service network of over 100 distributors and 2,000 service representatives with sales of ¥257 billion and 6,800 employees. Firm ownership has changed over the years, and in 1993, only three major shareholders remained, Isuzu Motors, Nissan Motors, and the Industrial Bank of Japan. Yokohama is split into three corporate divisions: injection pump, air conditioning, and hydraulics and pneumatics.

GLOSSARY OF TERMS

Activity-based costing (ABC): A highly accurate product costing system that assigns costs to products based on the causal relationships of the activities required to produce the product. ABC traces costs to products using many different activity measures that reflect the quantities of inputs consumed to manufacture the part.

Amoeba management system: A system developed at Kyocera that organizes the firm into a large collection of quasi-autonomous profit centers, or highly independent pseudofirms, responsible for selling a number of products both internally and externally.

Bunsha **philosophy:** An approach to managing firm size utilized by the Taiyo Kogyo Group founder Kuniyasu Sakai, who strongly believes that small firms are inherently more efficient and effective than large firms. *Bunsha,* meaning "to divide," refers to the spinning off of new venture firms from the parent firm.

Confrontation: A competitive strategy that assumes sustainable product-related competitive advantages are unlikely to be developed. Confronting competitors head on is achieved by rapidly matching the cost/quality/functionality improvements initiated by other firms while nurturing the ability to create temporary competitive advantages.

Cost-down programs: A disciplined corporatewide cost reduction campaign with a primary focus on finding ways to design costs out of products before they enter production. These programs also include methods for improving efficiency in the manufacturing process.

Cost leadership: A generic competitive strategy that requires the firm to establish itself as the lowest cost producer in an industry. Traditionally, cost leaders offer products that are low in price and functionality.

Current cost: The cost of a future product, assuming that it is manufactured today from existing components.

Dango: A Japanese term that refers to collusion among competitors. The term is associated with the practice of the Japanese construction industry, in which job orders are determined prior to competitive bidding.

Differentiation: A generic competitive strategy that relies on the provision of unique product offerings that closely satisfy customers' requirements. The differentiator's product offerings are usually high in both functionality and price.

Draft target cost: The unexpected cost of manufacture arrived at through target costing methods. The draft target cost is an updated allowable cost arrived at after computing the projected cost of each major subcomponent. It is primarily used to determine whether or not a product can be produced and sold profitably.

Expected cost: Used in cost-plus pricing approaches, the expected cost is determined by product designers who have no specified cost objective to achieve but are expected to minimize the cost of the new product as it is designed.

Expected selling price: Used in the product pricing methods associated with a cost plus approach, the expected selling price becomes the dependent variable and is determined by adding a target profit margin to the expected product cost.

Final target cost: The target cost set at the very end of the product design stage. It, unlike earlier target costs, includes both direct and indirect manufacturing costs.

First look VE: Focusing on the major elements of the product design, its objective is to create enhanced functionality by developing improved capability of existing functions.

Functional group management system: The Olympus Corporation's term for a bottom-up approach to identifying and achieving cost reduction targets carried out by self-directed work teams.

Hangen Game: One of several games employed at Higashimaru Soyu Company. Its purpose was to demonstrate that the number of workers in a group could be reduced to achieve the same objectives.

Human resource management (HRM): A performance-based compensation program used at Sumitomo Electric Industries. Salaries are determined using three separate criteria: base salary, bonus, and individual productivity enhancements. The latter is determined by multiplying the individual's base pay by the appropriate factor of productivity ratio.

Interorganizational cost management systems: A cost reduction program that is initiated by a core firm and carried out across the entire value chain. These systems contribute to the blurring of organizational boundaries as firms share information and resources to improve the efficiency of interfirm activities.

Just-in-Time (JIT): The ordering and delivery of parts as they are needed in the production process to achieve minimum inventory and waste.

Kaizen: A Japanese term that stands for continuous improvement. As applied in cost management practice, the term refers to a total commitment on behalf of the workforce to finding new ways to reduce costs and increase efficiency in the manufacturing process.

Kaizen **costing:** The application of *kaizen* techniques to reduce the costs of existing components and products by a prespecified amount. Its objective is to reduce a product's cost through increased efficiency of the production process.

Kaizen **variance analysis:** An operational control method used to determine whether cost reduction targets are being met. Using standards to evaluate *kaizen* costing systems, variances signal the need to achieve further cost savings in order to meet *kaizen* objectives.

Kyoto brewery system: A program that consisted of converting the

Kyoto brewery into a number of profit centers that rewarded center managers for improving profitability, not just reducing costs.

Lean enterprise: A new organizational form originating in Japan. It employs lean production methods, such as just-in-time production, total quality management, team-based work arrangements, supportive supplier relations, and improved customer satisfaction. The lean enterprise is capable of producing high-quality products economically in lower volumes and bringing them to market faster than mass producers.

Lean producer: A firm that relies upon lean production manufacturing techniques.

Mass producer: A firm that relies upon mass production manufacturing techniques similar to those pioneered by, among others, Henry Ford.

Maximum allowable price: The highest price the customer is willing to spend for the product irrespective of its quality and functionality.

Maximum feasible values (of a survival triplet characteristic): Determined by the capability of the firm, maximum feasible values are the highest values for product characteristics that a firm can achieve without violating the minimum or maximum values of the other characteristics.

Minimum acceptable profit: A preestablished minimum profit margin intended to prevent the launch of new products that cannot meet minimum profit criteria. See also Target costing.

Minimum allowable value (of a survival triplet characteristic): Determined by the customer, the minimum allowable level is the lowest value of each product-related characteristic that the customer is willing to accept.

Minimum cost investigation (MCI): A multilevel supplier meeting employing quality-price-function trade-offs used by Tokyo Motors to reduce the inefficiencies involved when multiple firms are engaged in the production of a purchased part.

Minimum feasible price: The lowest price that the firm is willing to accept for the product if it is at its minimum allowable quality and functionality levels.

Operational control: A method for obtaining feedback on how well costs are being controlled. By assigning responsibility to individuals for costs they control, responsibility centers become the primary unit of analysis to evaluate, through the use of variance analysis, how well costs are being controlled.

Plant management reporting system (PMRS): The operational control counterpart to the profit center orientation of the SOMRS at Kirin Breweries. The PMRS uses cost-oriented variance between actual and planned profit to evaluate plant performance. Under this system, workers have access to information that helps them to determine the impact of alternative cost saving activities on profitability.

Price control system: A method used at Higashimaru Soyu Company. It was designed to instill a profit-making attitude among work groups by organizing them into pseudoprofit centers that bought and sold resources consumed and produced within the firm.

Product costing: A systematic cost accounting method for assigning appropriate costs to products during the manufacturing process to determine product costs and monitor profitability.

Sales office management reporting system (SOMRS): A profit center control system developed at Kirin Brewery and designed to report the overall profitability of each sales office and the level of expenditures under the control of the sales manager in order to cope with the rapidly growing sales force and complexity of new product introductions.

Second look VE: Applied during the last half of the planning stage and the first half of the development and product preparation stage, its objective is to improve the value and functionality of existing components.

Sagyo-shigoto: A phrase coined at Higashimaru Soyu Company that translates as "job-work." The difference between the two is the commitment to improving one's performance contained in the latter term. The phrase was used to encourage workers to search for ways to improve their work performance.

Survival triplet: Three product-related characteristics: cost (price), quality, and functionality that must be managed to ensure that products remain within their survival zones.

Sustainable competitive advantage: The ability to sustain product-related advantages and thus high-profit margins for a lengthy period of time.

Target costing: A structured approach to determining the cost at which a proposed product with specified functionality and quality must be produced in order to generate the desired level of profitability at its anticipated selling price. A product's target cost is determined by subtracting its target profit margin from its target selling price.

Target margin: The target margin is set, based upon corporate profit expectations, historical results, competitive analysis, and in some cases, computer simulations. Target margins applied in target-costing procedures ensure products will be sold at a minimum acceptable profit.

Target price: The target price of a new product is determined primarily from market analysis. It is used to determine a target cost, which is applied during the design phase of new product development. It is also used as the basis for determining the purchase price of components and raw materials acquired externally.

Tear-down analysis: A method used to analyze competitive product offerings in terms of materials and parts used as well as ways in which they function and are manufactured.

Temporary competitive advantage: An advantage achieved over one's competitors that is not expected to last for long.

Total quality management (TQM): An integrated product development strategy that focuses on designing quality into products and ensuring that the production process is as defect free as possible.

Value engineering (VE): A systematic interdisciplinary examination of factors affecting the cost of a product in order to devise a means of achieving the required standard of quality and reliability at the target cost.

Zero defects (ZD): A quality program with the objective of reducing defects to zero.

Zeroth look VE: The application of VE principles at the concept proposal stage, the earliest stage in the design process. Its objective is to introduce new forms of functionality that have not previously existed.

Bibliography

Aoki, Masahiko. 1990. The participatory generation of information rents and the theory of the firm. In *The firm as a nexus of treaties,* edited by M. Aoki, B. Gustafsson, and O. Williamson. London: Sage Publications

———. 1988. *Information, incentives, and bargaining in the Japanese economy.* New York: Cambridge University Press.

———. 1987. The Japanese firm in transition. In *The political economy of Japan,* vol. 1, edited by Kozo Yamamura and Yasukichi Yasuba. Stanford: Stanford University Press.

Best, Michael. 1990. *The new competition: institutions of industrial restructuring.* Cambridge: Harvard University Press.

Blackburn, Joseph D. 1991. *Time-based competition.* Homewood, Ill.: Business One Irwin.

Blanchard, B. S. 1978. *Design and manage to life-cycle cost.* Portland, Ore.: M/A Press.

Borrus, Michael. 1988. *Competing for control: America's stake in microelectronics.* Cambridge, Mass.: Ballinger Publishing Company.

Byrne, John A. 1993. The horizontal corporation. *Business Week,* 20 December, 76–81.

Carsberg, B. 1985. *The economics of business decisions.* New York: Penguin.

The coming clash of logic. 1993. *The Economist,* 3 July, 21–23.

Cooper, R. 1995a. Shionogi and Co., Ltd. Case Study. Boston: Harvard Business School.

———. 1995b. Tokyo Motor Works, Ltd.: Target costing system. Unpublished case study. The Peter F. Drucker Graduate Management Center, Claremont Graduate School.

———. 1994a. Citizen Watch Company, Ltd: Cost reduction for mature products. Case Study 9-194-033. Boston: Harvard Business School.

———. 1994b. Higashimaru Shoyu Company, Ltd. (A): Price control system. Case Study 9-195-050. Boston: Harvard Business School.

———. 1994c. Higashimaru Shoyu Co., Ltd. (B): Revitalizing the organization. Case Study 9-195-051. Boston: Harvard Business School.

———. 1994d. Kirin Brewery Company, Ltd. Case Study 9-195-058. Boston: Harvard Business School.

———. 1994e. Komatsu, Ltd. (A): target costing system. Case Study 9-194-037. Boston: Harvard Business School.

———. 1994f. Komatsu, Ltd. (B): profit planning and product costing. Case Study 9-195-061. Boston: Harvard Business School.

———. 1994g. Kyocera Corporation: The amoeba management system. Case Study 9-195-064. Boston: Harvard Business School.

———. 1994h. Mitsubishi Kasei Corporation: Product line cost system. Case Study 9-195-066. Boston: Harvard Business School.

———. 1994i. Nissan Motor Company, Ltd.: Target costing system. Case Study 9-194-040. Boston: Harvard Business School.

———. 1994j. Olympus Optical Company, Ltd. (A): Cost management for short life cycle products. Case Study 9-195-072. Boston: Harvard Business School.

———. 1994k. Olympus Optical Company, Ltd. (B): Functional group management. Case Study 9-195-073. Boston: Harvard Business School.

————. 1994l. Sony Corporation: The Walkman line. Case Study 9-195-076. Boston: Harvard Business School.

————. 1994m. Sumitomo Electric Industries, Ltd.: The kaizen program. Case Study 9-195-078. Boston: Harvard Business School.

————. 1994n. The Taiyo Group: The bunsha philosophy. Case Study 9-195-080. Boston: Harvard Business School.

————. 1994o. Topcon Corporation: Production control system. Case Study 9-195-082. Boston: Harvard Business School.

————. 1994p. Yamatake-Honeywell Company, Ltd.: Activity-based costing system. Case Study 9-195-106. Boston: Harvard Business School.

————. 1994q. Yamanouchi Pharmaceutical Co., Ltd. Case Study 9-195-086. Boston: Harvard Business School.

————. 1994r. How Japanese manufacturing firms implement target costing systems: A field-based research study. Working paper, The Peter F. Drucker Graduate Management Center, Claremont Graduate School.

————. 1994s. The role of activity based systems in supporting the transition to the lean enterprise. In *Advances in management accounting,* vol. 3, edited by Marc Epstein. Greenwich, Conn.: JAI Press.

————. 1990a. Cost classification in unit-based and activity-based manufacturing cost systems. *Journal of Cost Management,* Fall, 4–14.

————. 1990b. Implementing an activity-based cost system. *Cost Management,* Spring, 33–42.

————. 1989a. The rise of activity-based costing—part three: How many cost drivers do you need, and how do you select them? *Cost Management,* Winter, 34–46.

————. 1989b. The rise of activity-based costing—part four: What do activity-based cost systems look like? *Cost Management,* Spring, 38–49.

————. 1988a. The rise of activity-based costing—part one: What is an activity-based cost system? *Cost Management,* Summer, 45–54.

————. 1988b. The rise of activity-based costing—part two: When do I need an activity-based cost system? *Cost Management,* Fall, 41–48.

Cooper, R., and M. Sakurai. 1990. New manufacturing cost management techniques. *Accounting* 42, no. 3:49–58.

Cooper, R., and T. Yoshikawa. 1994a Isuzu Motors, Ltd.: Cost creation program. Case Study 9-195-054. Boston: Harvard Business School.

————. 1994b. Kamakura Ironworks Company, Ltd. Case Study 9-195-056. Boston: Harvard Business School.

————. 1994c. Nippon Kayaku. Case Study 9-195-068. Boston: Harvard Business School.

————. 1994d. Yokohama Corporation, Ltd. (a): The Yokohama production system. Case Study 9-195-070. Boston: Harvard Business School.

————. 1994e. Yokohama Corporation, Ltd. (b): Cost management system. Case Study 9-195-108. Boston: Harvard Business School.

————. 1994f. Interorganizational cost management systems: The case of the Tokyo-Yokohama-Kamakura supplier chain. *International Journal of Production Economics* 37, no. 1.

Cooper, R., et al. 1992. *Implementing activity-based cost management: moving from analysis to action.* Montvale, N.J.: Institute of Management Accountants.

Crosby, Philip B. 1979. *Quality is free.* New York: McGraw-Hill.

Cusumano, M. A. 1985. *The Japanese automobile industry.* Cambridge: Harvard University, Council on East Asian Studies.

D'Aveni, R. 1994. *Hypercompetition.* New York: The Free Press.

Davidow, William H., and Michael S. Malone. 1992. *The virtual corporation.* New York: Harper and Row.

The five deadly sins of Japan's expanding "high tech syndrome." 1992. *Tokyo Business Today,* 34–36.

Fizzing. 1993. *The Economist,* 4 September, 63–64.

Friedman, David B. 1992. Getting industry to stick: Enhancing high value-added production in California. Paper presented at the UCLA Lewis Center Conference on Policy Options for the Southern California Economy, 19 November, University of California, Los Angeles.

Friedman, David B., and Richard Samuels. 1993. How to succeed without really flying: The Japanese aircraft industry and Japan's technology ideology. In *Regionalism and rivalry,* edited by J. Frankel and M. Kahler Chicago: The University of Chicago Press.

Fruin, W. Mark, and Toshihiro Nishiguchi. 1993. Supplying the Toyota production system. In *Country competitiveness: Technology and the organizing of work,* edited by Bruce Kogut. New York: Oxford University Press.

Gerlach, Michael. 1992. *Alliance capitalism.* Berkeley: University of California Press.

————. 1992. "The Japanese corporate network: A blockmodel analysis. *Administrative Science Quarterly* 37, no. 1:105–139.

Gordon, R. 1991. Innovation, industrial networks and high technology regions. In *Innovation networks: Spatial perspectives,* edited by R. Camagni. London: Belhaven.

Hamada, Kazuki, and Yasuhiro Monden. 1989. Profit management at Kyocera Corporation: The amoeba system. In *Japanese management accounting: A world class approach to profit management,* edited by Y. Monden and M. Sakurai. Cambridge, Mass: Productivity Press.

Hammer, Michael, and James Champy. 1993. *Reengineering the corporation.* New York: Harper and Row.

Harrison, Bennett. 1994. *Lean and mean: The changing landscape of corporate power in the age of flexibility.* New York: Basic Books.

Heldey, B. 1977. Strategy and the business portfolio. *Long Range Planning,* February, 12.

Hiromoto, Toshiro. 1988. Another hidden edge—Japanese management accounting. *Harvard Business Review,* July–August, 4–7.

Imai, Ken-ichi, Ikujiro Nonaka, and Hirotaka Takeuchi. 1985. Managing the new product development process: How Japanese companies learn and unlearn. In *The uneasy alliance: Managing the productivity-technology dilemma,* edited by Kim Clark et al. Boston: Harvard Business School Press.

Imai, Masaaki. 1986. *Kaizen: The key to Japan's competitive success.* New York: McGraw-Hill, Inc.

Ingrassia, Paul, and A. Nomani. 1993. Second thoughts: some fear backlash as Detroit prepares charges against Japan. *The Wall Street Journal,* 8 February.

Institute of Management Accountants. 1993. *Marketing, logistics and management accounting* (in Japanese). Tokyo: Institute of Management Accountants.

Johnson, Thomas H., and Robert S. Kaplan. 1987. *Relevance lost: The rise and fall of management accounting.* Boston: Harvard Business School Press.

Kagono, T., et al. 1985. *Strategic vs. evolutionary management.* New York: North Holland.

Kanter, Rosabeth Moss. 1992. Think like the customer: The global business logic. *Harvard Business Review,* July–August, 9–10.

Kaplan, Robert S. 1987. John Deere Component Works (A) and (B). Case Study 9-187-107/8. Boston: Harvard Business School.

Kaplan, Robert S. 1989. Texas Eastman Company. Case Study 9-190-039. Boston: Harvard Business School.

Kato, Y., G. Boer, and C. W. Chow. 1993. Target costing: Some key lessons from Japanese companies. Working paper, Vanderbilt University, Nashville, Tenn.

Kaufman, Jerry J. 1990. *Value engineering for the practitioner.* North Carolina: North Carolina State University.

Kester, Carl W. 1991. *Japanese takeovers.* Boston: Harvard Business School Press.

Krafcik, John F. 1988. Triumph of the lean production system. *Sloan Management Review,* Fall, 41–52.

Locke, E. A., and F. M. White. 1981. Perceived determinants of high and low productivity in three occupational groups: A critical incident study. *Journal of Management Studies,* vol. 18, 375–87.

Locke, E. A., and G. P. Latham. 1984. *Goal setting: A motivational technique that works!* Englewood Cliffs, N.J.: Prentice Hall.

Magnusson, Paul. 1993. Why Detroit hit the brakes: Fearing a backlash, it now wants Clinton to press Japan on dumping. *Business Week,* 22 February,

Makido, T. 1989. Recent trends in Japan's cost management practices. In *Japanese management accounting: A world class approach to profit management,* edited by Y. Monden and M. Sakurai. Cambridge, Mass.: Productivity Press.

Meyer, Christopher. 1993. *Fast cycle time.* New York: The Free Press.

Monden, Y. 1992. *Cost management in the new manufacturing age.* Cambridge, Mass.: Productivity Press.

Monden, Y., and K. Hamada. 1991. Target costing and *kaizen* costing in Japanese automobile companies. *Journal of Management Accounting Research,* Fall, 16–34.

Monden, Y., and M. Sakurai, eds. 1989. *Japanese management accounting: A world class approach to profit management.* Cambridge, Mass.: Productivity Press.

Monden, Y., and Y. Noboru. 1986. *Applying just-in-time: The American/Japanese experience.* Atlanta, Ga.: Institute of Industrial Engineers.

Morales, Rebecca. 1993. *Flexible production.* New York: Polity Press.

Morita, Akio. 1992. Partnering for competitiveness: The role of Japanese business. *Harvard Business Review,* May–June, 76–83.

Newbrought, E. T. 1967. *Effective maintenance management.* New York: McGraw-Hill.

Odagiri, Hiroyuki, and Akira Goto. 1993. The Japanese system of innovation: Past, present, and future. In *National innovation systems,* edited by Richard Nelson. New York: Oxford University Press.

Ohmae, Kenichi. 1982. *The mind of the strategist.* New York: McGraw-Hill.

Okimoto, Daniel. 1989. *Between MITI and the market.* Stanford: Stanford University Press.

Penrose, Edith. 1959. *The theory of the growth of the firm.* New York: John Wiley & Sons.

Pollack, Andrew. 1992. A lower gear for Japan's auto makers. *New York Times,* 30 August.

Porter, Michael. 1992. Capital disadvantage: America's failing capital investment system. *Harvard Business Review,* September–October, 65–82.

———. 1990. *Competitive advantage of nations.* New York: The Free Press.

———. 1985. *Competitive advantage.* New York: The Free Press.

———. 1980. *Competitive strategy: Techniques for analyzing industries and competitors.* New York: The Free Press.

Reitsperger, Wolf, D. Shirley, and A. El-Shaieb. 1990. "Quality is free": A comparative study of attitudes in the U.S. and Japan. *Journal of Purchasing and Materials Management* 26, no. 2.

Sakai, Kuniyasu, and Hiroshi Sekiyama. 1985. *BUNSHA (company division): What good is a stuffed tiger?* (in Japanese). Tokyo: Taiyo Industry Co., Ltd.

Sakurai, M. 1989. Target costing and how to use it. *Journal of Cost Management,* Summer, 39–50.

Samuels, Richard, Jr. 1994. Pathways of technological diffusion in Japan. *Sloan Management Review,* Spring, 21–34.

Saxenian, Annalee. 1994. *Regional advantage: Culture and competition in Silicon Valley and Route 128.* Cambridge: Harvard University Press.

Schreffler, Roger. 1990. Toyota Tahara: first they nailed the quality—now they're going after cost. *Automotive Industries* 170, no. 8: 42.

Sloan, Alfred P. 1963. *My years with General Motors.* New York: MacFadden-Bartell.

Stalk, George, Jr. 1988. Time—the next source of competitive advantage. *Harvard Business Review,* July–August, 41–51.

Stalk, George, Jr., and Alan M. Webber. 1993. Japan's dark side of time. *Harvard Business Review,* July–August, 93–102.

Stalk, George, Jr., and Thomas M. Hout. 1990. *Competing against time.* New York: The Free Press.

Tanaka, M. 1989. Cost planning and control systems in the design phase of a new product. In *Japanese management accounting: A world class approach to profit management,* edited by Y. Monden and M. Sakurai. Cambridge, Mass.: Productivity Press.

Tanaka, T. 1993. Target costing at Toyota. *Journal of Cost Management,* Spring, 4–11.

Thomas, Philip R. 1990. *Competitiveness through total cycle time.* New York: McGraw-Hill.

Toyota Motor Corporation. 1992. Toyota 1992 annual report. Toyota City, Japan.

U.S. General Accounting Office. 1993. *Intellectual property rights: U.S. companies' patent experiences in Japan.* A special report prepared at the request of the Honorable John D. Rockefeller and Dennis Deconcini, U.S. Senate. Washington, D.C.: Government Printing Office.

Williams, Jeffrey R. 1992. How sustainable is your competitive advantage? *California Management Review* 34 (Spring): 51.

Womack, James P., and Daniel T. Jones. 1994. From lean production to the lean enterprise. *Harvard Business Review,* March–April, 93–103.

Womack, James P., Daniel T. Jones, and Daniel Roos. 1990. *The machine that changed the world.* New York: Harper and Row.

Worthy, S. Ford. 1991. Japan's smart secret weapon. *Fortune,* 12 August, 72–75.

Yoshikawa, Takeo, et al. 1993. *Contemporary cost management.* London: Chapman & Hall.

INDEX

Product costing (*cont.*)
  Shionogi's, 226–229
  traditional, 211–214
  Yamatake-Honeywell's, 229–236
Product design, 131
  process and costs in, 131–134
  target costing in, 135–138, 163–164
    benefits of, 162–163
    factors affecting, 138–142
    systems of, 142–162
  value engineering in, 165–169, 182–183
    first and second look, 176–177
    at Isuzu, 169–172, 174–175
    other cost-reduction techniques of, 178–182
    teardown approaches to, 177–178
    zeroth look, 173
Product development, 138–140. *See also* Product design
Product differentiation. *See* Differentiation, product
Production yen, 219
Product life cycles, 95, 96–97, 98–99, 109
Product line cost systems, 215
  of Komatsu, 218–221
  of Mitsubishi Kasei, 221–222, 224–226
Product matrix, 55–56
Product mi
  in cost management, 95, 97–99, 109–110
    redesigning and outsourcing products, 104–106
    selling prices, 100–101
    unprofitable products, 101–104
  in product planning, 52–53

Product planning, 67
  impact of, on strategy, 61–66
  long-term consumer analysis in, 53–61
  nature of, 49, 67–68, 136
  short-term consumer analysis in, 49–53
Profit
  cost-plus pricing for, 100–101, 136–137, 149, 162, 163
  eliminating unprofitable products for, 101–104
  planning and control systems for, 269–276
  in product planning, 61–66
  redesigning and outsourcing products for, 104–106
  reflected in cost management, 94–95, 97–99
  See also Microprofit centers; Operational control systems
Profit centers. *See* Microprofit centers
Pseudomicroprofit centers
  Higashimaru's price control, 283
  imitation of, 40–41
  objectives of, 119–120, 121, 128
  process and function of, 285–290
  Kirin's Kyoto brewery, 290–294
  nature and role of, 106–107, 110, 279–282, 283–284, 300–301
  Olympus' functional group management, 294–299

Quality
  in affecting competition, 42–44, 48
  in cost management systems, 93–94, 109

in determining product survival
zones, 84–85
in auto industry, 22–29, 78–79
dark side of, 81–82
at Komatsu, 77–78
at Olympus, 70–75
at Sony, 79–80
at Topcon, 75–77
-function-price trade-off among
suppliers, 192, 193–197, 202–
203
in survival triplet, 14, 15, 17, 18,
33
managing, 30–32
See also Target costing
Quality-function-price (QFP) trade-
off, 192, 193–197, 202–203

Real microprofit centers
Kyocera's amoeba, 304–307
communication in, 311–313
cost systems of, 310–311
creating and disbanding, 307–
309
evaluating performance of, 313–
316
setting selling prices in, 309–310
nature and role of, 107–108,
110, 279–282, 303–304, 324–
327
Taiyo's *bushna*, 316–317
developing company presidents
under, 322–324
splitting the company under,
318–322
Responsibility centers
at Kirin Brewery, 269–276
nature of, 255, 258–260, 276–277
See also Operational control systems

Rewards. *See* Compensation systems
RINGI (cost-reduction proposal),
180

Sagyo-shigoto, 116–117, 127–128
Sakai, Kuniyasu, 303, 316–317,
318–319, 321, 322–323, 326,
345
Salaries. *See* Compensation systems
Sales office management reporting
system (SOMRS), 269–273
Sansei teaching, 40–41
Second look VE, 133, 169, 172,
176–177, 182
Sekiyama, Hiroshi, 345
Set-up time, 36
Shimada, Saburo, 233
Shimoyama, Toshiro, 2
Shinryo Heavy Equipment, 342
Shiono, Gisaburo, 344
Shionogi Pharmaceuticals, 6, 344
operational control at, 265–268
product costing at, 98–99, 215,
226–229, 237
Sloan, Alfred P., 23
Small-batch production, 36, 37
Sony Corporation, 6, 102, 344
product planning at, 50–51
product survival zones at, 79–80
target costing at, 139–140
technology diffusion at, 39–40
Standard costs, 255, 262–268
Static tear-down, 177, 178
Subcontractors, 138, 141–142.
See also Outsourcing; Suppliers
Sumitomo Electric Industries (SEI),
6, 112, 344–345
cost management at, 100–101,
104

team leaders in, 116–119
Japanese philosophy toward, 36, 46

Xerox, 13

Yamamoto, Juntaro, 343
Yamanouchi Pharmaceutical Co., 7, 345–346
operational control at, 262, 263–264
outsourcing at, 105–106
Yamatake-Honeywell Company, 7, 346
product costing at, 210, 215, 229–236, 237
Yokohama Corporation, 7, 342, 346

in Tokyo-Kamakura supplier chain, 187–188, 202–204
balance of power, 191–192
end-of-chain supplier, 198–202
information sharing, 188–191
minimum cost investigation, 197–198
trade-offs, 193–197
unprofitable products at, 101–102, 103–104
Yuasa, 190
Yukijirushi, 290

Zero defect (ZD) programs, 36, 45
Zeroth look VE, 133, 169, 173, 182